Eighteenth-Century British Premiers

Also by Dick Leonard

A CENTURY OF PREMIERS: Salisbury to Blair

NINETEENTH-CENTURY BRITISH PREMIERS: Pitt to Rosebery

THE BACKBENCHER AND PARLIAMENT (*edited with Val Herman*)

CROSLAND AND NEW LABOUR (*edited*)

THE ECONOMIST GUIDE TO THE EUROPEAN UNION (*10 editions*)

ELECTIONS IN BRITAIN: A Voter's Guide (*with Roger Mortimore*)

GUIDE TO THE GENERAL ELECTION

PAYING FOR PARTY POLITICS

THE PRO-EUROPEAN READER (*edited with Mark Leonard*)

THE SOCIALIST AGENDA: Crosland's Legacy (*edited with David Lipsey*)

WORLD ATLAS OF ELECTIONS (*with Richard Natkiel*)

THE FUTURE OF SOCIALISM by ANTHONY CROSLAND (*edited 50th Anniversary edition, 2006*)

Eighteenth-Century British Premiers

Walpole to the Younger Pitt

Dick Leonard

First published 2011 by
PALGRAVE MACMILLAN

Palgrave Macmillan in the UK is an imprint of Macmillan Publishers Limited, registered in England, company number 785998, of Houndmills, Basingstoke, Hampshire RG21 6XS.

Palgrave Macmillan in the US is a division of St Martin's Press LLC, 175 Fifth Avenue, New York, NY 10010.

Palgrave Macmillan is the global academic imprint of the above companies and has companies and representatives throughout the world.

Palgrave® and Macmillan® are registered trademarks in the United States, the United Kingdom, Europe and other countries.

ISBN: 978–1–4039–3908–1 hardback
ISBN: 978–0–230–28478–4 paperback

This book is printed on paper suitable for recycling and made from fully managed and sustained forest sources. Logging, pulping and manufacturing processes are expected to conform to the environmental regulations of the country of origin.

A catalogue record for this book is available from the British Library.

A catalog record for this book is available from the Library of Congress.

10 9 8 7 6 5 4 3 2 1
20 19 18 17 16 15 14 13 12 11

Printed and bound in Great Britain by
CPI Antony Rowe, Chippenham and Eastbourne

For Irène,
As always, my
Guide and inspiration

Contents

All illustrations by kind permission of the Government Art Collection
(GAC)

Introduction – The Road to the Prime Ministership

Historians are agreed that Sir Robert Walpole should be accounted the first British Prime Minister, though he never held the formal title, and nor did any of his successors until Sir Henry Campbell-Bannerman, in 1906–08. (The actual post to which Walpole was appointed, and for which he was paid a salary, was First Lord of the Treasury, a post held by all but two of his successors – Lord Chatham and the Marquess of Salisbury). It was George I, the first Hanoverian king, who chose Walpole in 1721, but both he and all his royal predecessors had previously employed ministers (not always known as such) who had advised them and helped in the administration of the kingdom. For substantial periods, individual ministers had been able to eclipse their colleagues and effectively become the 'chief minister' of the monarch. Writing in the 1920s, Clive Bigham identified 27 individuals who had filled this role, between the reigns of Edred (946–955) and Anne (1702–14). They held various titles, including Justiciar, Chancellor, Treasurer, Admiral, High Steward, Lord President, Marshal, Lord Lieutenant and Lord Great Chamberlain.* Bigham estimates that these men, whose average tenure was about 12 years, held power for rather less than half the nearly 800 years which separated Edred and Anne. 'Strong rulers', he writes, 'such as William I, William III or Oliver Cromwell, could do without them; weak ones, like Stephen, Edward II or Richard II, could never maintain them' (Bigham, 1925, p.4). Although these men wielded considerable,

---

* The 27 men were Dunstan, Godwin, Harold, Flambard, Roger, Becket, Marshall, de Burgh, de Montfort, Burnell, Stratford, Wykeham, Beaufort, Suffolk, Warwick, Morton, Wolsey, Thomas Cromwell, Somerset, Burghley (William Cecil), Salisbury (Robert Cecil), Buckingham, Strafford, Clarendon, Danby, Godolphin and Harley.

1

and sometimes arbitrary, power, they – with the partial exception of the last two or three names in the list – lacked many of the attributes which later became associated with the prime ministership, perhaps being more comparable to the vizier of a Moslem ruler. It required the developments of the previous half century – and particularly the Glorious Revolution of 1688–89 – to create the conditions which enabled Walpole, a man of considerable talent and resource, to fashion a new role for himself and his successors.

Politically, and constitutionally, the key achievement of the Glorious Revolution was the concept of a limited monarchy. Henceforth, the King (or Queen) would still govern the country, but only through and with the consent of Parliament. Even as naturally authoritarian a monarch as William III recognized this: his three successors – Queen Anne and the first two Georges – had little option, but to do so. A series of other developments, some of them preceding the Revolution, also contributed to the growing importance of Parliament, and the necessity for ministers to secure consistent support from both Houses if they were to survive in office. Chief of these was perhaps the emergence of political parties. This effectively dated from the reign of Charles II, and the attempt to exclude the King's younger brother, the Catholic James, Duke of York, from the succession. The opposition to James was led by the first Earl of Shaftesbury, whose Exclusion Bill failed to carry in 1680. His supporters were christened Whigs by their opponents, after the Whiggamores, Scottish Presbyterian rebels, who had opposed Charles I in 1648. The Whigs themselves happily accepted this appellation, claiming that Whig was an acronym for We Hope In God. They, in turn, branded their opponents, the supporters of the future James II, as Tories, after an Irish word meaning highwaymen or outlaws. It was largely the Whigs who presided over the replacement in 1688 of James II by his elder daughter, Mary II, and son-in-law William III, though the Tory Earl of Danby also played a significant role, and most Tories assented to the change. Party differences continued, however, mostly defined by attitudes to the monarchy, to religion and to foreign policy. It was the Whigs who were most in favour of limiting the monarchy, who believed most strongly in religious toleration, especially of Protestant Dissenters, and of prosecuting a warlike foreign policy, aimed at curtailing the ambitions of Louis XIV. The Tories retained a residual belief in the Divine Right of Kings. Though they accepted the accession of William, and later of Anne, they were divided about excluding the Stuart family from the succession after her death. They were fervent supporters of the Church of England, and opposed to any initiative to remove the disqualifications of Dissenters, let alone Catholics. Opponents of high taxation, they also emerged as the peace party, believing that the two long wars against France – the War of the Grand Alliance (1688–97), and the War of Spanish Succession (1701–13) – were ruinously expensive and were being fought more in the interests of the Netherlands than of Britain. There were social differences between the two parties – the Whigs were more aristocratic, while the Tories' strongest support came from the country gentry. The Whigs were less cohesive, being divided between the dominant 'court' faction, more interested in securing ministerial offices and other 'places' and the 'Country Whigs', whose interests often coincided with the Tories, though they were loath to cooperate with them.

Both Whigs and Tories lacked most of the attributes of modern political parties, but their development was fostered by the frequent electoral contests in the reigns of both William and Anne. Under the Triennial Act, passed in 1694, there were no fewer than ten general elections in the period up till 1715, after which the Septennial Act of 1716 brought the era of almost constant electoral activity to an end. Political activity was also fostered by the abolition of censorship in 1695, which led to the development of a lively periodical press, while the proliferation of coffee houses in London and the main provincial towns provided centres of debate for the growing intelligentsia. The fortunes of the parties fluctuated throughout the period – the Whigs gradually squeezing the Tories out of government during the reign of William III, but the accession of Anne, in 1702, giving the Tories a momentary boost. The largely apolitical Sidney Godolphin, who led the government until 1710, was supported predominantly by Whigs, notably John Churchill, the Duke of Marlborough, by far his most forceful colleague, whose influence was greatly bolstered by his stunning series of military victories over the French. His wife, Sarah, was a longtime favourite and confidante of the Queen, and constantly used her intimacy with her to promote her husband's interests, and those of his Whig allies. In the end, she over-did it, virtually browbeating Anne into appointing her son-in-law, Charles Spencer, Earl of Sunderland, as Secretary of State. Eventually, she fell out badly with Anne, who replaced her as her principal Woman of the Bedchamber by Sarah's cousin, Amelia Hill, who became Lady Masham, and a rather more discreet advocate for the Tories. In June 1710, the Queen girded herself up to dismiss both Marlborough and Godolphin, and a predominantly Tory administration was appointed, led by Robert Harley, later Earl of Oxford. In the subsequent general election, the Tories won a large majority in the Commons, though the Whigs were in control of the Lords. Harley proceeded to negotiate the Treaty of Utrecht, of 1713, ending the war with France, which the Whigs were in favour of continuing. On Harley's advice, the Queen took the unprecedented step of creating 12 new Tory peers in order to get the Treaty through the House of Lords.

The Tory triumph was short-lived: in the closing months of Anne's life, both Harley and his Tory colleague and bitter rival, Henry St. John, Viscount Bolingbroke, compromised themselves by entering into secret communications with James II's son, James Edward Stuart, the 'Old Pretender', trying in vain to persuade him to renounce Catholicism in order to succeed to the throne. On her deathbed, at the end of July 1714, Anne dismissed Harley and appointed the Duke of Shrewsbury as Lord Treasurer, who supervised the inauguration of the Elector of Hanover, George I, who arrived in England six weeks later. The Tories were irremediably tainted with Jacobitism, though most of them declared their loyalty to the Hanoverian dynasty. George immediately appointed a Whig administration, led by James, later Lord, Stanhope, and the Tories were condemned to opposition throughout his reign, and that of his son, George II, remaining in the wilderness until 1762, when the young George III appointed the Earl of Bute as Prime Minister.

Partly due to the expense of the wars which raged almost continuously during the reigns of William III and Anne, there was a constant need for Parliament to meet in order to vote Supply, which meant that the days when it met only occasionally – sometimes with a gap of several years – were long past. The monarch now had the need of a chief minister who would defend the policies of the government on a regular basis either in the Lords or in the Commons, which added a large new dimension to the role of the chief minister. Another important change was the development of cabinet government. From being individual advisers to the monarch, ministers were now summoned increasingly to meet together to give their collective view in a Council normally presided over by the monarch in person, though this was increasingly not the case with the accession of George I. Speaking little English, and often absent in his Hanoverian dominions, the cabinet, as it became known, met more and more often in his absence, with a leading minister in the chair, and this became the normal pattern when Walpole became First Lord of the Treasury in 1721. The fact that Walpole led his government from the Commons, rather than the Lords where most previous chief ministers had sat, both reflected and reinforced the growing predominance of the lower House of Parliament, which the Glorious Revolution had made possible. Walpole's long period in office – just short of 21 years – effectively bedded in the office of Prime Minister. Despite the fact that few of his successors were able to rival his qualities, all of them were expected to fulfill the various functions which he had accumulated – of being the monarch's chief adviser and administrator, of presiding over the cabinet and of ensuring majority support in both Houses of Parliament of the polices which the King wished to pursue.

The nation over which they ruled, earlier regarded as being a rather peripheral power, was poised to play an increasingly important role on the European and even the world stage. At the beginning of the eighteenth century, it was still an overwhelmingly rural country. The population of England and Wales, in 1700, was probably under 6 million, 85 per cent of whom lived in villages or small market towns. The population of Ireland was about 2.5 million and of Scotland, just over 1 million, making a total of around 9 million. Half a million of these lived in London, the second largest English town being Norwich with around 30,000 inhabitants, followed by Bristol with 20,000 and Newcastle with 15,000. Future major cities such as Liverpool, Manchester, Birmingham and Leeds, all had fewer than 10,000 inhabitants. In Ireland, Dublin had 60,000, while Edinburgh had 35,000 and Glasgow 12,000 inhabitants. The Act of Union of 1707 had united the parliaments and administrations of England and Scotland, though Scottish law and many of its customs remained distinct, with Presbyterianism being the established religion. Ireland retained its own Parliament and administration, but was effectively treated as a colony of England, and was dominated by its largely absentee Protestant Anglo-Irish aristocracy. Economically, Britain was now a fast developing country, though large-scale industrialization was still in the future. It was, however, already a major commercial and trading power, the union with Scotland making it the largest free trade area in Europe, while the establishment of the Bank of England, in 1694, greatly facilitated the raising of loans, for both government and private activity. Urbanization was to proceed rapidly throughout the century, so that by 1800 one-third of the population were town dwellers, though the big population growth of the major towns and cities was only just getting under way by then.

In 1700, already, Britain was becoming a significant imperial power, with its 13 North American colonies, a scattering of islands in the West Indies, a settlement in Gambia and an important presence in India, at Bombay, Madras and Calcutta. The treaty of Utrecht, in 1713, brought Hudson's Bay, Nova Scotia, Newfoundland, St Kitts, Gibraltar and Minorca under British rule, while the British Navy was probably already the most powerful in the world. Even its military strength was at its peak, with a large, standing army raised during the reigns of William and Mary, which was still nearly 150,000 strong at the accession of George I. It was then, however, rapidly run down, the country henceforth relying more on subsidizing the armies of its allies in the field, rather than employing large numbers of its own troops in the many European wars in which it engaged. Both politically and economically, Britain at the beginning of the eighteenth century was probably the most dynamic of the European powers. This was the inheritance that Sir Robert Walpole took over in 1721.

Works consulted

Bigham, Clive (1925), *The Chief Ministers of England 920–1720*, London, John Murray.

Cook, Chris and John Stevenson (1988), *British Historical Facts 1688–1760*, London, Palgrave Macmillan.

Cook, Chris and John Stevenson (1980), *British Historical Facts 1760–1830*, London, Palgrave Macmillan.

Eccleshall, Robert and Graham Walker, eds. (1998), *Biographical Dictionary of British Prime Ministers*, London, Routledge.

Englefield, Dermot, Janet Seaton and Isobel White (1995), *Facts about the British Prime Ministers*, New York, H.W. Wilson Company.

O'Gorman, Frank (1997), *The Long Eighteenth Century: British Political and Social History 1688–1832*, London, Arnold.

Turberville, A.S. (1964), *English Men and Manners in the 18th Century*, 2nd edition, New York, Oxford University Press.

1
Robert Walpole, First Earl of Orford – 'All These Men Have Their Price'

Despite his many qualities, Robert Walpole was not a particularly nice man. This is hinted at by the somewhat unwieldy title of the latest biography of him to appear, *The Great Man: Sir Robert Walpole – Scoundrel, Genius and Britain's First Prime Minister* (by Edward Pearce), and is amply corroborated by its text. But being nice has not been highly correlated with competence in high office: if it were, Lord Aberdeen would now rank higher than Gladstone, Baldwin higher than Churchill. Walpole was coarse, venal, ruthless and, at times, vindictive. Yet the fact that he was the longest serving, as well as the first, of Britain's 53 prime ministers (to date) strongly suggests that he was also one of the more effective.

Walpole was descended from a long line of country squires, who had been landowners in North Norfolk for 400 years. It was never one of the more prominent Norfolk families, but Robert's grandfather, Edward Walpole, a strong Royalist, was knighted at the restoration of Charles II in 1660 and was elected to the 'Cavalier' Parliament. He died prematurely, in 1667, leaving a 17-year-old son, Robert, to manage and extend the family estate, which he did to good effect, raising the annual rent-roll from £750 to £2500 over his lifetime. The elder Robert, usually known as Colonel Walpole because of his service in the Norfolk militia, was also knighted like his father, and for the last 11 years of his life represented the nearby constituency of Castle Rising in the House of Commons, thanks partly to the sponsorship of the Duke of Norfolk and his brother, Thomas Howard, who largely controlled the nomination for the seat. A man of some learning, he built up a notable library at his house at Houghton, and his wife, Mary Burwell, the daughter of another – more affluent – Norfolk squire, also had intellectual tastes. They had 17 children, 8 of whom died in infancy. The younger Robert Walpole, who was the fifth child and third son, was born at Houghton on 26 August 1676. Intended, as a younger son, for the Church, he was sent to board at the age of six, with the Rev. Richard Ransome, who ran an elementary school at Great Dunham, Norfolk, from where he proceeded to Eton, as a King's Scholar, at the age of 13, though his age was falsely listed as 12, so as to qualify for the scholarship. While at Eton, he became close friends with his cousin, Charles Townshend, the scion of a much grander Norfolk family, who inherited a viscountcy while still in his teens. Townshend was to marry Robert's sister, Dorothy, and was later to become an important influence in his brother-in-law's political career. In 1696, at the age of 20, Robert went up to King's College, Cambridge, but resigned his scholarship two years later, when his elder brother Edward died, and his father summoned him home to run the family estates. He was now his father's heir, the second son – Burwell, a naval cadet – having died in 1690, aged 14, at the Battle of Beachy Head, in which the French defeated the combined Anglo-Dutch fleet. All thoughts of entering the Church were now quickly forgotten, and when Colonel Walpole died suddenly, on 18 November 1700, his son moved quickly to ensure that he took over his parliamentary seat. Within a week he had secured the backing of Thomas Howard, for what was expected to be an early by-election. A general election intervened, however, and in January 1701, he and Howard were elected unopposed as the two MPs for the borough. Howard was a Whig, as Walpole's father had been, and the new 24-year-old MP wore the same party colours.

Six months earlier, Walpole had got married to the 18-year-old Catherine Shorter, daughter of a Baltic timber merchant, from Kent, who had aristocratic connections through her mother. It was effectively an arranged marriage, Colonel Walpole having searched far and wide for a suitable consort for his son, who would bring in a sizeable dowry, and consolidate his social position. Yet Walpole was undoubtedly in love with his new wife, who was described by Walpole's first biographer, Archdeacon Coxe, writing in 1797, as 'a woman of exquisite beauty and accomplished manners' (Taylor, 2004). It did not, however, turn out to be a successful marriage. Catherine's extravagant tastes matched those of her husband's, and he soon got deeply into debt, not least because soon after inheriting Houghton Hall from his father, he embarked on extensive improvements to the house, which he was later to pull down to erect a far grander Palladian mansion in its place. Most of the time, however, he spent in London, where the couple lived, initially, in an apartment in Berkeley Street, in the house of Catherine's grandmother, Lady Philipps, where they entertained on an impressive scale. Catherine produced two sons and two daughters during the first six years of their marriage, but after that they drifted apart, both having numerous affairs. It was widely suspected that Robert may not have been the father of Catherine's fifth child, Horace Walpole (the noted author and aesthete), born in 1717, though he acknowledged him as his son.

As a young MP, Walpole soon established himself as an up-and-coming man. He was rapidly accepted in leading Whig circles, largely through the influence of his schoolboy friend, Charles Townshend, already the Lord Lieutenant of Norfolk, and of his wife's aristocratic relatives. He was also to benefit from his connection to Sir Charles Turner, who had married his elder sister Mary. Turner's father, Sir John, a wealthy wine merchant, was the 'proprietor' of the two King's Lynn parliamentary seats, which he jointly represented with his son, Charles. As a favour to the Turners, Walpole, who soon mastered the procedures of the House of Commons, undertook the arduous task of steering through Parliament a Private Bill establishing a workhouse at King's

Lynn. This proved a farsighted move, when, in 1702, he was forced to seek a new constituency. He desperately needed to raise money to pay his debts, and required the consent of his Uncle, Horatio Walpole, who was a trustee of his father's estate, to sell family property in Suffolk. Horatio agreed to this only on condition that he could take over his seat at Castle Rising. To this, Walpole reluctantly agreed, even though Horatio was a Tory, but Sir John came to his rescue, standing down at King's Lynn, which enabled Walpole to share the borough's representation with Charles Turner. They were returned unopposed, as Walpole was on 16 subsequent occasions. At two general elections, those of 1701 and 1710, however, he also contested the much more prestigious county constituency of Norfolk, but lost each time to Tory opponents.

The general election of 1702 was consequent on the death of William III, and the accession of Queen Anne. Unlike William, who was predisposed to the Whigs, the new Queen was known to favour the Tories, who obtained a significant majority in the election, leading to the eviction of Whig ministers from the government, which continued to be led by the virtually non-party Sidney (now Lord) Godolphin, as Lord High Treasurer. As most of the more prominent Whigs – including the surviving members of the 'Junto' who had dominated the government for much of William's reign* – were in the House of Lords, there was a dearth of talent on the Whig benches of the Commons, and Walpole soon assumed a prominent role. This was not only because of his superior debating skills and his easy mastery of parliamentary procedure but also because of his high popularity, which spread far beyond his core following of Whiggish Norfolk squires. As the historian Geoffrey Holmes put it:

> The young Robert Walpole was a man of easy temper and almost limitless good humour, endowed with what James Brydges [Paymaster-General in 1705–13] once called 'the most friendly nature I have known'. (Holmes, 1967, p.231)

Walpole became a particular protégé of one of the 'Junto' lords,* Edward Russell, Earl of Orford, and his already close relationship with the steadily rising Lord Townshend was further consolidated when, in 1705, he and Catherine moved into larger premises, in Dover Street, and invited his younger sister Dolly, 20 years old and a noted beauty, to stay with them for the winter season. She immediately attracted the

---

* The five 'Junto' lords, three of whom were unsuccessfully impeached by their Tory opponents in 1701, were the Marquis of Wharton, the Earl of Orford, the Earl of Sunderland, the Earl of Halifax and Lord Somers.

attention of a number of notorious rakes, including another 'Junto' lord, the Marquis of Wharton. Catherine quarrelled with her, and she took herself off to the Wharton household, where Lady Wharton was well known for condoning her husband's infidelities. A furious Walpole raced round to Wharton's house, and peremptorily removed his sister, lodging her instead with the Townshends. Lady Townshend died soon afterwards, and within two years Townshend made Dolly his second wife. Townshend was also responsible for enrolling Walpole into the exclusive Kit-Cat club, the apex of Whig 'High Society'.

In the 1705 general election, the Whigs made extensive gains, finishing up on nearly equal terms with the Tories. Some prominent Whigs joined the Cabinet, and Walpole had his first taste of junior office, being appointed a member of the Council of the Lord High Admiral. This cabinet post was held by Prince George of Denmark, the Queen's husband, though the fleet was actually commanded by Admiral George Churchill, the brother of the Duke of Marlborough who, as Captain-General was the most powerful figure in the government. This appointment carried a salary of £1000 a year, which – though welcome – did not go very far towards relieving the debts, which both Robert and Catherine had accumulated due to their continuing extravagance. However, it brought Walpole into closer contact with leading governmental figures, including both Godolphin and Marlborough, who were impressed by his appetite for administration, and the clear and forthright way in which he expressed his views. He also continued to be an effective debater for the Whigs in the House of Commons, though there was some cooling of his relations with the 'Junto', who resented their continued exclusion from the cabinet, and who feared that Walpole was becoming a mere creature of Godolphin's. However, both Walpole and the Junto proved to be beneficiaries of the Act of Union with Scotland, forced through in 1707 against some resistance from the Tories. In the ensuing general election, in 1708, the Whigs were victorious, partly owing to their sweeping successes in the Scottish constituencies, and the Junto Lords returned to the Cabinet after an eight-year interval, while Walpole was appointed to the important post of Secretary-at-War, on the strong recommendation of Marlborough. In January 1710, he was appointed simultaneously to the post of Treasurer of the Navy, potentially a highly profitable office. This time – or so she claimed – it was at the strong urging to the Queen of Sarah, Duchess of Marlborough. Walpole thus assumed parliamentary responsibility for both the armed forces at a crucial period during the War of Spanish Succession.

Walpole took a prominent part in the impeachment proceedings against Dr Henry Sacherevell, a High Church and High Tory clergyman, who, in November 1709, preached a fiery sermon in St Paul's Cathedral in which he was held to have challenged the legitimacy of the Glorious Revolution and appeared to be advocating the claims to the throne of the 'Old Pretender', James Edward Stuart, the Catholic son of James II. Heavily applauded by his fellow Whigs, he made by far the most effective speech against Sacherevell in the Commons debate, which led to his trial before the House of Lords. A major *cause célèbre*, the move proved to be a serious miscalculation by the overconfident Whigs. A backlash soon built up in Sacherevell's favour: the London mob rioted on his behalf, he was widely seen as a martyr and even his strongest critics regarded the Commons' decision as an overreaction. When the case reached the House of Lords, which then had a strong Whig majority, their lordships took fright, and though they found him guilty, imposed only the mildest sentence. Public opinion swung against the Whigs, who were already losing support because of their insistence in continuing an unpopular war, and this finally emboldened the Queen to take decisive action against her increasingly over-bearing ministers. She had already replaced her long-standing friend and confidante, the Duchess of Marlborough, as her Chief Woman of the Bedchamber by the Tory-supporting Mrs Masham, and, in August 1710, she dismissed both Godolphin and Marlborough, forming a new and almost exclusively Tory government, led by Robert Harley (soon to become Earl of Oxford), with Henry St John (later Viscount Bolingbroke) as a Secretary of State. Walpole lost his post as Secretary-at-War, but continued for a few months more as Treasurer of the Navy, before resigning in sympathy with his fellow Whigs. No sooner was he in office, than Harley began secret negotiations with France, which led eventually to the Treaty of Utrecht, bringing an end to the war nearly three years later. A general election, held soon after, led to a crushing victory for the Tories, and Walpole, who chanced his arm by contesting, for a second time, the Norfolk county constituency, came bottom of the poll, though he was re-elected at King's Lynn.

The Tory government, after having unsuccessfully tried to tempt Walpole away from his fellow Whigs, soon proved nasty, and launched an investigation into his financial probity. The commissioners of public accounts reported to Parliament that he had accepted bribes from a friend, the banker Robert Mann, to whom he had awarded, while War Secretary, two lucrative forage contracts for the army in Scotland. He was expelled from the House of Commons and committed to the Tower of London in January 1712, a fate which actually seems to have given his political career a significant boost, as the historian Stephen Taylor suggests:

> Imprisonment turned Walpole into a national political figure and a Whig martyr. He was visited daily by the leading Whigs, a ballad composed in his honour described him as 'the Jewel in the *Tower* ... and at the King's Lynn by-election he was triumphantly returned, defeating a local Tory. The Commons promptly declared his re-election void. (Taylor, 2004)

He was released from the Tower in July 1712, and remained out of Parliament until the general election of 1713, when he was returned unopposed for King's Lynn. Whether he was guilty as charged is doubtful, but the fact that – like many other ministers in this period – he left office a much wealthier man than when he entered suggests that there were ample grounds for suspicion. On his return to Parliament, Walpole resumed his role as one of the leading Whig speakers, and was well placed to benefit from the discomfiture of the Tories, after the death of Queen Anne, in August 1714. The Tory leaders, including both Oxford and Bolingbroke, had compromised themselves by entering into correspondence with the Pretender, and George I was determined, from the outset, to govern only with the Whigs, pushing the Tories into opposition for a period which was to last for 48 years. His first administration was effectively headed by General James Stanhope, as one of the two Secretaries of State, the other being Townshend, Walpole's brother in-law. Three of the 'Junto' lords, Wharton, Halifax and Sunderland, were included in prominent posts, while Marlborough regained his position as Captain-General, and sat in the Cabinet as Master of the Ordnance. Largely due to Townshend's advocacy, Walpole secured the highly lucrative post of Paymaster-General.

The new government, with Walpole taking the lead, lost no time in settling scores with its Tory predecessors. Oxford, Bolingbroke and the Duke of Ormonde (who had succeeded Marlborough as Captain-General in 1710) were impeached for treason. Ormonde and Bolingbroke fled to France, where the latter served for some time as Secretary of State with the Pretender, but Oxford was committed to the Tower. He was eventually acquitted when he came up for trial in 1717. No sooner had the three Tory leaders been impeached, than the 1715 Jacobite rebellion, in support of the Pretender, broke out in Scotland and Lancashire. It was easily defeated – the Pretender attracting very little support in the face of his refusal to give up his Catholic religion. Six peers had, however, assisted in the uprising, and Walpole, who had been promoted to First Lord of the Treasury and Chancellor of the Exchequer in October 1715, strongly urged their attainment and execution. George I, however, was inclined to clemency, and eventually only two of their number, Lords Derwentwater and Kenmure, were beheaded. Walpole made his implacable opposition to Jacobitism a central theme of his political career, and in truth was something of a 'witch-hunter'. He saw Jacobite plots everywhere, and cynically used the issue to discomfort his opponents, implying that all Tories – even those most publicly loyal to the Hanoverian succession – were Jacobites at heart.

Walpole remained a minister for three years – from August 1714 to October 1717 – during which time he accumulated a large sum of money, estimated by J.H. Plumb at over £100,000 (roughly equivalent to £20m today). He suddenly became one of the richest men in the country, paying off his enormous debts and later enabling him to pull down Houghton Hall and build a magnificent Palladian replacement, which he filled with a fantastic array of paintings and other artistic treasures. Most of these finished up in the hands of Catherine the Great of Russia, when his grandson, George, sold them off in 1779. Today, they form the core of the Hermitage collection in St Petersburg. Walpole was by no means the only minister in British history to make money for himself by managing the country's finances. Yet he did it on a more exorbitant scale than any of his predecessors or successors, and of Britain's 53 Prime Ministers, to date, he remains the only one who raised himself to plutocrat status by this means. During this period, Walpole was the principal ministerial spokesman in the Commons, especially after Stanhope took a peerage, becoming Viscount Stanhope of Mahon. Yet he was probably no higher than number five or six in the unofficial ranking order of ministers, coming behind Stanhope, Townshend, the Earl of Sunderland and perhaps one or two others. Due to ill health, he played little part in the passage of the Septennial Act, in 1716, though this legislation, which increased the parliamentary term of office from three years to seven, was later to prove a major factor in enabling him to remain in power as Prime Minister for a record 21 years.

Throughout his reign of nearly 13 years, George I, who remained Elector of Hanover, made lengthy periodic visits (seven in all) to his German dominions, causing some concern to his British subjects, many of whom felt he was subordinating British interests to those of Hanover. This was particularly true of the visit which he made between July 1716 and the following January, when he took Stanhope with him, and they were later joined by Sunderland. Hanover had joined Charles XII of

Sweden in the Great Northern War against Peter I of Russia, Christian V of Denmark and Augustus of Saxony-Poland, as George was hopeful of annexing new territories to his Electorate. Anxious to protect his rear, he sought an alliance with Britain's traditional enemy France, whose Regent following the death of Louis XIV, the Duke of Orleans, was happy to comply. Stanhope sent instructions to Townshend to negotiate such an alliance, which would also include the Netherlands. Townshend, who doubted the wisdom of the move, was somewhat dilatory in carrying it out. Stanhope, prompted by Sunderland, who lusted after Townshend's position as Secretary of State, wrote to him saying that the King wished to relieve him of the post and offering instead the Lord Lieutenancy of Ireland. Townshend reluctantly accepted, but was dismissed from this post a few months later, in April 1717, when he voted against a government bill in the Lords. Walpole then resigned in sympathy with his brother-in-law; his post as First Lord of the Treasury and Chancellor of the Exchequer being taken by Stanhope, while Sunderland and the essayist Joseph Addison became the two Secretaries of State. This was effectively a new government, known to history as the Stanhope-Sunderland administration. It was thoroughly Whig, but the Whigs were now split, as Townshend and Walpole carried their own faction, which included Lord Orford, William Pulteney, Paul Methuen and the second Duke of Devonshire, all former ministers, into opposition with them. The following three years were marked by growing bitterness between Walpole and Stanhope and Sunderland. He did everything he could to undermine their power in the hope of forcing his own return to office, while carefully avoiding giving gratuitous offence to the King.

In opposing the government, the Walpolites did not disdain from cooperating with the Tories on several occasions. They also benefited from the support of the Prince of Wales, the future George II, who was at odds with his father, and who encouraged his own band of supporters in the Commons to vote with the 'opposition Whigs'. One issue on which they succeeded in defeating the government was on the repeal of the Corporation and Tests Acts, dating from the reign of Charles II, which barred Protestant Dissenters (later known as Non-Conformists) from public office. The Whigs had traditionally been supporters of religious toleration, and Stanhope proposed a Bill to restore the Dissenters' rights, but Walpole – nothing if not an opportunist – calculated that the weight of opinion of the Church of England (which was vehemently opposed to repeal) was very much greater. He therefore sided with the Tories in opposing the government's measure, which it was forced to withdraw. A much more serious defeat for Stanhope's government was over the Peerage Bill of 1719. This was an attempt by Stanhope and his associates to perpetuate their rule by freezing the current membership of the House of Lords, where they enjoyed a comfortable majority. In perhaps the outstanding parliamentary performance of his entire career, Walpole rallied the Commons to stand up for its own rights, which he maintained would be prejudiced by creating a permanent oligarchy in the Upper House, responsible to nobody, neither the electors nor, indeed, the King. Perhaps his conclusive argument, so far as many MPs were concerned, was his appeal to their own self-interest and ambitions. Walpole had already published a swingeing attack on the Bill in a pamphlet entitled *Thoughts of a Member of the Lower House,* in which he quoted the words of a typical 'country' Member: 'Shall I consent to the shutting the door upon my family ever coming into the House of Lords?' He returned to this theme in his speech. The result was a humiliating rebuff to Stanhope, whose Bill was defeated by 269 votes to 177, with the aid of numerous defections from normally loyal supporters of the government.

Stanhope concluded that in order to safeguard his ministry, he would have to lure back the opposition Whigs, and, in June 1720, both Townshend and Walpole, and a handful of their supporters, rejoined the government. Several of their prominent followers, however, notably William Pulteney, who had been Walpole's able 'lieutenant' in the Commons, were left out, much to their chagrin. Even Townshend and Walpole had to content themselves with more menial offices than they had held before. Townshend now became Lord President of the Council, but Walpole was fobbed of with the Paymaster-Generalship, a lucrative but not very senior post. Their position in the government was not a strong one – they were deeply distrusted by both Stanhope and Sunderland, and also – to some extent – by George I.

It now appeared as if Stanhope, who enjoyed the full confidence of the King, was set to remain in power for many years. If this had been the case, he – and not Walpole – would almost certainly have gone down in history as Britain's first Prime Minister. It was not to be – largely because of the events which came to be known as the 'South Sea Bubble'. The South Sea Company had been established in 1711, with the support of Harley (Oxford), and was initially seen as a Tory rival to the Whig-sponsored Bank of England and East India Company. It was assured of large profits by the Treaty of Utrecht (1713), which awarded Britain the *assiento* (the monopoly of the slave trade with Spanish America) and the right to send one ship a year to trade with the Spanish colonies. In

February 1720 Parliament approved a measure, promoted by Stanhope and Sunderland, designed to reduce the rate of interest on the National Debt, which had become a heavy burden as a result of the two long wars against France. The proposal was that three-fifths of the debt should be converted into South Sea Company stock, the remainder being held by the Bank and the East India Company. The directors of the South Sea Company proceeded to 'talk up' the value of their stock, which led to a feverish bout of speculation, in which many other new companies of doubtful provenance were formed, and their shares also were snapped up by large numbers of people anxious to get rich quick. Many already wealthy people, including George I, who invested, and lost, the enormous sum of £56,000 (over £11million in today's money), also bought into the Company, seeing their investments rise to dizzy heights, and then fall vertiginously when, inevitably, the bubble burst. The directors of the company paid bribes to ministers and court officials on a large scale and were undoubtedly guilty of a wide range of fraudulent practices.

Thousands of people were ruined, and some, at least, of those who had profited illegally from their transactions now had to face the reckoning. The House of Commons took the lead in demanding retribution, not least on those who were themselves Members of the House. Chief among these was the Chancellor of the Exchequer, John Aislabie, who was expelled from the House and sent to the Tower of London, after the passage of a motion that he had been guilty of 'most notorious, dangerous and infamous corruption'. He was stripped of all his ill-gotten gains, though he was eventually allowed to keep all the property he had owned before becoming Chancellor, and retired to live quietly on his estate in Yorkshire. The Postmaster-General, James Craggs the elder, committed suicide when faced with criminal charges, while his son, James Craggs the younger, one of the two Secretaries of State, who was also deeply implicated, fortuitously died of smallpox at the same time. William Stanhope, the Secretary of the Treasury, escaped censure by only three votes after George I had intervened on his behalf. His cousin James Stanhope, the effective leader of the government, was less lucky. Though himself innocent of any wrong-doing, he faced fierce criticism in the House of Lords, and burst a blood vessel while making an impassioned speech in his own defence, dying of a stroke shortly afterwards.

The chief beneficiary of the 'Bubble' was undoubtedly Walpole, who had originally strongly opposed the scheme to sell off the National Debt to the Company, though he had then unwisely invested in it and narrowly avoided financial ruin when his banker failed to act on his instructions sharply to increase his stake a few days before the final crash. He was called in by George I to resume his earlier posts as First Lord of the Treasury and Chancellor, and calmly proceeded to introduce measures to restore some stability to financial markets. Their apparent success greatly added to his reputation, and he was now seen for the first time as one of, if not yet *the*, leading ministers of the King. Walpole did not restrict himself to trying to restore the damage to the national finances, but also sought, wherever possible, to protect the reputations of fellow ministers and royal courtiers suspected of accepting bribes from the Company. Chief among these was his great rival, John Spencer, the Earl of Sunderland, who aspired to take over James Stanhope's role at the head of the government. Sunderland was very close to the King, and Walpole presumably calculated that it would do him no harm in the King's eyes if he threw him a lifebelt. Accordingly, when Sunderland was charged with corruption before the House of Commons, Walpole sprang to his defence, and in a brilliant speech – on 15 March 1721 – secured a vote for acquittal by 233 votes to 172. For this, and several other efforts which he made to 'screen' suspected villains, Walpole acquired the nickname of 'Skreenmaster-General'. This did him no good with the more high-minded Whigs, but won him invaluable support in high places. Then in April 1722, Sunderland suddenly died, which removed another serious rival from his path. There were now only two other ministers who might challenge his seniority in the government. These were the two Secretaries of State, Townshend and John, Lord Carteret, the very able former Ambassador to Sweden, who had negotiated an end to the Great Northern War in 1719–20. An excellent linguist, Carteret was on the inside track with George I, with whom he was able to converse in fluent German.

Traditionally, Walpole's period as 'Prime Minister' has been dated from his appointment, for the second time, as First Lord of the Treasury, on 3 April 1721. By this reckoning, his total time as PM was almost 21 years. In reality, his primacy was established only later, perhaps after both these ministers had resigned, or been ejected from the government, Carteret in 1724, and Townshend in 1730, though the death of Sunderland, on 19 April 1722, has also been suggested as a plausible date (see Plumb, 1956, p.378, and Taylor, 1998, pp.3–5). Where Walpole was pre-eminent, right from the beginning, was in the House of Commons, where he had no rival. (Indeed, throughout his period in office he was either the only Cabinet minister in the Commons, or – at most – shared this distinction with only one other.) Walpole was adamant that he must lead the government from the Commons, and strongly resisted pressure from George I to accept a peerage. In 1724, however, he persuaded the monarch to bestow the honour instead on his eldest son, Robert, who became Baron Walpole of Walpole.

Initially, Walpole's relationship with George I was rather distant, but he set himself assiduously to earn the goodwill of his monarch. This was greatly assisted by his assiduity in pursuing Francis Atterbury, the Bishop of Rochester, who was involved in a plot to assist a Jacobite invasion in 1722, led by the Duke of Ormonde. The plot came to nothing, and the case against Bishop Atterbury was too slender for him to be prosecuted for treason. Instead, Walpole introduced a 'bill of pains and penalties' into Parliament, for the passage of which it was only necessary to secure a parliamentary majority rather than submitting the partly manufactured evidence, which Walpole had assembled, to a court of law. The vote went against Atterbury, and he was stripped of his bishopric and exiled to Brussels, and then to France, where he shortly entered the service of the Pretender, thereby virtually acknowledging his guilt. Within the ministry, a largely silent struggle began for influence with the King, pitching the Townshend–Walpole faction against the followers of the late Earl of Sunderland, of whom the effective leader was Carteret. The two Secretaries of State, Townsend and Carteret, were jointly responsible for foreign policy and fierce rivalry opened up between them. They openly quarrelled over relations with both France and Russia, and particularly over plans to marry off the daughter of the King's mistress, the Countess Von Platen, into a leading French aristocratic family. Carteret's protégé, the British Ambassador to the French court, Sir Luke Schaub, was blamed by George I for mishandling the negotiations and was dismissed in April 1724, and replaced by Walpole's younger brother Horatio, while Carteret himself was sacked two months later, but was compensated by being appointed Lord Lieutenant of Ireland.

William Pulteney, who had been Walpole's chief supporter in the House of Commons was grievously disappointed not to have been appointed to replace Carteret as Secretary of State, and bitterly blamed Walpole for not using his influence on his behalf. Instead, Walpole successfully pushed the claims of the young Duke of Newcastle, whose initial appeal to Walpole rested largely on his control, as a landed grandee, of a string of several parliamentary constituencies. Walpole's neglect of Pulteney, as well as his hostility to Carteret, has often been attributed to his unwillingness to accept men of high talent as his colleagues, fearing that they would become serious rivals to him. Instead, he preferred men of rather lesser ability, on whose personal loyalty he could rely. Newcastle, and his more able younger brother, Henry Pelham, both of whom held senior posts throughout the remainder of Walpole's long period in office, were the most prominent of these. As for Pulteney, he became completely estranged from Walpole, and set himself up as the leader of a growing group of 'opposition' or 'country' Whigs, who consistently harassed the government in a similar fashion to Walpole's own conduct against Stanhope's administration in 1717–20. Pulteney received heavyweight support from Bolingbroke, who returned to Britain with a royal pardon in 1723, having broken with the Pretender. Walpole succeeded in maintaining Bolingbroke's exclusion from the House of Lords, but he remained an influential figure through his writings, particularly in the magazine *The Craftsman*, to which Pulteney was also a leading contributor, and which ceaselessly and pungently criticized the 'corruption' of Walpole's administration.

The corruption of which they complained was, above all, linked to his successful methods for obtaining and keeping control of the House of Commons. Every possible inducement was offered to those prepared to sell their votes – either at a constituency level – or within the Commons. As his latest biographer puts it:

> There had been places and placemen before, but Walpole was the most systematic and unfastidious player of that game electorally and inside the House of Commons itself... He operated a species of private interest/public expenditure mini-welfare state for anyone able to elect a Member or persuade one to vote right. (Pearce, pp.207, 383)

Nor did Walpole neglect the House of Lords, over whom he, in practice, exercised greater control than he was ever able to achieve in the Commons. Large number of peers were granted places or pensions either for themselves or for their relatives or friends, and Walpole for long achieved conspicuous success in 'fixing' the election of Scottish Representative Peers, who contributed 16 of the 200-odd members of the Upper House. Another 26 seats were held by Archbishops and Bishops, and Walpole was able to ensure, through his adviser on ecclesiastical appointments, Bishop Edmund Gibson, that virtually all bishoprics and other senior Church appointments went to convinced Whigs. By this means, Walpole was also able to counteract the influence within the Church of the lower clergy, the great majority of whom were Tories. The more ambitious of these soon learnt on which side their bread was buttered and moderated or dissimulated their opinions.

The expression 'every man has his price' has been widely attributed to Walpole, who was undoubtedly a cynic of a high order. His actual words, referring to a specific group of opposition MPs were 'All these men have their price.' In partial mitigation, it should be remembered that this was nearly 200 years before MPs were paid a salary, and long before peers received attendance allowances. Many upright citizens at that time took the view that it was acceptable for them to make some profit from their political activities. It would be a mistake, however, to conclude that it was only through corruption that Walpole was able to maintain his parliamentary primacy for so long. At no time did he have an assured majority in the Commons, where a substantial number of Members did not have any firm party allegiance or venal motive for supporting the government. Time and again Walpole was able to win the support of a majority of these 'independent' members, through his persuasive if seldom brilliant oratory, his commonsense arguments and the trouble he took to maintain good relations with even the humblest of MPs. Most of these were country squires, and Walpole presented himself as a typical plain, blunt Norfolk squire, more interested in hunting and shooting than in intellectual pursuits.

Walpole characterized himself as 'no saint, no Spartan, no reformer'. His policy objectives were relatively modest, and have been best summarized as 'security, stability and low taxation' (O'Gorman, 1997, p.80). The key to all three of these was, in Walpole's view, peace, and the need to keep Britain out of foreign conflicts, following the almost continuous two decades of war against France after the 'Glorious Revolution', which had left the country a heavy burden of debt. Throughout the 1720s, Townshend as Secretary of State was primarily responsible for conducting foreign policy, but initially at least, he and Walpole were at one in their desire to maintain peace and to prioritize the pursuit of friendship with Britain's traditional enemy France, with whom a treaty of alliance had been signed, under Stanhope, in 1717. The maintenance of peace enabled Walpole to concentrate on economic and financial improvements, and to abate the heavy level of taxation which he had inherited. Deft management of the national debt (including the establishment of a 'sinking fund', some half a century before the Younger Pitt adopted the same device to help reduce the large accumulated debts from the American War of Independence) allowed him to reduce the interest paid by the government from 5 per cent to 4 per cent. During his ministry the total debt was reduced by £6.25 million, and the annual interest charge fell from £2.57 million to £1.89 million (Taylor, 2004). He was particularly anxious to reduce the Land Tax, which bore heavily on his own class of country landowners, and he sought to achieve this by reducing public expenditure, cracking down on smuggling and transferring the tax burden from direct to indirect taxation. In 1731–32, he was able to bring the Land Tax down to 1s. in the pound, the lowest it had ever been since its introduction under William III. (Prior to this it had fluctuated between 2s. and 4s. in the pound.) He was only able to achieve this by re-imposing a salt duty, which affected everybody, but bore down most heavily on those with the smallest incomes.

In the final years of George I's reign, he came more and more to depend on Walpole, and their relations became much warmer. In 1725, he was made a Knight of the Bath, and two years later, of the Garter, the large star of which he proudly bore on his breast in all the numerous portraits which were painted of him. By contrast, however, the Prince of Wales, who was often (like most Hanoverian heirs to the throne) at loggerheads with his father, and ran an 'alternative' court based at Leicester House (the site of the modern Leicester Square), became increasingly hostile to him. Walpole, however, was careful to build up a good relationship with his shrewd and highly intelligent wife, Caroline of Brandenburg-Anspach. Other ambitious politicians made the mistake of cultivating instead the Prince's mistress, Henrietta Howard, whose influence over the Prince did not extend beyond the bedchamber. When George I unexpectedly died, aged 67, during a visit to Hanover, on 11 June 1727, the general expectation, shared by Walpole himself, was that the new King George II would rapidly dispense with his services. This seemed to be confirmed when he received a cold message from the King to 'Go to Chiswick and take your directions from Sir Spencer Compton.' Compton, who was more of a courtier than politician, was Speaker of the House of Commons, and had been Treasurer to the Prince of Wales. It was certainly the King's intention to appoint him in Walpole's place, but he failed abysmally to live up to expectations. Asked to draft the King's declaration to the Privy Council on ascending the throne, he found this beyond his capacity and called in Walpole to do it for him. The King also sought Walpole's advice on seeking parliamentary approval for a new Civil List, and was delighted when Walpole proposed that he should ask for £800,000 a year – £100,000 more than what his father had received – plus £100,000 for the Queen. Within three weeks, Compton threw in his hand, and Walpole's government was confirmed in office, with Compton (who was created Lord Wilmington), later becoming Lord Privy Seal, and then Lord President of the Council. Walpole's survival was generally attributed to Caroline's spirited pleas to her husband, who – spurning her as a lover – was the more disposed to follow her advice on public affairs.

The early years of George II's reign proved to be the zenith of Walpole's power and influence. One mark of this was his eclipse of Townshend, who, from being his close friend and sponsor, had sometimes become a fractious rival, particularly the death of Dolly Townshend, in 1726, severed their warm familial relationship. Walpole is reported by Lord Macaulay as saying: 'The firm is now going to be the firm of Walpole and Townsend, and not the firm of Townshend and Walpole as it used to be.' On one occasion the two men actually came to blows and even put their hands on their swords, only to be restrained by onlookers. Their views on foreign policy also began to diverge gradually, Townshend believing that the new alliance with France should take preference over all other considerations, even to the extent of siding with her against Britain's traditional ally, Austria. This Walpole, and Townshend's fellow Secretary of State, the Duke of Newcastle, refused to do, and they succeeded in over-ruling him, with the support of the Queen, leading to Townshend's resignation in 1730. He retired to his Norfolk estate, where he spent the eight remaining years of his life in pioneering experiments in crop rotation, earning himself the nickname of 'Turnip Townshend'. Walpole seized his opportunity, and persuaded George II to appoint one of his own cronies, Lord Harrington, in his place. He even prevailed upon the reluctant King to dismiss Carteret from his post as viceroy (Lord Lieutenant) of Ireland, and from now on the ministerial team consisted predominantly of Walpole's men. His closest collaborators were the Pelham brothers – the Duke of Newcastle continuing as the other Secretary of State, and Henry Pelham, the only other cabinet minister in the Commons, as Paymaster-General. It was now that Walpole became a popular public figure, much better known than any other politician, and his features became generally familiar, owing to the new vogue of publishing prints, whose display in shop-windows meant that they were seen by many more people than actually purchased them. He was widely dubbed as 'the Great Man', not altogether an ironic comment on his wide girth, and the term of 'Prime Minister', previously employed pejoratively by his critics, and those of earlier dominant ministers, such as Godolphin and Harley, now became a more neutral description, used as much by his friends as his enemies.

George II, essentially a lazy man, who took little interest in administration, and who was mainly interested in military and foreign affairs, as well as in his beloved Electorate of Hanover, came to depend heavily on Walpole, and strongly backed him, despite his initial dislike. One of their few disagreements was over the War of Polish Succession, which broke out in 1733, with France backing the claims of Stanislaw

Leszcynski, the father-in-law of Louis XV, while Austria and Russia supported Augustus II of Saxony. Britain was obliged to go to the support
of Austria, under the Treaty of Vienna, signed in 1731, and George II
was anxious to do so, sensing the possibility of adding to his German
dominions at the expense of other German states allied to France. There
was also considerable backing in Parliament for British intervention, not
only from Tories but also from many Whigs. Yet Walpole was adamant
that no British interest was involved in the conflict, and succeeded in
carrying the point. When the War ended within two years, Walpole was
able to boast that 50,000 had been slain during the conflict, but that
not a drop of British blood had been spilled. Augustus was confirmed
as King of Poland, but France and Spain both made territorial gains at
Austria's expense, including the Duchy of Lorraine, which was given to
Stanislaw as compensation for the loss of his throne, but was to revert
to France on his death.

Up until 1733, Walpole's reputation rested largely on his handling
of financial affairs, and his success in reducing taxation. In that year,
however, he overreached himself with his proposal to end customs
charges (largely circumvented by smuggling) on tobacco and wine
and the substitution of excise duties. This was substantially based on
his much earlier legislation concerning tea, coffee and chocolate. The
proposal was that all imports should be put into bonded warehouses
and only released when excise duties were collected. He estimated that
government revenue would increase by some £300,000 a year, helping him to keep the Land Tax low. Yet he seriously underestimated the
degree of opposition which his proposal would provoke. The tobacco
merchants, many of whom were deeply implicated in fraud, organized
a spirited campaign against his Tobacco Excise Bill, claiming it would
lead to a massive expansion of the Excise Service, with 'arbitrary powers of search', which would be an attack on 'English liberties' (Taylor,
2004). Their arguments resonated with many MPs, and Walpole saw
his parliamentary majority (normally over 100) plunge to a mere 17
votes on a motion to receive a petition against the Bill from the City of
London. He promptly dropped the Bill, a personal humiliation, from
which he extricated himself with some skill. He remained in office for
a further eight years, but in retrospect it appears as the first in a long
series of setbacks which eventually led to his downfall.

In the subsequent general election, of 1734, Taylor writes: 'There
is little doubt that, in what was one of the most contested elections
of the century, most of the electorate voted against Walpole's ministry' (Taylor, 2004). He was saved by the fact that most of the 'rotten

boroughs', in particular those in Cornwall and Scotland, returned MPs who were his supporters. His majority – just over 90 – remained substantially intact, but the opposition was clearly strengthened in the new Parliament, where it was reinforced by the election of several forceful younger MPs, such as William Pitt (later Lord Chatham) and his brother-in-law, George Grenville, both later prime ministers. It nevertheless remained seriously divided, and was seldom able to mount an effective challenge to Walpole in the Commons. Even on those occasions when it was able to pass Bills restricting the number of placemen in Parliament, Walpole was able to reverse the decision when the Bills reached the Lords.

Outside Parliament, the government's critics (both Tories and Opposition Whigs) had greater success in denting its reputation and that of Walpole, in particular. Their periodicals, notably but not only *The Craftsman*, were more lively and better written than those, often helped by lavish government subsidies, which supported Walpole, while most of the leading authors of the time, joined in lampooning the over-mighty Prime Minister, including Defoe, Swift, Pope, Fielding and Dr Johnson. He was ridiculed both as Peacham, and MacHeath in John Gay's *The Beggar's Opera*, and as Flimflam in *Gulliver's Travels*. They largely succeeded in implanting the notion that Walpole's rule was based on corruption, and dubbed his system of government 'the Robinocracy'. Nevertheless, some of Walpole's most inveterate enemies began to tire of the struggle. Bolingbroke packed up and went back to France in 1736, while Pulteney hedged his bets by hinting at a willingness to end his differences with Walpole in exchange for being re-admitted into the government. Despite this, no deal was, however, concluded.

In 1736, the system of personal support which Walpole had painstakingly constructed began to unravel. In arithmetical terms, the most serious was the undermining of his previous dominance over the Scots, which contributed largely to his majority in both Houses of Parliament. The trigger for this was a riot in Edinburgh, which had been forcefully put down by Colonel John Porteus, the commander of the Edinburgh city guard, whose soldiers fired on and killed six demonstrators. He was subsequently tried, found guilty of murder and sentenced to death, but received a royal reprieve. A mob then stormed the gaol in which he was held, seized him and hanged him in the street. Ministers then drew up a 'bill of pains and penalties' to punish the city of Edinburgh, which was toned down by Walpole, so that the only penalty actually imposed was the barring from office of the City Provost, Andrew Wilson. In the process, however, Walpole fatally alienated the Duke of Argyll and his brother, the Earl of Ilay, on whom he had previously relied for organizing the Whig electoral interest in Scotland.

Almost equally serious was the alienation of Frederick, Prince of Wales, who – like his father before him – was at daggers' drawn with both the King and the Queen – and was organizing an alternative court at Leicester House, to which opposition politicians flocked. His main disagreement with his father was over what he regarded as a mean provision for himself in the Civil List, but he widened this out into general opposition to government policies. As Duke of Cornwall, he controlled a large number of parliamentary boroughs in the county, whose MPs normally deferred to his wishes in casting their votes. In the same year, Walpole fell out with his close collaborator on Church affairs, Edmund Gibson, now Bishop of London, and with several other bishops, on whose support in the House of Lords he had previously depended. They were upset by three government bills, with which they disagreed, particularly the Quaker Tithe Bill, which was designed to give limited relief to members of the Society of Friends who suffered because of their conscientious objection to paying tithes to the Church of England. The Bill was defeated in the House of Lords, with all the bishops present voting against, and Gibson promptly resigned as Walpole's ecclesiastical adviser. The following year, Queen Caroline, who had been his strongest and most consistent supporter at Court, died. George II continued to favour Walpole, but no longer so firmly as hitherto. Another death occurred in 1737 – that of Walpole's long-estranged wife Catherine. After the minimum 'decent' interval – a mere six months – Walpole married a second time, to his long-time mistress, Molly Skerrett, who had borne him a daughter, Maria, 13 years earlier. Walpole was devoted to Molly, but they were to enjoy barely three months of marital bliss. She died in childbirth, in June 1738, aged 36. Walpole was devastated, and never fully recovered from his loss.

Yet the main factor leading to Walpole's eventual loss of power was the breakdown of his 'peace at any price' policy, which had left Britain dangerously isolated in Europe, after his refusal to take sides in the War of Polish Succession. In the following years tension built up between Britain and Spain, whose coastguards in the Caribbean enforced the right of search over British ships suspected of smuggling or piracy. Often the searches were carried out in a brutal fashion, with damage to British lives and property. British merchants began to petition the House of Commons for support, amid strident demands, led by the opposition Whigs, for war on Spain. The pressure became almost irresistible, when a Captain Robert Jenkins appeared before a committee of the House brandishing his own severed ear, which he alleged had been cut off by Spanish coastguards who had boarded his ship. Walpole sought to head off the demands by seeking an amicable settlement with Spain, which resulted in the Convention of Pardo, negotiated in January 1739. This was only narrowly passed in both Houses of Parliament. When the Convention broke down, with neither side having fulfilled all its obligations, Walpole could no longer resist pressure from his Cabinet colleagues and acquiesced in a declaration of war, in October 1739. The 'War of Jenkins' Ear', as it was popularly known, soon merged into the War of Austrian Succession, in which France, Spain and Prussia contended with Austria and Britain. It lasted until 1748, and ended with the inconclusive Treaty of Aix-la-Chapelle, the main consequence of which was the confirmation of 'great power' status for Prussia. Walpole grumpily refused to take responsibility for prosecuting the war, saying to the Duke of Newcastle, 'This war is yours, you have had the conduct of it, I wish you joy of it.' Nevertheless, the early stages of the war went very badly, and this inevitably contributed further to the attrition of Walpole's authority.

If there was a dominant issue in the general election which took place in the early summer of 1741, it was for or against 'Robin' Walpole. Heavy losses in Cornwall and Scotland, influenced respectively by the Prince of Wales and the Duke of Argyll, cut heavily into the government's nominal majority, which was now estimated at 16, with 23 seats vacant or contested, and to be determined by the Commons itself. The House was not due to meet until December, but already by the autumn there were credible rumours that senior ministers, notably Newcastle and Lord Hardwicke, the Lord Chancellor, were negotiating with Carteret and Pulteney to form a broader government, excluding Walpole. When Parliament did meet, Walpole with 'an impressive and memorable speech' (Taylor, 2004) just held off a motion for a secret committee to investigate the conduct of the war, which was effectively a motion of no confidence. But the margin was only 253 votes to 250, and within a couple of weeks he resigned, on 11 February 1742, following two defeats on an election petition concerning the Chippenham constituency. He had accepted a peerage, becoming the Earl of Orford, a title which he took over from his former 'Junto' mentor, who had died without surviving issue in 1727. He soon made clear his lack of esteem for the Upper House: meeting up with Pulteney who had been ennobled shortly after, he said 'My Lord Bath, you and I are now two as insignificant men as any in England' (Turberville, 1957, p.220).

Nevertheless, he used his influence with the King to secure a warrant recognizing the legitimacy of his daughter by Molly Skerrett, who was henceforth known as Lady Maria Walpole, and subsequently married into the Churchill family.

The removal of Walpole after more than two decades in office was an event of the highest public significance. The intrigues leading up to it were almost certainly parodied in the famous nursery rhyme, *Who killed Cock Robin?* the first written record of which dates from 1744 (Opie and Opie, pp.130–3). George II reverted to Sir Spencer Compton, now Lord Wilmington, his first choice in 1727, to replace Walpole as First Lord of the Treasury. He became the nominal head of the new government, but the dominant figure was Carteret, who reclaimed his place as a Secretary of State. Otherwise, the main posts continued to be held by Walpole's senior ministers. Pulteney, now the Earl of Bath, declined for the moment to serve, in the evident hope that he would eventually be asked to form a government of his own. Walpole retired to Houghton to live among the splendours of his art collection, but continued to bombard his former close associates, notably the Pelham brothers, with advice as to how they should conduct the government, and in particular on how to ensure that the succession, as Wilmington's health rapidly deteriorated, went to one of them rather than to Pulteney. In return, they exerted themselves to head off parliamentary enquiries designed to arraign the former Prime Minister for abuses of power and for enriching himself at the public expense. His health was not good, he suffered from kidney stones and he was weakened by responding to an appeal from the King to travel to London to advise him during a cabinet dispute between Carteret (now the Earl of Granville) and the Pelhams, which was resolved, before his arrival, by Granville's resignation, in November 1744 (see Chapter 3). Too ill to return to Norfolk, Walpole died at his London home in Arlington Street, Mayfair, from kidney failure, on 18 March 1745.

Modern readers instinctively recoil from Walpole's methods, but few would now deny that – within the limits he set himself – he was remarkably successful in achieving his aims of peace, stability and economy. He left the country – and the Hanoverian dynasty – in a much stronger position than he had found it. The relative ease with which it met the greatest challenge it had faced in nearly six decades – the 1745 rebellion of the Young Pretender – within a few months of his death is a tribute to the soundness of his policies. His claim to be accounted as the first Prime Minister has on occasion been questioned, but few can deny that he re-moulded and largely enhanced the office so that he was able to play the dual role of representing the King in Parliament and Parliament 'in the [royal] closet' (Holmes, 1974, p.46). His long tenure set a pattern which was to be followed by all his successors, even though few of them were as dominant as he. Perhaps the most perceptive estimate of his qualities was that made by a much later Prime Minister, and one who was far less successful, the Earl of Rosebery. Writing in his biography of the Elder Pitt, he wrote of Walpole:

> He had the advantage of being brought up as a younger son to work, and thus he gained that self-reliance and pertinacious industry which served him so well through long years of high office. From the beginning to the end he was primarily a man of business. Had he not been a politician it cannot be doubted that he would have been a great merchant or a great financier. And, though his lot was cast in politics, a man of business he essentially remained... His first object was to carry on the business of the country in a business spirit, as economically and as peacefully as possible... a hard-working man with practical knowledge of affairs and strong common sense; a sagacious man who hated extremes. He had besides the highest qualities of a parliamentary leader ... he had dauntless courage and imperturbable temper. (Rosebery, 1910, pp.144–6)

Works consulted

Black, Jeremy (2001), *Walpole in Power*, London, Sutton Publishing.

Cannon, John (2004), 'George II (1683–1760)', *Oxford Dictionary of National Biography*, Oxford, OUP.

Hill, Brian W. (1989) *Sir Robert Walpole: 'Sole and Prime Minister'*, London, Hamish Hamilton.

Holmes, Geoffrey (1967), *British Politics in the Reign of Anne*, London, Palgrave Macmillan.

Holmes, Geoffrey (1974), 'Sir Robert Walpole', in Herbert Van Thal (ed.), *The Prime Ministers*, Volume I, London, Allen & Unwin.

O'Gorman, Frank (1997), *The Long Eighteenth Century*, London, Arnold.

Opie, Iona and Opie, Peter (1973), *The Oxford Dictionary of Nursery Rhymes*, Oxford, Clarendon Press.

Pearce, Edward (2007), *The Great Man: Sir Robert Walpole – Scoundrel, Genius and Britain's First Prime Minister*, London, Jonathan Cape.

Plumb, J.H. (1956), *Sir Robert Walpole: The Making of a Statesman*, London, Cresset Press.

Plumb, J.H. (1960), *Sir Robert Walpole: The King's Minister*, London, Cresset Press.

Plumb, J.H. (1967), *The Growth of Political Stability in England 1675–1725*, London, Palgrave Macmillan.

Rosebery, Lord (1910), *Chatham*, London, A.L. Humphreys.

Taylor, Stephen (1998), 'Robert Walpole, First Earl of Orford', *Biographical Dictionary of British Prime Ministers*, London, Routledge.

Taylor, Stephen (2004), 'Walpole, Robert, First Earl of Orford (1676–1745)', *Oxford Dictionary of National Biography*, Oxford, OUP.

Turberville, A.S. (1957), *English Men and Manners in the 18th Century*, New York, OUP.

Wilson, Harold (1977), *A Prime Minister on Prime Ministers*, London, Weidenfeld & Nicolson.

2
Spencer Compton, First Earl of Wilmington – 'George II's Favourite Nonentity'

The man usually credited with having been Britain's second Prime Minister is a somewhat shadowy figure. No full-length biography of him has ever appeared, and most accounts of his career have largely depended on passing – and usually acerbic – references in the memoirs of such contemporaries as Horace Walpole, Lord Hervey, Lord Chesterfield and Mr Speaker Onslow. The almost unanimous conclusion has been that he was not really up to the job, and that he owed his preferment almost entirely to the inflated view which King George II held of his abilities.

Spencer Compton was born in 1673 – the exact date is unknown – at the family seat at Compton Wynyates, in Warwickshire. His father, James Compton, was the third Earl of Northampton, his mother being his second wife, Mary Noel, daughter of the third Viscount Camden. Altogether, there were ten children from the two marriages, most of whom died in infancy. Spencer was the youngest child, and of his siblings only his elder brother, George (who became the fourth Earl) and a sister, Mary, who was to marry the sixth Earl of Dorset, reached adulthood. The third Earl came from a wealthy family, long established in both Warwickshire and Northamptonshire, who were strong Royalists during the Civil War and afterwards. A fervent Tory, he died in 1681, but subsequent events pushed members of his family in the direction of the Whigs. One of the Earl's brothers became Bishop of London under Charles II, but joined in the movement to exclude the Catholic James, Duke of York, from the succession. When James II came to the throne, he suspended Bishop Compton, but he was reinstated under William III and Mary, and indeed was responsible for crowning the new King and Queen, when the Archbishop of Canterbury refused to take the oath of allegiance. Meanwhile, Spencer's brother, George Compton, the fourth Earl, had married into a leading Whig family, becoming the brother-in-law of Henry Fox (later the first Lord Holland, and the father of Charles James Fox). So the young Spencer grew up in a family with strong Tory roots, but with some at least of his close relatives now having Whig connections.

Very little is known of Spencer's childhood and youth. He was educated at St Paul's School, and Trinity College, Oxford, and enrolled at the Middle Temple, becoming a barrister. Aged 22, he contested the 1695 general election, as a Tory, at East Grinstead, but came bottom of the poll. Three years later, while travelling on the Continent, in an early version of the 'Grand Tour', he was elected unopposed, still as a Tory, in a by-election in the Suffolk constituency of Eye. This was a 'pocket' borough controlled by the Cornwallis family, and Spencer continued to represent it until 1710, though in 1701 he switched his allegiance to the Whigs, soon hitching his wagon to that of the rising young star, Robert Walpole, three years his junior.

A poor and pedantic speaker, Compton's parliamentary career soon prospered, however, due to the assiduity with which he mastered Commons procedures, his strong aristocratic connections and his ingratiating manner. In 1705, he was appointed chairman of the important Elections and Privileges Committee of the House of Commons, a key position as he was expected by the government, then led by Lord Godolphin, to ensure that the many disputed elections were normally settled in favour of the government's candidates. Two years later, while retaining the chairmanship, he achieved office as Paymaster of the Queen's Pensions, which he doubled up with acting as Treasurer to the household of Prince George of Denmark, the Queen's husband, who sat in the Cabinet as Lord High Admiral. In 1709, he was appointed, together with Walpole, to draw up the articles of impeachment against Dr Henry Sacheverell (see Chapter 1). Normally a mild-mannered man, he attacked Sacheverell with the greatest severity in several speeches, so much so that even his friends felt he had gone rather 'over the top'. One person who was displeased by Compton's performance was Lord Cornwallis, who withdrew his support in the Eye constituency, which meant that he was unable to contest the 1710 general election. So he was out of the House for three years, though the predominantly Tory government led by Edward Harley (later Lord Oxford) allowed him to retain his Paymaster's office. His other post with Prince George had lapsed, when the latter died in 1708.

Compton returned to Parliament in the 1713 general election, being returned unopposed for the East Grinstead constituency of Sussex, in which county he had recently acquired an estate. Two years later, in the general election following George I's accession, he contested one of the county seats, and – coming in second place – was elected as one of the two county MPs – more prestigious than sitting for a borough. Compton was disappointed not to be included in the Whig ministry appointed by the new Hanoverian king, but received ample compensation when he was chosen as Treasurer of the household of the Prince of Wales (later George II), as well as being elected as Speaker of the House of Commons, on 17 March 1715. This was largely a reward for his earlier work as Chairman of the Elections and Privileges Committee and a tribute to his mastery of parliamentary procedure. He continued as Speaker for 12 years, presiding with great dignity and punctiliousness and not a little self-importance. His much more distinguished successor as Speaker, Arthur Onslow, described him as 'very able in the chair...but [he] had not the powers of speech out of it' (Hanham, 2004). He was remembered for a famous put-down, when a Member complained of noisy interruptions, and claimed the right to be heard. 'No Sir', replied the Speaker, 'You have a right to speak, but the House have a right to judge whether they will hear you.'

Compton was put in a potentially invidious position in 1717, when a violent dispute between the Prince of Wales and his father coincided with a split in the Whig Party, leading to the exit from the government of Lord Townshend, Robert Walpole and several other leading figures, who then set themselves up as a Opposition faction, with the support of the Prince. Despite his position in the Chair, Compton proclaimed himself a supporter of the Opposition Whigs, but this did not seem to affect the acceptance of his authority by MPs as a whole. In 1721, Walpole was restored to office as First Lord of the Treasury and Chancellor of the Exchequer, but the Prince's feud with his father continued, and he again became openly hostile to the king's ministers, including Walpole. He made no secret of his intention to replace him, as Prime Minister, by his loyal treasurer when he should succeed to the throne. In the meantime, Walpole tried to buy Compton off, by supporting his re-election as Speaker in 1722, and appointing him, in addition, as Paymaster-General, a highly lucrative office, from which Compton was reputed to have made £100,000 over the next eight years. He was also appointed, on Walpole's recommendation, as a Knight of the Bath, in 1725.

When George I died during a visit to Hanover on 11 June 1727, it seemed as though Compton's hour had come. As recounted in Chapter I, Walpole hastened to Richmond to inform the Prince of Wales, bowing deeply and saying, 'I am come to acquaint your Majesty with the death of your father.' He was received coolly by the new monarch, whose only reply was: 'Go to Chiswick and take your directions from Sir Spencer Compton.' This Walpole did, and according to the memoirs of Lord Hervey, addressed Compton with great humility, saying:

> I put myself under your protection, and for this reason I expect you to give it. I desire no share of power or business; one of your white sticks, or any employment of that sort, is all I ask as a mark from the Crown that I am not abandoned to the enmity of those whose envy is the only source of their hate. (Sedgwick, 1931, vol. 1, p.23)

Compton proved himself incapable of rising to the opportunity which now opened out before him. Instructed by the new King to draft his declaration to the Privy Council on assuming the throne, he felt unequal to the task, and asked Walpole to do it for him. As his most distinguished biographer put it, 'Walpole took up the employment immediately retiring to another room, and naturally slipped in a charming and appreciative tribute to the ability of the late ministry' (Plumb, 1960, p.165). The first issue which had to be settled under the new reign was the size of the Civil List, for which Parliamentary approval would be sought. The King consulted Compton, who displeased him by suggesting that the new Queen's allowance should be set no higher than £50,000. He then discussed it with Walpole, who proposed to double the amount, and the King concluded that the retiring Prime Minister would have a better chance of obtaining a generous settlement from Parliament than his projected successor. Queen Caroline herself had spared no effort in persuading the King both of Walpole's abilities and of Compton's shortcomings, and within three weeks Compton concluded that the game was up, and withdrew himself from the King's counsels. He felt humiliated, and bore a lasting grievance against Walpole, which he was careful to conceal until the closing stages of Walpole's premiership more than a decade later.

Reinstated as the King's chief minister, Walpole hastened to placate Compton by nominating him for a peerage, and he became Baron Wilmington, which title was upgraded to an earldom in 1730. He was also made a Knight of the Garter, in 1733. He joined Walpole's cabinet as Lord Privy Seal, in May 1730 – probably at the King's behest, and on the last day of that year became Lord President of the Council, a post he held until 1742. Punctilious in his duties, in a low-key manner, he was outwardly loyal, but privately intrigued against Walpole on several occasions. A now wealthy bachelor, Wilmington never married, though, according to Horace Walpole's memoirs, he was 'a great lover of private debauchery'. He was reputed to have fathered several illegitimate children, one of whom – a daughter – was to marry James Glen, a Governor of South Carolina. His sister, Mary, was married to Charles Sackville, the sixth Earl of Dorset, who was close to him and apparently anticipated (wrongly) that he and his family would inherit Wilmington's fortune. Dorset's three sons were all in the House of Commons and, together with their father, constituted the bulk of the small parliamentary faction personally loyal to Wilmington. Despite Wilmington's ministerial office, he remained much more of a courtier than a politician, and his basic loyalty was to the King rather than Walpole. Indeed, he privately expressed the view that Walpole's use of his powers was excessive, and that 'the true interest of England was to have no chief minister...that every great office should be immediately dependent on the king and answer for it' (Egmont Diary, quoted by Hanham, 2004). Nevertheless, he continued to brood on his earlier humiliating failure and felt increasingly that if there had to be a chief minister it should be him.

When Walpole finally resigned, in February 1742, it was a severe blow to George II, an essentially lazy man who had grown used to his heavy dependence on the man who had been his chief minister throughout the (then) nearly 15 years of his reign. He was shocked that there was no longer a stable parliamentary majority available for Walpole, but wished to continue with his administration with the least possible disruption. He therefore resolved to keep the bulk of his ministers in place, but to recruit from the opposition sufficient additional support for them to retain power. Determined to maintain the exclusion of the Tories, he focused on two distinct groups of opposition Whigs – those associated with Lord Carteret and William Pulteney, and the followers of his estranged son, Frederick, Prince of Wales, with whom he now sought an accord. On the advice of the Duke of Newcastle, the senior of his two Secretaries of State, and of Lord Hardwicke, the Lord Chancellor, the post of First Lord of the Treasury was offered to Pulteney, who reluctantly declined, feeling bound by his previous declarations that he had not sought office for himself in pursuing his opposition to Walpole. Nevertheless, he agreed to cooperate in the formation of a new, broadened government, and evidently hoped that after a decent interval he would himself take over its leadership. Carteret had expected that Pulteney would support his own claims, but – recognizing his general unpopularity – he declined to do so, and George seized the opportunity of offering the post to the man who had long been dubbed his 'favourite nonentity'. Wilmington thus became First Lord of the Treasury, and nominal head of the government, but this role was effectively played by Carteret, who became – with Newcastle – a Secretary of State. The most able and decisive man in the cabinet, Carteret had the additional qualification of being close to the King, with whom he was able to converse in fluent German. Proud and disdainful, Carteret had a low opinion of the House of Commons, in which he had never served. The additional support in the Commons, from Pulteney's followers and those of the Prince of Wales (who had been bought off by an increase in his Civil List provision) amounted to 43 MPs, who became known as 'New Whigs'. No member of the Cabinet now sat in the Commons, and the effective leader of the House became Newcastle's younger brother, Henry Pelham, who was Paymaster-General. After a little while it was apparent that close liaison with the Commons was essential to the government's survival, and Pelham was invited to attend Cabinet meetings and became, in effect, one of its most influential members. Pulteney then made the crucial blunder of accepting a peerage, becoming the first Earl of Bath. His previous standing owed much to his being perhaps the most effective debater in the Commons, and his influence soon declined, as Walpole shrewdly anticipated, with his transfer to the Upper House. Moreover, he was now cut off from his former followers in the Commons, and many other 'opposition Whigs' were resentful that he had not also brought them into the governmental fold, so that they could share in the 'spoils'.

Wilmington himself had been in favour of a more 'broad-bottomed' government, bringing in not only all the Whig factions, but leading Tories as well, a view strongly held by the Duke of Argyll, previously a strong Walpolite and the leader of the Scottish Whigs, who had violently fallen out with his leader following the Porteus riots in Edinburgh in 1736 (see Chapter 1). Wilmington protested to the King about the narrowness of the government's base, and the promotion of Carteret without his being consulted, even threatening to resign, but without avail, and quietly reconciled himself to being merely a figurehead Prime Minister. Even his powers as the chief Treasury Minister were effectively removed from him, with the appointment of Samuel (later Lord) Sandys as Chancellor of the Exchequer (previously Walpole had combined both posts). Already 69, and in poor health – he suffered from kidney stones – his government had few achievements to its credit. The only significant Bill to be passed was the Place Act, of 1742. In a bid to restrict the government's powers of corrupting MPs, this excluded Members of Parliament from being appointed to various public offices.

Otherwise, apart from the passage of the Spirituous Liquors Act, of 1743, which increased the duties on spirits in an attempt to combat public drunkenness, overwhelming priority was given to Britain's participation in the War of Austrian succession. This had broken out in 1740, following the death of the Hapsburg Emperor, Charles VI. He had left no male heir, and his daughter, Maria Theresa, while recognized as Queen of Hungary, was not eligible to be elected Holy Roman Emperor, which title had been monopolized by the Austrian Arch-Dukes since the fifteenth century. In the hope of wresting Hapsburg territories in Germany and Italy, France, Spain, Prussia and Bavaria promptly attacked Austria, whose allies were Britain and Holland. George II took a keen interest in the war, his main concerns being to protect his Hanoverian electorate from French or Prussian attacks and his own desire for military glory. Skilful diplomacy by Carteret succeeded in establishing that Hanover would remain neutral in the conflict, but a large military force, known as the 'Pragmatic Army' made up of British, Austrian, Dutch, Hanoverian and Hessian troops was assembled in the Netherlands, under the personal command of George II. It crossed the Rhine and defeated the French army at Dettingen, in June 1743. George II, who exposed himself to great personal danger while fighting on foot, emerged as a hero from the battle, while Carteret discreetly observed the conflict from the comfort of his heavily upholstered coach at a respectful distance. Despite this victory, the war continued, with many ups and downs, for another five years, before it ended inconclusively, with the Treaty of Aix-la-Chapelle in 1748 (see Chapter 3).

Wilmington played no part in these stirring events. He was already a dying man, and expired at his house in St James's Square, while still in office, five days after the battle, on 2 July 1743. He was probably aged 70. Altogether, he had served for one year and 136 days. He was unlamented by most of his contemporaries, who seem to have had little respect for him, Lord Hervey's view being not untypical:

> A plodding heavy fellow with great application but no talents, and vast complaisance for a court without any address; he was always more concerned for the manner and form in which a thing was done than about the propriety or expediency of the thing itself. His only pleasures were money and eating; his only knowledge form and precedents; his only insinuations bows and smiles. (Bigham, 1924, p.30)

Nor has posterity been much kinder in its verdict. As previously noted, there has been no biography, but the fullest appreciation was penned, as long ago as 1924, by Clive Bigham, whose words of extenuation were strictly limited:

> Yet Wilmington filled for nearly thirty years the four highest places in the State to which a layman can aspire. He seems to have been honest, conscientious, well-meaning and precise, perhaps even loyal as the times went, but as to character and talents he was little more than a cipher. (Ibid., p.31)

In Britain, he is a totally forgotten figure, though in the United States there remain small sparks of fame. There are three places called Wilmington – in Massachusetts, North Carolina and Delaware. It is doubtful if many of their inhabitants know anything at all about the man after whom their home towns were named.

Works consulted

Bigham, Clive (1924), *The Prime Ministers of Britain 1721–1924*, London, John Murray.

Cannon, John (2004), 'George II (1683–1760)', *Oxford Dictionary of National Biography*, Oxford, OUP.

Cruickshanks, Eveline (1998), 'Spencer Compton, First Earl of Wilmington', in *Biographical Dictionary of British Prime Ministers*, London, Routledge.

Hanham, A.A. (2004), 'Compton, Spencer, Earl of Wilmington (c. 1674–1743)', *Oxford Dictionary of National Biography*, Oxford, OUP.

Hill, Brian W. (1989), *Sir Robert Walpole: 'Sole and Prime Minister'*, London, Hamish Hamilton.

O'Gorman, Frank (1997), *The Long Eighteenth Century*, London, Arnold.

Owen, John B. (1957), *The Rise of the Pelhams*, London, Methuen.

Plumb, J.H. (1960), *Sir Robert Walpole: The King's Minister*, London, Cresset Press.

Romney, Sedgwick (ed.), (1931), *Some Materials towards Memoirs of the Reign of King George II*, by John, Lord Hervey, three volumes, London, Eyre & Spottiswoode.

Van Thal, Herbert (1974), 'The Earl of Wilmington and the Carteret Administration under Wilmington', in Herbert Van Thal (ed.), *The Prime Ministers*, Volume I, London, Allen & Unwin.

3
Henry Pelham – Pragmatic Heir to Walpole

Henry Pelham is invariably listed as Britain's third Prime Minister, but a case can certainly be made that he was virtually the second, given the ineffectiveness of his predecessor as First Lord of the Treasury, the Earl of Wilmington (see Chapter 2). The offspring of a landed family based mainly in Sussex, which had sent representatives to Parliament continually since Elizabethan times, he was born in London on 25 September

1694. His father, Thomas, the first Baron Pelham, was married twice, and fathered 11 children, two from his first marriage, and nine from the second. Henry was the third son, and ninth child. The first son, John, was to die in infancy, but the second, also named Thomas, who was only 14 months his senior, was to play a crucial, and indeed determining, role in his life and career. Their mother, formerly Lady Grace Holles, was the daughter of the third Earl of Clare, and sister of John Holles, Duke of Newcastle. The brothers were unusually close and loved each other dearly, though this did not prevent them from having many disputes, or Thomas from becoming obsessively jealous of Henry, later in life.

Both brothers were educated at Westminster School, but Thomas then proceeded to Cambridge, while Henry enrolled at Hart Hall, Oxford, in September 1710, which he was to leave without taking a degree. Both his parents died when he was still young, his mother in 1700, when he was nearly five, and his father, in 1712, when he was not yet 18. His father left him £5000 and some small annuities, but the bulk of his large estate went to Thomas, who had already inherited a substantial fortune from his uncle, the Duke of Newcastle, on condition of changing his name to Pelham-Holles. Thomas was to inherit the Pelham barony from his father and later the Earldom of Clare from his grandfather. He provided Henry with an additional annuity of £1000 a year, and was to settle further sums on him on several subsequent occasions. The Pelham family were staunch Whigs, and strongly supported the accession of George I in 1714. The two brothers raised a troop of horse in Sussex during the Jacobite rebellion of 1715, and Henry went off to fight at the Battle of Preston. As a reward, the Newcastle dukedom, which had lapsed with his uncle's death without a direct male heir, was revived in Thomas's favour, and he attained the highest rank of the peerage at the age of 22. He was related by blood or marriage to many of the great Whig families, including that of Robert Walpole, and he consolidated these links in 1717, by marrying Lady Henrietta Godolphin, the granddaughter both of the Duke of Marlborough and of Queen Anne's former chief minister, Sidney Godolphin.

Thomas, who had immediately taken his seat in the House of Lords within days of his twenty-first birthday, now held property in no less than 11 counties, which gave him a strong influence in the representation of a large clutch of parliamentary constituencies. He lost no time in providing a 'pocket borough' for Henry, who was returned unopposed for the Sussex constituency of Seaford in a by-election in February 1717, at the age of 22. Henry, who had returned from an early version of the 'grand tour' to fight the seat, thus owed the opportunity of a political career entirely to his brother, and his wider family connections. His rapid promotion up the political ladder was also due primarily to the continued support of Thomas, who had quickly established himself as a leading Whig magnate.

Newcastle joined the government, jointly led by James Stanhope and the Earl of Sunderland, in April 1717, as Lord Chamberlain of the Royal Household, and in this capacity was able to appoint his brother as Treasurer of the Chamber, a junior ministerial post, three years later. This brought Pelham into close contact with Robert Walpole, who was Paymaster-General and later First Lord of the Treasury and Chancellor of the Exchequer. Walpole appointed Pelham as a Lord of the Treasury in 1721. He was deeply impressed by Pelham's administrative abilities, his discretion and his ability to argue the government's case in the House of Commons, virtually all the other ministers, apart from Walpole himself, being in the Lords. Something of the quality of the relationship which was to grow up between the two men was caught in the usually caustic memoirs of Lord Hervey, who – together with Horace Walpole – was one of the two leading contemporary chroniclers of politics during the reign of George II. 'Mr. Pelham', he wrote,

> was strongly attached to Sir Robert Walpole, and more personally beloved by him than any man in England. He was a gentleman-like sort of man, of very good character, with moderate parts, in the secret of every transaction, which, made him at last, though not a bright speaker, often a useful one; and by the means of a general affability he had fewer enemies than commonly falls to the share of one so high a rank. (Newman, 1974, p.63)

Both Newcastle's and Pelham's position was greatly strengthened in 1724, when Walpole succeeded in evicting the ambitious Lord Carteret from his post as one of the two Secretaries of State (see Chapter 1). These positions, regarded as the most senior posts in the government, after that of First Lord of the Treasury, were mainly concerned with Foreign Affairs, the Northern Department being responsible for relations with countries in Northern and Central Europe, and the Southern with the Mediterranean powers. Newcastle replaced Carteret (who was exiled to become Lord Lieutenant of Ireland), as Secretary of State (South), and became effectively the number three man in the government, after Walpole and Lord Townshend, who was Secretary of State (North).

Pelham was promoted to the post of Secretary at War, one of the most senior posts outside the Cabinet. Steps were also being taken at this time to ensure his financial security, and diminish his dependence on his brother. In the words of his biographer:

> As early as 1723 the solution was decided upon: Henry Pelham was to marry someone who would bring him a dowry of £30,000 in cash, which he could exchange for the family estates in Lincolnshire. Such a marriage was arranged in 1726 with the Duke of Rutland, who gave the required sum with his daughter, Lady Katharine Manners. The Lincolnshire estates, thus obtained, were the main financial resources of Henry Pelham and his family for the rest of his life, though the Duke of Newcastle often supplemented the income of his brother. It is interesting to observe that the marriage, contracted in this calculating manner, proved to be a supremely happy one. (Wilkes, 1964, p.3)

It was to produce six daughters and two sons, both of whom were to die, on successive days in 1739, from a throat infection, at the ages of ten and three – the greatest tragedy in Pelham's life.

Pelham was to remain a member of Walpole's administration for the whole of his period in power, becoming personally closer to him than any other minister. Walpole acted as his mentor, as well as his friend, and taught him everything he knew, so much so that by the time that he finally resigned in 1742, his pupil had completed, in his biographer's view, 'the most thorough preparation for office of any man of the eighteenth century'(Wilkes, p.25). In 1730, when Walpole reconstructed his ministry following the resignation of Lord Townshend (see Chapter 1), Pelham was appointed Paymaster-General to the Forces, a post he continued to hold until 1743. Traditionally, its holders used the office greatly to enrich themselves, which Pelham conspicuously failed to do. This earned him a reluctant tribute, after his death, from his long-time enemy, Horace Walpole (Sir Robert's putative son), who wrote: 'He lived without abusing his power, and died poor' (Wilkes, p.214). Although he remained outside the Cabinet, Pelham eventually became one of the most influential of Walpole's ministers, along with his brother, Newcastle, and Philip Yorke, Earl of Hardwicke, the Lord Chancellor. He was also his most loyal follower, opposing him only once during his 21 years as a minister, on the issue of reforming the national debt in 1737. Nor, unlike Newcastle (see Chapter 4) and other leading ministers, did he engage in any intrigues with opposition figures trying to displace Walpole during his declining years. Indeed, it was only through his gentle mediation between Walpole and Newcastle (both of whom trusted him implicitly) that he was able to prevent a breach between the two men.

Pelham was notably lacking in charisma, and came across as a pleasant, mild man, well organized and skilful in his handling of parliamentary colleagues. Beneath his bland exterior, lay steely determination and moral and physical courage. He almost fought a duel with William Pulteney after an altercation in the Commons, in 1732, and 'the next year he came boldly forward when quite alone and protected Sir Robert [Walpole] from the attack of a crowd of his opponents outside the House. He drew his sword and stood out, saying, "Now, gentlemen, who will be the first to fall?"' (Bigham, 1924, p.36). It was he who took the lead in defending Walpole from censure motions in the House of Commons in the final year of his premiership, and in heading off subsequent attempts to impeach him.

When Walpole finally resigned, in 1742, and was replaced by the ineffective Lord Wilmington as First Lord of the Treasury, Pelham was the only senior minister sitting in the House of Commons, and when Pulteney unwisely accepted a peerage, as the Earl of Bath, became its uncontested leader. He was still, initially, outside the Cabinet, and Carteret, who as Secretary of State (Northern), and an intimate of George II, dominated the government, strongly resented his growing influence. On one occasion, he expostulated: 'He [Pelham] was only a chief clerk to Sir Robert Walpole, and why should he expect to be more under me, I can't imagine: he did his drudgery and he shall do mine.' Nevertheless, as the man whose task it was to present the Cabinet's policies to the Commons it was illogical for Pelham not to be a member, and he was soon to be admitted, despite Carteret's objections. Within the Cabinet, he formed part of a triumvirate, along with his brother and Lord Hardwicke, who provided the strongest resistance to the overbearing Carteret. It was only a matter of time before there would be a decisive showdown between these three, supported from the outside by Walpole (now Lord Orford), who still had the King's ear, and Carteret, who was his undoubted favourite. A crucial moment came when Wilmington died, in July 1743. For almost two months, George II hesitated about appointing a successor as First Lord of the Treasury. Bath, backed by Carteret, aspired to the post, but the choice eventually fell on Pelham, the King having reluctantly decided that it was better to have somebody from the Commons. Newcastle outwardly supported his brother's promotion, but was clearly in two minds about it.

He regarded himself as the leader of the 'Old Corps' of Whigs who had dominated the Walpole government, and he did not enjoy the prospect of having to play second fiddle to his brother.

Pelham was appointed on 27 August 1743, but it was another year or two before he came to be regarded as 'Prime Minister', in the sense that Sir Robert Walpole had been. Before that could happen, two further conditions had to be met. He had to assert his dominance over Lord Carteret, and to win the full backing of George II. The first objective was made easier by the insensitivity of Carteret, who became the Earl of Granville, in October 1744. Basing himself entirely on his close relationship with George II, with whom he was able to chat cosily in German, he totally failed to build up a reservoir of parliamentary support and unnecessarily antagonized many would-be supporters by his apparent disdain. His conduct of the War of Austrian Succession, which Britain had joined in 1741, as a consequence of its existing struggle with Spain and France in the War of Jenkins' Ear (see Chapter 1), brought him great unpopularity, especially among landowning MPs. They blamed him for the high taxation which this brought, and also because they believed he was giving too much weight to the King's Hanoverian dominions at the expense of Britain's own interests. Granville's policies were relentlessly criticized in the Commons by, among others, William Pitt the Elder, the greatest orator of his day, and Pelham and his colleagues believed that it would no longer be possible to maintain a parliamentary majority unless he was removed from the Government. In November 1744, they persuaded a deeply reluctant George II to agree to the dropping of his favourite, and Pelham, who by now had – like Walpole before him – added the post of Chancellor of the Exchequer to that of First Lord of the Treasury was given (almost) a free hand in restructuring the government. He determined to form a 'broad bottomed' administration, bringing in as many weighty figures as possible from the former Opposition in order to ensure that – unlike under Walpole – the government's position would not be progressively undermined by parliamentary attrition. He even brought in a few Tories, mostly into fairly junior posts, but mainly he was instrumental in bringing in 'dissident' Whigs, including the followers of such influential grandees as the Duke of Bedford, the Earl of Chesterfield and Lord Cobham. Pelham wanted to include William Pitt, but George II, inflamed by his earlier attacks on Hanover, refused to countenance this.

The King greatly resented the formation of a government containing so many of his erstwhile critics, and withheld full confidence from them, continuing to consult with Granville, whom he hoped to be able to restore to office at an early date.

It was this government which had to contend with the 1745 Jacobite uprising. This began on 22 June 1745, with the landing on the Hebridean island of Enniskay of 'Bonnie Prince Charlie', the elder son of the Old Pretender, James Edward Stuart. Accompanied by seven followers, and a consignment of arms and ammunition supplied by the French, he made his way to the mainland and soon raised mass support among the Highland clans, capturing Edinburgh on 17 September, and defeating a British force under Sir John Cope at Prestonpans four days later. The Scottish authorities, led by the Secretary of State, Lord Tweeddale, the only supporter of Granville remaining in the Cabinet, grossly underestimated the danger and totally failed to take adequate steps to contain the uprising. General panic now afflicted the government, as fears raged of a French invasion across the Channel in support of the Jacobites, but Pelham kept his head and calmly decided that salvation would come through the withdrawal from Flanders of the powerful British army led by the King's younger son, the Duke of Cumberland. The Duke was highly reluctant, but eventually returned with ten battalions and marched north to face the troops of the Pretender. By then Charles Stuart had squandered his great opportunity by wasting several weeks in elaborate celebrations in Scotland, before crossing the border into England. It was 4 December before his exhausted troops reached Derby, a mere 128 miles from London, but – disheartened by the absence of either an English uprising or a French invasion – they then turned back in the hope of consolidating Stuart rule in Scotland. Cumberland set off slowly in pursuit, and despite reverses at Penrith on 18 December, and Falkirk on 17 January 1746, totally routed the Pretender's army at Culloden, on 16 April 1746. Earning himself the sobriquet of 'Butcher' Cumberland, the Duke then proceeded brutally to suppress the Highland clans, one of the most disreputable episodes in British military history. Pelham strongly disapproved of Cumberland's actions, but was determined to prevent any recurrence of Jacobite activity north of the border. He embarked on a programme of 'carrots' and 'sticks', the former being a policy of clemency towards the survivors of the uprising, the latter a substantial centralization of the Scottish legal system, depriving clan chiefs of their hereditary jurisdictions. Only two treason trials were held of the Pretender's chief supporters. One was of the Earls of Kilmarnock and Cromarty, and of Lord Balmerino. All were found guilty, but Cromarty was reprieved as a sign of the King's mercy. A separate trial was held later for Simon, Lord

Lovat, who had earlier been reprieved for his role in the 1715 uprising. This time he was less lucky. Found guilty by a unanimous vote of the House of Lords, by 117 votes to 0, he was the last person in Britain to suffer death by beheading. With his death, the Jacobite cause expired, and an issue which had lingered on for nearly six decades was finally laid to rest. One consequence was a boost to the standing of the Tories, who had long suffered from the taint of Jacobitism, sedulously spread by Walpole and other leading Whigs. The fact that not a single prominent Tory declared for the Pretender meant that this was no longer a tenable accusation.

In February 1746, Pelham and his closest colleagues had decided that it was now essential to reinforce the government by including William Pitt, preferably as Secretary at War. When George II, egged on by Lord Bath, refused to contemplate this, the Cabinet decided, at a secret meeting on 9 February 1746 to force the issue by collective resignation. Next day, Newcastle and his fellow Secretary of State, Lord Harrington, submitted their resignations, followed by Pelham and a bevy of other ministers a day later. The King responded by appointing Bath to replace Pelham, and Granville in place of both Newcastle and Harrington, and invited the two men to form a new government. Their attempt to do so proved farcical – they failed to recruit men of sufficient standing to fill the other Cabinet offices, their following in the Commons was derisory and the City of London made it clear that little financial support would be forthcoming for a government not led by Pelham. The 'Bath government' was stillborn, and within two days George II was pleading with Pelham and his colleagues to come back. A contemporary satire, entitled *A History of the Long Administration,* concluded with the words:

> And thus endeth the second and last part of this astonishing Administration which lasted 48 hours and 3 quarters, seven minutes and eleven seconds; which may truly be called the most honest of all administrations; the minister to the astonishment of all wise men never transacted one rash thing; and, what is more marvellous, left as much money in the treasury as he found in it. (Wilson, 1977, p.11)

In a masterstroke, Pelham and his colleagues insisted that they resumed office on their own terms, and not those of the King. In a secret meeting on 13 February, held in the house of the Duke of Dorset, the Lord President of the Council, they drew up a memorandum to present to the King, a copy of which, in the handwriting of the Lord

Chancellor, Lord Hardwicke, is in the archives of the British Library. It is in the following terms:

> That, out of Duty to the King, & Regard to the Public, It is apprehended that His Majesty's late Servants cannot return into his Service, without being honour'd with that degree of Authority, Confidence, & Credit from His Majesty, which the Ministers of the Crown have usually enjoy'd in this country, & which is absolutely necessary for carrying on his Service.
>
> That His Majesty will be pleas'd entirely to withdraw his confidence & countenance from those Persons, who have of late, behind the Curtain, suggested private Councills, with ye view of creating difficulties to his Servants, who are responsible for every thing, whilst those Persons are responsible for nothing.
>
> That His Majesty will be pleased to demonstrate his Conviction of mind that Those Persons have deceiv'd or misled Him by representing that they had sufficient Credit & Interest in the Nation to support & carry on the public affairs, & that he finds They are not able to do it.
>
> That in order to these Ends, his Majesty will be pleas'd to remove [Granville's followers]....
>
> That he will be graciously pleased to perfect the Scheme lately humbly propos'd to Him for bringing Mr. Pitt into some honourable Employment, & also the other persons formerly nam'd with him.
>
> That His Majesty will be pleased to dispose of the vacant Garters in such manner, as to strengthen, & give a public mark of his Satisfaction in, his Administration.
>
> That, as to foreign affairs, His Majesty will be pleased not to require more from His Servants than to support the Plan, which He has already approved. (Wilkes, p.144)

Modern readers may be astonished at the temerity of Pelham's ministers in presenting such a document to the King, and even more surprised that he meekly accepted it. Nor did this hitherto rather slippery customer subsequently attempt to renege on the assurances which he had given. The previously unpretentious Pelham now emerged as one of the strongest characters ever to hold the role of Prime Minister, and the extent of his power now rivalled or exceeded that of Walpole in his prime. He had demonstrated that, with a largely united Cabinet and solid support in the House of Commons, a Prime Minister could have his way over a reluctant monarch. This was an important precedent for the future, though one which George II's headstrong grandson and successor, George III, was able to ignore on a number of occasions, notably in 1783 (see Chapter 13) and in 1807 (see Leonard, 2008, chapter 3).

The immediate consequence was that Pelham, who returned to office on 14 February 1746, was able to take even further his desire to form a broad-bottomed administration, bringing in Pitt as Paymaster-General, Pitt's brother-in-law, George Grenville, as a Lord of the Admiralty, and a little later, the fourth Duke of Bedford as one of the two Secretaries of State, along with Newcastle. Bedford had been the leader of a large dissident Whig faction, and his adhesion to the government – though he proved an ineffective minister – greatly helped to boost its parliamentary majority. Pelham moved sharply to consolidate his advantage by springing a snap election – one year before it was due under the Septennial Act, in June 1747, catching the opposition off guard, and substantially increasing his majority. There was now – apart from the Tories, who were much reduced in numbers – no significant opposition grouping left in the Commons, apart from the faction supporting the interest of Frederick, Prince of Wales, who – permanently at odds with his father – was constantly stoking discontent. His following was considerable, partly because of the large number of 'pocket' boroughs he controlled, notably in the Duchy of Cornwall, but mainly because, as his father grew older and in less than splendid health, ambitious politicians increasingly looked forward to his succession to the throne to further their own fortunes. This 'Reversionary interest' was a recurrent factor under each of the first three Hanoverian kings, all of whom had bad relations with their eldest sons. Pelham acknowledged the difficulty he often faced from Frederick, and his 'Leicester House circle', saying in a letter to Newcastle, in May 1750:

> The House of Commons is a great unwieldy body, which requires great Art and some Cordials to keep it loyal; we have not many of the latter in our power; the Opposition is headed by the Prince, who has as much to give in the present as we have, and more in Reversion. This makes my task an hard one, and if it were not for that I should sleep in quiet. (Newman, 1974, p.68)

The 'Cordials' which Pelham mentioned referred to the system of patronage and bribery, which Walpole had perfected during his long period in power. Although both Pelham and Newcastle personally refrained from enriching themselves from the public service (apart from drawing their ministerial salaries), they had few scruples in continuing with Walpole's methods, though they did it more discreetly and on a somewhat smaller scale. Frederick's unexpected death, in 1751, at the age of 44, removed this particular difficulty, as his group of followers rapidly disintegrated, many of them hastening to make peace with the government. Henceforward Pelham had no difficulty whatever in controlling the Commons, as the leader of the House, Henry Fox (later the first Lord Holland), indicated in a letter in November 1751: 'There never was such a session as this is likely to be…. A bird might build her nest in the Speaker's chair, or in his peruke; There won't be a debate that can disturb her' (Hanham, 1998, p.23).

As a faithful disciple of Walpole, Pelham shared most of his objectives, notably the desire to bring peace and stability to the country, and to lower taxation. As Prime Minister, he had little direct control over foreign affairs, in which the King took great interest, and which was the special concern of the two Secretaries of State, of whom the more influential was his brother, Newcastle. Pelham earlier took the view that Britain had little to gain from a continuation of the War of Austrian Succession, which was a serious drain on the country's finances. Yet the King still hankered after military glory, following his personal participation in the Battle of Dettingen, in 1743 (see Chapter 2), a rare victory over France in continental Europe, and Newcastle rashly promised renewed subsidies to Britain's allies to keep them in the war. Yet it continued to go badly, with the French Marshal Saxe gaining a series of striking victories at Fontenoy, Roucoux and Lauffield in 1745, 1746 and 1747, and the only British successes being at sea. Pelham eventually had his way, and the compromise Treaty of Aix-la-Chapelle concluded the war in October 1748. Only France's ally Prussia, which retained its conquests of Silesia and Glatz, emerged with any significant gains. Britain had little to show for its participation, other than belated recognition by France of the Hanoverian succession.

Partly driven by the cost of the war, Pelham was determined to reform the national finances, and to reduce the burden of the national debt. By 1748, this had risen to the then regarded astronomical sum of £76 million, the interest thereon absorbing some 44 per cent of the annual budget. 'Over the next two years', according to a parliamentary historian,

> He succeeded in scaling down government expenditure from £12 million to £7 million. This was greatly facilitated by the cutting of the army back from 50,000 to its peacetime level of 18,850 men, and the navy from 51,550 to 8,000. His wholesale reduction in the size

and cost of the government's fiscal bureaucracy was probably the most extensive undertaken by an eighteenth-century prime minister. (Hanham, 1998, p.26)

This enabled him to cut the land tax from four shillings in the pound in 1749 to three, and again to two shillings in 1752, a highly popular move among land-owning backbenchers. Even more important were his fiscal reforms, which allowed interest on the national debt to be reduced from 4 per cent to 3.5 per cent in 1750, and down to 3 per cent in 1757. Among those who expressed their admiration for Pelham's achievement was the King, who in conversation with Newcastle, in 1752, compared him favourably to Walpole. 'With regard to money matters', he said, 'your brother does that, understands that, much better' (Hanham, p.22). It had taken the King some time to warm to Pelham, whom he had initially disliked. But within a year or two of Pelham's *démarche* in 1746, he had become so dependent on him to deliver quiet and orderly government that he had utterly lost any desire to replace him. Much of the power had soon slipped away from the Cabinet as a whole, whose meetings became little more than a formality. Almost everything was settled by Pelham, in close consultation with Newcastle and the Lord Chancellor, Lord Hardwicke. The ever-jealous Newcastle even began to complain that he was left out of the loop, complaining to Hardwicke in September 1751: 'The truth is everything passes through my brother's hands, and I am with regard to the King as much a stranger as if I was not in the ministry' (Hanham, p.24). Newcastle constantly quarrelled with his brother, and it was up to the ultra-conciliatory Hardwicke to patch things up. In fact, Pelham, though intensely irritated by his unreasonable attitude, deferred to Newcastle on numerous occasions. For years – against his better judgment – he tolerated Newcastle's policy of paying subsidies to German states, such as Bavaria and Saxony, in order to ensure that they would vote for the Austrian Hapsburg candidate for the Holy Roman Emperor, despite substantial parliamentary opposition. He also eventually supported Newcastle's campaign to enforce the resignation of his fellow Secretary of State, the Duke of Bedford, and very reluctantly agreed, in 1751, to the readmission to the Cabinet of Granville, as Lord President of the Council. Newcastle represented that he was now a 'changed man', and would not represent a threat to their primacy. So it proved, and Granville remained a member of successive governments until his death in 1763, though his now ingrained alcoholism largely undermined his effectiveness. Despite their frequent quarrels, the mutual love and affection of the two brothers continued until the end. The childless Newcastle was devoted to Pelham's young family, and arranged for his own title to pass, on his death, to the Earl of Lincoln, who married Pelham's eldest daughter, Catherine, in 1744.

Apart from his financial policies, Pelham left no great reputation as a reformer. Nevertheless, a number of useful pieces of legislation were enacted under his leadership. Most important may have been the over-due proposal of the Earl of Chesterfield to adopt the new Gregorian calendar, which had replaced the Julian calendar in most of the rest of Europe as long ago as 1582. Under this Act, the New Year was to begin on 1 January, instead of 25 March, and 11 days were omitted between 2 and 14 September 1752, provoking mob riots with the slo-gan 'Give us back our eleven days.' Another reform was the Marriage Act of 1753, proposed by Lord Hardwicke, which prohibited clandestine and runaway marriages. This caused great controversy, and seriously upset the leader of the Commons, Henry Fox, who had himself eloped with a Duke's daughter. Subsequent generations of scholars, and armies of tourists, have had reason to be grateful to Pelham's government for passing an Act in 1753, establishing the British Museum.

It said much for Pelham's religious toleration, and perhaps also for his gratitude to Jewish financiers who helped in the restructuring of the national debt, that he sponsored the Jewish Naturalization Act of 1753. It said rather less for his courage that he later agreed to its repeal in the face of anti-Semitic agitation in advance of the general election scheduled for April 1754. He did not live to fight the election, dying, while still in office, on 6 March 1754, aged 59. He had served for 10 years and 191 days, succumbing finally to an attack of the inflam-matory disease, erysipelas. His health had not been good since 1748, when he suffered a severe attack of shingles, and three years later had proposed to retire from office and take a sinecure. George II would not hear of this, and he had carried on, declaring only a few weeks before his death that 'I am now, thank God, as well as I ever was in my life' (Kulisheck, 2004).

Newcastle was devastated by Pelham's death, and 'was sunk for sev-eral days in violent grief, unable and unwilling to attend to any busi-ness at all' (Newman, p.70). Within a week, however, he was able to exert himself sufficiently to ensure that he would be his brother's suc-cessor. As for George II, his first words, as recorded by Horace Walpole, were 'Now I shall have no more peace.' Prophetic words, for the stabil-ity which Pelham had been able to establish did not long survive his departure from the scene. Of the many tributes he received from his contemporaries, that from the *Memoirs* of the second Earl of Waldegrave seems most apposite:

> Mr. Pelham died in March 1754; and our tranquility, both at home and abroad, died with him.
>
> He had acquired the reputation of an able and honest minister, had a plain, solid understanding, improved by experience in business, as well as by a thorough knowledge of the world; and without being an orator, or having the finest parts, no man in the House of Commons argued with more weight, or was heard with greater attention.
>
> He was a frugal steward to the public, averse to continental extravagance and useless subsidies; preferring a tolerable peace to the most successful war; jealous to maintain his personal credit and authority; but nowise inattentive to the true interest of his country. (Wilkes, p.215)

Squeezed between the premierships of Walpole and the Elder Pitt (Chatham), Pelham's achievements have often been overlooked. Infinitely less flamboyant than either of these rivals, he nevertheless must share with them the credit of having been one of the three most effective political leaders of the eighteenth century.

Works consulted

Bigham, Clive (1924), *The Prime Ministers of Britain 1721–1924*, London, John Murray.

Browning, Reed (1975), *The Duke of Newcastle*, New Haven, Yale University Press.

Hanham, Andrew (1998), 'Henry Pelham', in Robert Eccleshall and Graham Walker, eds., *Biographical Dictionary of British Prime Ministers*, London, Routledge.

Kulisheck, P.J. (2004), Pelham, Henry (1694–1754), *Oxford Dictionary of National Biography*, Oxford, OUP.

Leonard, Dick (2008), *Nineteenth Century British Premiers*, Basingstoke, Palgrave Macmillan.

Newman, A.N. (1974), 'Henry Pelham (1743–54)', in Herbert Van Thal, ed., *The Prime Ministers*, Volume I, London, Allen & Unwin.

Owen, John B. (1957), *The Rise of the Pelhams*, London, Methuen.

Wilkes, John W. (1964), *A Whig in Power: The Political Career of Henry Pelham*, Evanston, Northwestern University Press.

Wilson, Harold (1977), *A Prime Minister on Prime Ministers*, London, Weidenfeld & Nicolson and Michael Joseph.

4

Thomas Pelham-Holles, Duke of Newcastle – Mighty Panjandrum, Feeble Premier

Britain's roll-call of 53 Prime Ministers, to date, contains two sets of fathers and sons (Pitts and Grenvilles), but only one pair of brothers. Thomas Pelham's case was the more unusual, in that he was to succeed his *younger* brother (Henry Pelham). As recounted in the previous chapter, they were the two surviving sons of Thomas, first Baron Pelham, and his second wife, Lady Grace Holles, the sister of John Holles, Duke of Newcastle-upon-Tyne. The Duke had no male children, though he had a daughter, and several other nephews who were older than young 'Tommy' Pelham, but he took a fancy to him and made him his heir, much to the chagrin of his widow, his daughter and other potential inheritors. When he was 18, Tommy was to change his name to Pelham-Holles, in accordance with the terms of this legacy. He was born in London on 21 July 1693, and lost his mother at the age of 7, and his father when he was 18. His childhood, however, was hardly a lonely one – he had seven sisters or half-sisters and a younger brother – Henry. Moreover, he was educated at a day school – Westminster – before moving on to Clare Hall (later Clare College), Cambridge, which – like Henry, at Oxford – he was to leave without taking a degree. According to his biographer, he was 'In fine, no scholar, but in light of his later facility with French and his ability to conform to the epistolary standards of the age by invoking relevant classical allusions, neither was he a dunce' (Browning, 1974, p.2).

Tommy was to remember Cambridge with great affection, and eagerly accepted nomination as University Chancellor in 1748, having induced George II to persuade the rival candidate, Frederick, Prince of Wales, to withdraw from the contest. By the time he left the University his life and financial circumstances had changed beyond recognition. The death of his father, in 1712, left him as the second Baron Pelham, and the inheritor of the larger part of his father's estate, after provision had been made for Henry and each of his five surviving sisters. A year earlier, he had received a far larger inheritance from his uncle. The Duke's will was fiercely contested by his widow, the Dowager Duchess, and by his daughter, Lady Henrietta Holles. Together with other relatives – some quite distant – they fought a long, but losing legal battle for several years, but Thomas was anxious to reach a compromise settlement, even expressing his willingness to marry Lady Henrietta. This offer was not accepted, but after the death of the Dowager Duchess in 1716, the daughter, now married to Lord Harley, son of the Earl of Oxford, formerly Queen Anne's chief minister, struck a deal giving her Welbeck Abbey, the great Nottinghamshire estate, and numerous other lands, but leaving Pelham-Holles with the great bulk of his uncle's holdings, which – together with his father's legacy – yielded him an annual income of some £32,000 a year (perhaps equivalent to £6.4m in modern terms). According to Browning (1975, p.5), 'this figure placed him somewhat below the rank of the wealthiest landlords in the kingdom'. It should, however, have been sufficient for him to live a life of luxury, with no material cares, but the new Duke, as he became in 1715, was recklessly extravagant, abnormally generous and an extremely bad manager of his own resources. He was in debt for the greater part of his long life, and by the time of his death, in 1768, his income had shrunk to barely £6000 a year and his debts amounted to £114,000.

As Lord Pelham, Thomas took his seat in the House of Lords, a few days after his twenty-first birthday in August 1714, and it immediately became clear that he was interested in following a political career. An ardent Whig, and follower of the new Hanoverian monarch, George I, he bribed a London mob to demonstrate noisily in his favour on the day of his proclamation, and the new monarch was not tardy in repaying his debt. Two months later he was raised in the peerage to become Viscount Houghton and Earl of Clare, both titles previously held by his uncle, and was appointed Lord Lieutenant of both Middlesex and Nottinghamshire. In the general election, which followed George's accession to the throne, he threw his weight behind the new Whig ministry, in which his brother-in-law, Lord Townshend, was a Secretary of State. Thomas was now a landowner in no less than 11 counties, and in 3 of these – Sussex, Nottinghamshire and Yorkshire – he had significant influence in the choice of MPs. In this election, in January 1715, he was credited with securing the election of no fewer than 14 MPs, which made him the biggest 'boroughmonger' in the country. An impressed George I once more showed his gratitude, by restoring the Dukedom of Newcastle-upon-Tyne, and bestowing it on Thomas, shortly after his twenty-second birthday, in August 1715. A month later, the Jacobite Rebellion of 1715 broke out, and Newcastle, as he was now known, hastened to organize militia in both Middlesex and Nottinghamshire, as well as in his native Sussex, and dispatched his brother Henry to take part in the Battle of Preston, where the supporters of the Old Pretender, Prince James Edward Stuart, were decisively defeated.

The final step which Thomas took in his progress towards becoming a grandee was his marriage, on 2 April 1717, to Lady Harriet Godolphin: he was 23, she 16. This united Newcastle with two of the grandest Whig families, one of Harriet's grandfathers being Lord Godolphin, the chief minister during most of Queen Anne's reign, and the other, the Duke of Marlborough. It was, in fact, Marlborough's wife, Sarah, who negotiated the marriage of her granddaughter. She offered to provide a dowry of £10,000, but the already cash-strapped Newcastle demanded £30,000.

Eventually a figure of £20,000 was agreed, and the fact that the normally avaricious Sarah agreed to part with this sum 'suggests that [she] was pleased to get her dull and unattractive granddaughter married off so well' (Browning, 1975, p.12). A chronic invalid – or at least a hypochondriac – Harriet hardly proved an asset to her husband's career. Yet, he was devoted to her, and apparently – highly unusually for a Whig magnate at this period – remained entirely faithful to her. His hopes of siring progeny descended from the great Duke of Marlborough were not, however, to be realized. Harriet had a miscarriage shortly after the marriage, and was not thereafter able to conceive. Newcastle compensated for his childlessness by quite extraordinary devotion to other members of his family, particularly the children of his brother, Henry, but also extending it to a wide network of cousins, nephews and nieces, many of whom became beneficiaries of the extensive patronage which he was later able to dispense.

Newcastle's perpetual financial worries have been attributed to the large sums he expended in order to ensure the election of his nominees in Parliament for the constituencies (varying between 14 and 17, over a period of 40 years), where his influence was predominant (see Ray A. Kelch, 1974). In fact, he spent far more on endless improvements to his many houses, notably Claremont, the fine Surrey mansion built by John Vanbrugh. Both here, and in his grandiose London residence, Newcastle House, in Lincoln's Inn Fields, he embarked on a ceaseless round of entertainment for his large number of friends and associates of every kind. Everybody who was anybody benefited at one time or another from the Duke's hospitality.

Newcastle's political career took off in 1717 when, still at the age of 23, he was appointed Lord Chamberlain, with responsibility for George I's household – then an important political office, though outside the Cabinet. This brought him into frequent contact with the King, and a close friendship developed between the two men. When, later in the year, a son was born to the Prince of Wales (later George II), the King insisted that Newcastle should be named as his godfather. The younger George had other ideas and had a violent argument with the Duke when he personally conveyed the message to him, leaving Newcastle with the impression that he was challenging him to a duel. This was, apparently a misunderstanding, due to the Prince's inadequate knowledge of the English language, but the King angrily banished his son from the Court, and relations between the Lord Chamberlain and the heir to the throne remained extremely frosty for some years.

When the Cabinet split later in the same year, with the eviction of his brother-in-law, Lord Townshend, and of Robert Walpole (see Chapter 1), Newcastle sided with their opponents – Lord Stanhope and the Earl of Sunderland. Yet he was able to mend his fences with them, when they returned to power, with Walpole becoming First Lord of the Treasury and Townshend, Secretary of State (North), in 1721. This enabled Newcastle to appoint his brother, Henry Pelham, as Treasurer of the Chamber, and the two brothers now both became close associates of Walpole. So far as the latter was concerned, Newcastle's greatest assets were his closeness to the King, his great assiduity in carrying out his duties and his willingness (indeed, eagerness) to take on any additional task that might be assigned to him, his unquestioning acceptance of Walpole's judgment and – not least – his control of more than a dozen parliamentary constituencies. When Walpole succeeded in removing his rival, Lord Carteret, from the post of Secretary of State (South) and banishing him to the Lord Lieutenancy of Ireland, the general expectation (certainly shared by Pulteney himself) was that he would propose to the King the appointment of William Pulteney, his chief supporter in the House of Commons. But Pulteney was a man of independent judgement, and very considerable ability, and thus a new potential rival, so Walpole played safe by proposing Newcastle instead. This was to make a deadly enemy out of Pulteney, but bound Newcastle to him with ties of steel.

The two Secretaries of State shared responsibility for foreign affairs, and there were often serious disagreements and rivalry between them. Yet – at least in the early years – Newcastle readily accepted his junior status in relation to Townshend and goodnaturedly deferred to him, allowing him to set the broad outlines of foreign policy. Townshend gave over-riding priority to fostering good relations with France, after 20 years of almost continuous warfare between the two traditional enemies, and – with the close co-operation of Cardinal Fleury, France's chief minister during the minority of Louis XV, an informal alliance was formed, somewhat to the detriment of Britain's long-standing association with Austria. In 1725, however, the unexpected conclusion of an alliance between Austria and Spain, under the Treaty of Vienna, posed an added threat to British interests. On the one hand, Austria, through its development of ports in the newly acquired Austrian Netherlands, and the creation of an aggressive new trading company, based in Ostend, was beginning to present a direct challenge to the East India Company. On the other hand, Spain was blockading Gibraltar, and represented an ever-present threat to British possessions in the Caribbean. Townshend and Newcastle were agreed that the new alliance must be broken up, but disagreed strongly about how to go about it. Townshend regarded the Austrian threat as more serious, and advocated taking a pacific approach towards Spain to detach her from her new ally. Newcastle was adamant that Spain represented a far greater danger, and strongly urged the reconstitution of the earlier close ties with Austria.

Meanwhile, in 1727, the sudden death of George I threatened to put an immediate end to Newcastle's ministerial career. The new King, George II, initially intended to dismiss Walpole and his fellow ministers, and install a rival team under Spencer Compton, later Lord Wilmington (see Chapter 1). Partly persuaded by Queen Caroline, however, he soon changed his mind, and Walpole, together with both Newcastle and Townshend, resumed office, the King not seeming to harbour any resentment against Newcastle from their contretemps of ten years earlier. His disagreement with Townshend over relations with Austria and Spain now re-surfaced, and Walpole exerted himself to resolve the issue. His formerly close family ties with Townshend had been loosened by the death in 1726 of his favourite sister, Dolly (the second Lady Townshend), and he came down decisively on Newcastle's side. A disillusioned Townshend resigned, to spend the remainder of his life conducting agricultural experiments on his Norfolk estate.

Townshend's replacement as Secretary of State (North) was the inoffensive Lord Harrington, who readily accepted that Newcastle should henceforth play the dominant role in foreign policy. 'With this latest ministerial reshuffle, Newcastle was the second most powerful politician in the kingdom' (Browning, 2004). His influence was to grow even greater as the 1730s and 1740s progressed and, as he amassed an unprecedented degree of patronage. This covered not only the bulk of appointments in the diplomatic service and in the colonies, but also in Scotland, for which he had assumed responsibility for the administration after the suppression of the post of Secretary of State for Scotland, and ecclesiastical appointments, which he controlled after Bishop Edmund Gibson felt out with Walpole in 1736 (see Chapter 1). In addition to this was his ability to provide parliamentary seats for those who sought his favour. He also acted as leader of the House of Lords, where he was the government's chief spokesman. In fact, Newcastle became the Grand Panjandrum of the Walpole administration, with his finger in every pie, and his willingness to spend long hours in boring administrative duties. He was fussy and pompous, and regarded by many as a figure of fun, but both Walpole and the King came to see him as an indispensable wheel in the government machine. His main weakness was an inability to say no, which arose in part from his genuine good nature. This meant that though he had many critics he had very few enemies, of whom Horace Walpole, his leader's putative son, was the most persistent. Never an easy colleague, he was extremely touchy, and inclined to be jealous of others' success, including his brother, who eventually surpassed him, partly due to greater ability, but also because – like Walpole until his last years – he chose to remain in the House of Commons rather than accept a peerage. One of Newcastle's saving graces was that, though he was more than willing to use his vast patronage powers for political purposes, he was – like his brother Henry Pelham – personally incorruptible, and never used his 40-year-long ministerial career to enrich himself, despite his chronic shortage of cash.

Throughout the greater part of his long career, Newcastle's closest associate was Philip Yorke, later the first Earl of Hardwicke. A promising and highly ambitious young lawyer, two years his junior, Yorke was first elected to Parliament in 1719, under Newcastle's aegis for the Sussex borough of Lewes, transferring to another seat in the Duke's gift – Seaford – three years later. As a strong Walpolite, he became successively Solicitor-General, Attorney-General, Lord Chief Justice, and, finally, in 1737, Lord Chancellor, a post he was to hold for almost 20 years. During the final years of Walpole's rule, he formed, with Newcastle and Henry Pelham, a triumvirate of 'Old Corps Whigs' who contested the ministerial succession with such formidable rivals as Lord Carteret (later the Earl of Granville) and William Pulteney (later, Earl of Bath). An exceptionally level-headed man, Hardwicke was the sheet-anchor of this alliance, mediating between the two brothers who were often quarrelling, and also between them and King George II, who blew hot and cold in his relations with the two men. Newcastle, in particular, came to rely heavily on Hardwicke for advice, which was freely given and almost always sound.

Newcastle remained Secretary of State, first of the Southern, then of the Northern Department, for 30 years – from 1724 to 1754 – a record unlikely ever to be equalled. For all of this period, except for the first half dozen or so years when he was subordinate to Lord Townshend, he was the dominant influence in determining British foreign policy – only the Prime Minister or, of course, the King, being in a position to over-rule him. One such occasion was the outbreak, in 1733, of the War of Polish succession, which pitched Austria and Russia against an alliance between France, Spain and Piedmont-Sardinia, who were supporting Stanislaus Leszczynski (the father-in-law of Louis XV), against the rival claims of Frederick Augustus II of Saxony. Newcastle, who had negotiated the Treaty of Vienna two years earlier, which pledged mutual support in war between Britain and Austria, felt that Britain was now obliged to intervene on the Austrian side. Walpole, however, who felt that no important British interest was at stake, was determined to keep out of the war, and succeeded in imposing his view, even though many, including the King, sympathized with Newcastle's opinion. The Duke was resentful, feeling, not without some justification, that Austria would, in its turn, be reluctant to support Britain in any future conflict.

Newcastle, however, supported Walpole's efforts to reach a peaceful agreement with Spain over the mounting number of maritime disputes between the two countries. With the negotiation of the Convention of Pardo (see Chapter 1), in January 1739, it seemed that they had succeeded. Yet the failure of both sides fully to implement it, and the incessant pressure by British trading companies and sea captains, led to an overwhelming public demand for war, which Newcastle and a majority of his Cabinet colleagues felt unable to resist. The War of Jenkins' Ear began in October 1739, Walpole, having resisted to the last, saying to Newcastle: 'This war is yours, you have had the conduct of it, I wish you joy of it.' In his biographer's words, 'this transformed Newcastle from *de facto* foreign minister to *de facto* minister of defence' (Browning, 2004). Under his guidance, the war did not go well – an initial success with the British capture of Porto Bello being over-shadowed by the failure of an attack on Cartagena, with heavy loss of life. The following year the death of the Emperor Charles VI, without a male heir, led to the War of Austrian Succession, in which Britain sided with Maria Theresa (Charles's daughter) in her war against Frederick the Great of Prussia, and his Bourbon allies, France and Spain. The War of Jenkins' Ear was merged with this greater struggle, which continued spasmodically until 1748 (see Chapter 3).

During the last couple of years of Walpole's premiership, there was a certain cooling of relations between the two men, and Newcastle was suspected of conspiring with opposition Whigs, notably Lord Carteret and William Pulteney, in moves to displace the Prime Minister. That he had contacts with them (as did many other Cabinet ministers) is undeniable, but it is doubtful if he did anything actively to undermine his chief. When Walpole finally resigned, in February 1742, having effectively lost his parliamentary majority, Newcastle remained as Secretary of State (South) in the administration formed by the Earl of Wilmington, which included Carteret as Secretary of State (North).

Newcastle accepted with reasonable grace that Carteret's influence on foreign and defence policy should be greater than his own, but – with encouragement from Walpole (now retired as Earl of Orford) – worked together with his brother, Henry Pelham, and the Earl of Hardwicke to prepare for what they regarded as an inevitable showdown with their brilliant but erratic rival. Newcastle certainly regarded himself as the leader of the 'Old Corps' of Whigs, and as Walpole's political heir. With the death of Wilmington, in July 1743, he found it difficult to reconcile himself to the fact that his brother's appointment as First Lord of the Treasury made him, at best, only the number two man in the government, which he effectively became, with the ousting of Carteret, in November 1744 (See Chapter 3). Throughout the ten years of Pelham's premiership, they had a difficult relationship, with Newcastle being openly jealous of his brother's superiority and trying to act on the basis that the government was really a diarchy. Pelham was greatly irritated, but often deferred to his brother – especially on foreign policy issues, and the conduct of the War of Austrian Succession – even against his own better judgment. Although they frequently quarrelled, there was a deep bond of love and affection between the two men, and when Pelham died, on 6 March 1754, the Duke was devastated.

Within a week, however, he was persuaded (or persuaded himself) that as the unchallenged leader of the Whig party it was his duty also to take charge of the government. He might have preferred to do this while remaining Secretary of State, but as the post of First Lord of the Treasury had effectively become synonymous with the Prime Ministership, he determined to take it himself. 'With that decision taken', his biographer writes, 'a major problem loomed, for three vacancies needed filling' (Browning, 1974, p.195). There were highly capable candidates for each of the three posts involved, but Newcastle declined to choose them, thereby in large part contributing to the disastrous failure of his own premiership. The most important of the posts was the leadership of the House of Commons, and, according to Horace Walpole, there were three outstanding candidates for the post – William Pitt, Henry Fox and William Murray, the Solicitor-General. Newcastle, however, was chary of awarding the post to a man of the highest ability, lest he should emerge as a rival leader to himself, and chose instead the mediocre Sir Thomas Robinson, who doubled up as Secretary of State (South), the second of the two vacancies to be filled. Before this could be effected, however, Newcastle had to contend with the difficulty that both King George II and majority parliamentary opinion clearly expressed a preference for Fox. Newcastle and Hardwicke accordingly 'devised the plan of offering him a restricted leadership, with conditions such as to make likely his rejection of the offer' (Browning, 1975, p.197). An emissary, Lord Hartington (later the fourth Duke of Devonshire), 'was dispatched to Fox on 12 March to offer him the post of southern secretary with direction of affairs in the Commons'. Fox enthusiastically accepted, but when he met Newcastle the following day, he learnt that he would have no right to nominate people for office and would have no knowledge of which MPs were in receipt of secret service money (essential for maintaining a majority in crucial divisions). He angrily withdrew his acceptance, and asked, instead, to retain his previous post of Secretary at War.

As Chancellor of the Exchequer, a much more significant position when the First Lord of the Treasury was in the Lords, he chose Sir William Lee, a clearly inadequate choice, whom he replaced a month later with Henry Bilson Legge. Legge was a competent figure, but Newcastle withheld authority from him, and the effective head of the Treasury was one of the under-secretaries, James West, a crony of Newcastle. Having grossly mishandled his major ministerial appointments, on 16 March 1754 Newcastle embarked on his first premiership, which lasted for some two-and-a-half years. By general consent, it proved to be a catastrophe, not least because, under Newcastle's feeble leadership, Britain slipped into what became known as the Seven Years' War, utterly unprepared for the struggle.

It was the young Colonel George Washington who fired the first shots in the war, on 3 July 1754, even though Britain and France were still at peace. With the encouragement of the British governor of Virginia, he led a force of 350 troops in an ill-judged attack on Fort Duquesne (later renamed Pittsburgh), a French fortress dominating the Ohio valley. Defeated and captured by the French, his humiliation led Newcastle to conclude that a major reinforcement of British forces in North America was necessary. Vice-Admiral Edward Boscowen and Major-General Edward Braddock were dispatched, after much hesitation, but the former was unable to prevent the landing of French troops at Louisbourg, in Nova Scotia, while the latter was killed, fighting alongside Washington, in yet another abortive attack on Fort Duquesne, in July 1755.

It was only in May 1756 that war was officially declared between the two countries, in what to most Britons appeared as a continuation of the War of Austrian Succession, which had come to an end eight years earlier. There had, however, been a substantial *renversement des alliances*, largely due to maladroit diplomatic initiatives by Newcastle, who succeeded in alienating Britain's former ally, Austria, and the newly powerful Russia under Catherine the Great. France abandoned its earlier alliance with Protestant Prussia in favour of Catholic Austria, its traditional foe. These two countries now joined Russia, Sweden and Saxony in a struggle against Prussia and Great Britain. At first, the war went very badly for Britain, an early setback being the French conquest of Minorca, which had been under British rule since 1708.

Newcastle, and his ministers, now faced severe criticism, led by William Pitt in a series of coruscating speeches in the House of Commons, which Sir Thomas Robinson and other government spokesmen were quite unable to combat. In desperation, Newcastle made another approach to Henry Fox, who in November 1755 accepted the post of Secretary of State (South), combined with the leadership of the Commons. Though hardly Pitt's equal as an orator, he was an effective parliamentary performer, and under his guidance the government's business in the Commons began to proceed more smoothly. Outside Parliament, however, the barrage of criticism of ministers over the loss of Minorca continued unabated. Newcastle did everything he could to deflect it to Admiral John Byng, the unfortunate commander of the naval force which had been sent to relieve the siege of the island. Byng was accused of dilatoriness in arriving at the scene and of failing to engage the French forces with sufficient commitment. When a deputation from the City of London visited Newcastle to complain about Byng's conduct, he said to them: 'Oh! Indeed he shall be tried immediately – he shall be hanged directly' (Browning, 1975, p.236). In what Browning describes as 'the most shameful chapter of his personal life', Newcastle hastened to convene a court-martial, taking good care to suppress the presentation of evidence which might have exonerated Byng. The admiral was acquitted of cowardice and disaffection, but was found guilty of neglect of duty and condemned to death, with a recommendation of mercy. George II refused to exercise clemency, and Newcastle made no attempt to persuade him to do so. Byng was executed aboard ship by firing squad on 14 March 1757. This sordid incident gained added notoriety from Voltaire's famous comment in *Candide* that 'In England it is thought well to kill an admiral from time to time to encourage the others.'

By the time of Byng's execution, Newcastle was no longer in office. The scapegoating of the admiral had not sufficed to ease the criticism of the Duke for his inept conduct of the war, and William Pitt's repeated oratorical onslaughts led to the gradual attrition of his parliamentary support. Eventually, in October 1756, Henry Fox decided he had had enough, and resigned his post to join Pitt in opposition. Unable to find an effective replacement, and belatedly recognizing that Pitt was now the inevitable war leader, Newcastle himself resigned a month later. To his great distaste, George II – who had consistently refused to give high office to him – was now forced to appoint Pitt as Secretary of State (South), with the fourth Duke of Devonshire as a figurehead Prime Minister.

It looked as though Newcastle's political career was now over. His premiership was almost universally seen as a disaster. An indispensable support – as a number two – to Walpole and then to Pelham, he had proved incapable of providing leadership himself. Chronically afraid of accepting responsibility, he was also too jealous of the success of others to devolve power to those who might have been able to use it to good effect. Yet the one extraordinary talent which he did possess – his mastery of patronage – was sorely needed by the incoming Devonshire government, which collapsed after less than eight months, in June 1757 (see Chapter 5). The King toyed with the idea of appointing the Earl of Waldegrave, but after three days abandoned the attempt, and turned again to the Duke, being reluctantly persuaded that he needed not only Pitt, but also Newcastle, if a stable government was to be formed. So, on 29 June 1757, he again became First Lord of the Treasury, and thus at least nominally Prime Minister. The government, however, is known to history as the Pitt-Newcastle government, with Pitt undoubtedly seen as the senior partner. Yet it was a true partnership – with Pitt triumphantly directing the war effort (see Chapter 9), while Newcastle, with the assistance of able colleagues in the Treasury, raising unprecedented sums to finance Pitt's expensive campaigns, as well as using his patronage powers to assure strong support for the government in both Houses of Parliament.

Newcastle's principal means of maintaining control of Parliament was the payment of bribes or pensions to peers and MPs, or to their family connections, out of Secret Service funds. Newcastle kept assiduous notes of the payments made, and accounted for every penny spent in periodic reports which he made directly to the King. These reports were to be a principal source for Sir Lewis Namier's groundbreaking work, *The Structure of Politics at the Accession of George III*, first published in 1957. This included a 56-page appendix setting out every payment made during Newcastle's two terms as Prime Minister. Typical examples are the payments made during the month of May 1759:

		£
May 2d	To Mr. Martin towards Camelford election	300
8th	To Mr. Medlycott for one year	600
11th	To Lord Saye and Sele, one year to Lady Day	600
	To Mr. Hamilton, the late Duke of Hamilton's relation, ½ a year due at Lady Day	100
	To Mr. Henry Fane, for Lyme as usual	100
17th	To Sir Francis Poole, one year due at Christmas	300
18th	To Mr. Dodd, one year	500
25th	Retained to myself by Your Majesty's special command, one quarter	1050
	To Lord Malpas, remainder	300
29th	To Orford, rent, ½ a year due at Midsummer last	100
	To Mr. Offley, ½ a year to Christmas	200

(Namier, 1957, p.457)

On most issues Newcastle was obliged to defer to Pitt, and though they had occasional disagreements, their partnership worked extremely well, while Pitt's energetic direction of the war led to a series of major victories in Canada, India, Germany, the Caribbean, West Africa and the high seas. The year 1759, dubbed the 'year of victories', was without doubt the most successful in British military history. There seemed no reason to believe that the Pitt-Newcastle government would not be set for a long and glorious tenure. Then, on 25 October 1760, George II died suddenly, just short of his 77th birthday. Newcastle had never been close to him, but – after many misgivings – George had come to depend on him as an anchor of stability for his government during his final years. On his death, Newcastle wrote to Hardwicke's son, Joseph Yorke, that he had lost 'the best king, the best master & best friend that ever subject had' (Browning, 1975, p.271). His tribute may not have been totally sincere, but perhaps betrayed a fear that his relationship with his successor would be a great deal less satisfactory. So it was to prove.

George III was 22 years old, and had very different ideas on how to reign than his grandfather, George II, and great-grandfather, George I. He considered that they had supinely allowed royal prerogatives to be appropriated by a Whig oligarchy, and was determined to put the process into reverse. He had been influenced by the Tory philosopher and former politician, Lord Bolingbroke, whose work *The Idea of a Patriot*

King had fostered in him a deep aversion to party politics. He regarded parties as divisive, if not subversive, but his particular dislike was focused on the Whigs. Ministers should be appointed, in George's view, because of their 'virtue' not their political views. Devoted to his former tutor, the Earl of Bute, to whom he invariably referred as 'my dearest friend', he was determined to promote this royal favourite to the highest ranks of his administration. Initially, he was appointed to the largely honorific post of the Groom of the Stole, which hardly did justice to the great influence which he wielded from the day of George's accession. It should have been evident to both Pitt and Newcastle that the eruption of Bute was likely to undermine the position of both men, and that in self-defence they should work closely together. Unfortunately, Newcastle appeared not to realize this, and – in the hope of ingratiating himself to the King and to Bute – he connived in the appointment of the latter as the Secretary of State (North), without previously consulting Pitt, who was far from amused. Sharp differences now appeared between Pitt and Newcastle on the continuation of the war. Newcastle, acutely aware of the costs of the conflict was in favour of negotiating a quick peace with France, on the basis of the great territorial gains which had already been made. Pitt, however, was determined to continue the struggle until Britain's hereditary enemy had been brought to its knees. Bute was able to play off each of them against the other, and the government became seriously split on the issue, and also on the priority which should be given to waging the war in Germany, which was no longer a great royal concern, as George III placed much less value on his Hanoverian possessions than his predecessor.

The issue came to a head over the determination of Pitt to extend the war to Spain, which had recently concluded a treaty of alliance with France. Pitt believed that Spain would eventually come in on the French side, and that it was better for Britain to make a preemptive strike before its forces were properly mobilized. He was over-ruled by his Cabinet colleagues, led by Bute, and, declaring that 'I will be responsible for nothing that I do not direct' flounced out of the government in October 1761. With Pitt gone, Newcastle's position soon became untenable. He grumbled that 'My advice or opinion are scarce ever ask'd, but *never* taken. I am kept in, without confidence, and indeed without communication' (Browning, 1975, p.283).

He submitted his resignation in May 1762. The King, who had taken a thorough dislike to him and had been heard to remark 'The more I know of this fellow the more I wish to see him out of employment', was delighted, and offered him a pension. Newcastle proudly refused, saying that if his fortune had suffered in service to the royal family 'it was my honour, my glory and my pride' (Browning, 1975, pp.288–9).

Newcastle was now nearly 69, and a comfortable retirement might well have beckoned. But the still energetic Duke's whole interest in life centred on politics and administration, and he did not think for a moment of giving up. Grossly over-estimating his own continuing influence, he calculated that 'over 40 per cent of the House of Lords and thirty-five per cent of the members of the House of Commons would stand with him' (Browning, 1975, p.291), and set himself the task of either controlling the government from the outside, or of evicting the new Prime Minister, Bute, from power. He was soon to be disillusioned. In October 1762, Bute dismissed the Duke of Devonshire, a close associate of Newcastle's, from his post as Lord Chamberlain. An enraged Newcastle then called on all his presumed followers to resign from office in protest. Few of them did so, and Bute, encouraged by Henry Fox, who was now again Leader of the House of Commons, sensing Newcastle's impotence, moved against his remaining supporters – in what became known as 'the slaughter of the Pelhamite innocents'. A goodly number of officials, high or low, who owed their initial appointments to one or other of the Pelham brothers, were peremptorily dismissed, while Newcastle himself was unceremoniously stripped of his Lord Lieutenancies of Middlesex and Nottinghamshire.

Unabashed, Newcastle now set himself the dispiriting task of organizing the Whig Party, which had monopolized office for the best part of five decades, as an opposition force. Though his prodigious hospitality helped the process along, he gradually lost influence to a group of younger men, notably his protégé, the second Marquess of Rockingham. Rockingham succeeded in forming a government in 1765, in which Newcastle served as Lord Privy Seal, but was seen more as an elder statesman than as one of the more activist ministers. The government lasted barely a year, after which, in July 1766, George III was finally persuaded to appoint the Elder Pitt (now Lord Chatham) as Prime Minister, and the latter – almost as reluctantly – agreed to serve (see Chapter 9). On leaving office, Newcastle was again offered a pension (of £4000 a year), but again refused. He lived for another two and a half years, constantly engaged in political intrigues, dying, aged 75, after a stroke, on 17 November 1768.

Altogether, Newcastle served for 7 years and 204 days as Prime Minister, but his total ministerial career was one of the longest in British history, some 46 years, including 30 continuously as a Secretary of State, and effectively number two or three in the government. Only Palmerston, who served – rather less continuously – for a total of 47 years has surpassed his record. The surprising fact about Newcastle is that he was able to survive for so long, when contemporary views of him were so negative. These views have been conveyed by the three principal chroniclers of the reign of George II – Horace Walpole, Lord Hervey and the Earl of Waldegrave. All three, however, were rival (and less successful) politicians, and each had a personal grudge against him, as the historian H.T. Dickenson has pointed out (Van Thal, Vol. I, 1974, p.75). Walpole, he writes, described Newcastle as:

> A Secretary of State without intelligence, a Duke without money, a man of infinite intrigue, without secrecy or policy, and a Minister despised and hated by his master, by all parties and Ministers, without being turned out by any.

Waldegrave's view was just as damning:

> Talk with him concerning public or private business, of a nice or delicate nature, he will be found confused, irresolute, continually rambling from the subject, contradicting himself almost every instant.

Another contemporary politician, with literary inclinations – Lord Chesterfield – saw matters more in perspective. His view is cited by Lewis Namier, and goes a long way towards explaining why, despite his many faults, Newcastle was long regarded as being indispensable by those who worked with him:

> The public put him below his level: for though he had no superior parts, nor eminent talents, he had a most indefatigable industry, perseverance, a court craft, and a servile compliance with the will of his sovereign for the time being. (Namier, 1961, p.7)

Perhaps the final word should go to Reed Browning, who set out fairly the case for and against Newcastle in his distinguished biography of 1975. Writing a generation later, he was forced to conclude that 'Newcastle was not always guilty of poor judgment. But, leaving longevity aside, it is hard in surveying the entirety of his career to find substantive arguments for regarding it as anything other than an exercise in political mediocrity' (Browning, 2004).

Works consulted

Bigham, Clive (1924), *The Prime Ministers of Britain 1721–1924*, London, John Murray.

Black, Jeremy (1998), 'Thomas Pelham-Holles, Duke of Newcastle', in Robert Ecceleshall and Graham Walker, eds, *Biographical Dictionary of British Prime Ministers,* London, Routledge.

Brooke, John (1972), *King George III,* London, Constable.

Browning, Reed (1975),,, *The Duke of Newcastle,* Newhaven, Yale University Press.

Browning, Reed (2004), 'Thomas Pelham-Holles, Duke of Newcastle (1693–1768)', in *Oxford Dictionary of National Biography,* Oxford, OUP.

Clark, J.C. D. (1982), *The Dynamics of Change; The Crisis of the 1750s and English Party Systems,* Cambridge, CUP.

Dickinson, H.T. (1974), The Duke of Newcastle (1754–56; 1757–62) in Herbert Van Thal, ed., *The Prime Ministers,* Volume I, London, Allen & Unwin.

Kelch, Ray A. (1974), *Newcastle: A Duke without Money,* London, Routledge & Kegan Paul.

Nulle, Stebelton H. (1931), *Thomas Pelham-Holles, Duke of Newcastle: His Early Political Career 1693–1724,* Philadelphia, University of Pennsylvania Press.

Namier, Lewis (1957), *The Structure of Politics at the Accession of George III,* London, Macmillan.

Namier, Lewis (1963), *England in the Age of the American Revolution,* 2nd ed., London, Macmillan.

Owen, John B. (1957), *The Rise of the Pelhams,* London, Methuen.

Turberville, A.S. (1929), *English Men and Manners in the 18th Century,* 2nd edition, New York, Galaxy Books, OUP.

5
William Cavendish, Fourth Duke of Devonshire – 'I Have No Motive but the King's Service'

William Cavendish, 4th Duke of Devonshire
Prime Minister 1756-1757

Although he came from the very highest ranks of the aristocracy, surprisingly little is known of the early years of Britain's fifth Prime Minister. His date of birth was not recorded, though it was almost certainly in 1720, the year in which he was baptized (in St. Martin-in the

Field Church on 1 June), nor is there any information about his schooling. It is assumed that he was educated at home by private tutors, and there is no record of his attending a university. William Cavendish was the second child and eldest son in a family of four boys and three girls. His father, the third Duke of Devonshire, was descended from a family which derived from the small town village of Cavendish Overhall in Suffolk – one of his ancestors, Sir John Cavendish, was Lord Chief Justice under Edward III, and was beheaded by a mob during the Peasants' Revolt, in 1381. The family came into great prominence in Tudor times, and the Earldom of Devonshire dated from 1618. It was the fourth Earl of Devonshire, one of the original 'Whigs' who tried to exclude the Catholic Duke of York (James II) from the throne, who established the family as a political dynasty. When James ascended the throne in 1685, he set out to ruin Devonshire, fining him £30,000, and exiling him from his court to his stately home at Chatsworth (Derbyshire). The Earl soon had his revenge, being one of the seven notables who invited William III to invade England, and himself seized the city of Nottingham in William's interest. The new King showed his gratitude by creating him the first Duke, and he and his son and grandson all held office in Whig administrations. William Cavendish also had distinguished Whig ancestry through the female line, his grandmother, being the daughter of Lord William Russell, revered as the first 'Whig martyr', being beheaded in 1683 for his alleged participation in the Rye House Plot against Charles II. His own mother, Catherine Hoskins, came from less eminent or adventurous stock. She was the daughter of a steward to the Duke of Bedford, and William's father may well have been thought to be marrying 'beneath' himself, in choosing her in an evident love-match.

With this background, it is no surprise that William Cavendish grew up as a very committed Whig, and a strong supporter of the Hanoverian monarchy. When he was nine years old, in 1729, his father became the third Duke, and subsequently held high office under Robert Walpole, successively as Lord Privy Seal, Lord Steward of the Household, and – for the unusually long period of seven years – as Lord Lieutenant of Ireland. William, who was now known by the courtesy title of the Marquess of Hartington, departed on the Grand Tour in his late teens, returning to be elected, very shortly after his coming of age, as one of the two MPs for Derbyshire, a family seat. This was in the April 1741 general election, and he was to remain an MP for ten years. A strong supporter of Robert Walpole, Hartington transferred his loyalties to the Pelham brothers (Henry Pelham and the Duke of Newcastle), who were his kinsmen, when Walpole was forced to resign in February 1742. Henry Pelham, who became Leader of the House of Commons, under Walpole's successor, Lord Wilmington, invited Hartington to move the loyal address after the King's Speech at the opening of Parliament in October 1742, a clear sign that the young Marquess was already being seen by the Whig hierarchy as having a promising political future.

On 27 March 1748, the 28-year-old Hartington married Lady Charlotte Elizabeth Boyle, aged 16. It was a good match. His bride was the daughter and heir of the third Earl of Burlington, and was also a peeress in her own right, as Baroness de Clifford. Her inheritance brought to Hartington vast landownings in Yorkshire, including Bolton Abbey and Londesborough, and equally large holdings in Ireland, including Lismore Castle, in County Waterford, as well as both Chiswick House and Burlington House in London. It boosted the Devonshires' already great political influence, and gave them control of 'pocket' boroughs in both the London and Dublin parliaments. The marriage had been arranged several years earlier by the third Duke, when Lady Charlotte was still a child. Hartington's mother, who had married for love, did not approve, and left her husband for a period, subsequently boycotting the marriage and remaining on distant terms with her son and his wife. Nevertheless, the marriage turned out to be a happy one, and four children were born in the seven years until Lady Charlotte (who never became the Duchess of Devonshire) died from smallpox, at the age of 23, in December 1754.

Hartington did not appear to be a very active Member of Parliament, but from the outset mixed freely with the most senior Whigs, becoming a close friend of Henry Fox and on good terms with William Pitt, though remaining somewhat wary of him. In 1749, following his marriage, he was translated to the House of Lords, assuming one of his father's subsidiary titles, as Baron Cavendish of Hardwicke. Around this time, he was sounded out about becoming tutor to the young Prince George, whose father, Frederick, Prince of Wales, had recently died. Devonshire declined, which had serious consequences, as the prince was instead to fall under the nefarious influence of the Earl of Bute (see Chapter 6). Two years later, he joined Henry Pelham's cabinet as Master of the Horse, and was sworn of the Privy Council. Pelham died in March 1754, to be succeeded by his brother, the Duke of Newcastle, who, the following year rewarded Cavendish with the prestigious post of Lord-Lieutenant of Ireland. It was an unusual appointment, as his father had recently served in the same capacity, and it was not customary to choose a major Irish landowner to the post. In fact, Hartington (who became the 4th Duke of Devonshire the following year, on the death of his father), proved an ideal choice. He had close family connections with each of the two factions vying for control of the Irish Parliament and administration. By a mixture of firmness and tact, he was able to reconcile the factions – at least temporarily – and when he returned to England, in October 1756, he was acclaimed as a successful viceroy, who had succeeded in putting the Irish administration on a firmer basis.

Now a widower, who had been devastated by the death of his young wife, and left with four young children to bring up, Devonshire did not expect – nor indeed did he aspire to – any other senior appointment. But his return came at a very convenient moment for George II. The war with France was going badly, the Newcastle government had just collapsed, and Henry Fox's attempt to form an administration had failed. The King was reluctantly persuaded that William Pitt, who had been his *bête noire*, must play a major role in any new government, in order to dynamize the war effort, but was unwilling to appoint him as Newcastle's successor. Pitt himself proposed the answer: who better to take the lead than the charming and unambitious Devonshire, whom everybody liked and who had all the right political connections? George II leaped at the suggestion, but Devonshire was highly reluctant, refusing to commit himself to serve beyond the end of the current parliamentary session. It was on this basis that, on 16 November 1756, he became First Lord of the Treasury, with Pitt, as Secretary of State (South), acknowledged as the dominant figure in the government, with responsibility for prosecuting the Seven Years War, which pitched Britain and Prussia against France, Austria, Russia, Sweden, Saxony and Bavaria.

Newcastle, who commanded the allegiance of a majority of Whig MPs, remained in opposition, so the parliamentary position of the new government was precarious from the outset. It could, however, rely on at least the benevolent neutrality of the Tories, who admired Pitt's ultra-patriotic stance, and of the Leicester House faction – the supporters of the late Frederick, Prince of Wales, who under the leadership of the Earl of Bute, had transferred their loyalty to his son, the young Prince George, still a minor but widely courted as the heir to the throne. On this basis, the new government's ambitions were strictly limited. It could attempt no controversial legislation, and confined itself to holding the ring until such time as the three dominant political actors, Pitt, Henry Fox and the Duke of Newcastle, should have resolved which of them – or what combination – would take control of the nation's affairs. Newcastle, in particular, was in no hurry to bring matters to a head. Hanging over him and his former colleagues (including Fox, who sought to dissociate himself as far as possible from them) was the threat of a parliamentary enquiry into their conduct of the war against France. Newcastle was determined that Admiral John Byng should be the main, or if possible, the sole scapegoat for the disasters which occurred under his premiership, and wanted to wait until after his trial and punishment before mounting any challenge to the Pitt-Devonshire government, as it was widely dubbed.

The principal significance of this government, which lasted only for 225 days – the shortest term during the eighteenth century – was the opportunity it gave to Pitt to show his mettle as a war leader. In short order, 'America was set forth as a strategic priority, a militia for home defence was established, a continental army was assembled, and naval raids against the French coast were organized' (Schweizer, 2004). It was widely noted that Pitt had dropped his earlier opposition to a major British commitment on the European continent and to the payment of subsidies to Britain's Prussian ally. Lord Lyttelton reported in a letter to a kinsman that Pitt's contribution to the debate on the King's speech in December 1756 was 'modest and discreet ... In short, he spoke like a minister; and unsaid almost all he had said in opposition' (Clark, p.305). Nevertheless, Pitt proved himself less than a totally satisfactory colleague to most of his fellow ministers. He was a firm decision-taker, but was reluctant to consult with them. His health was bad, and he was frequently absent through attacks of gout. Sometimes their reality was doubted, and it was suspected that he used them as a pretext to avoid entering into discussions. Devonshire was largely a figurehead leader, and his chief functions seemed to be liaising with the King through their frequent meetings in 'the closet', and the tactful way in which he kept his rather heterogeneous team of ministers in reasonable harmony.

The first three months of the government were dominated by the trial of Admiral Byng for his alleged responsibility for the fall of Minorca to the French (see Chapters 4 and 9). Public opinion – and George II – was strongly against Byng, but the government itself was deeply divided, with Pitt and his brother-in-law, Lord Temple, the First Lord of the Admiralty, confidently expecting him to be acquitted, and then exerting themselves to persuade the King to exercise clemency, in the face of the unanimous recommendation by the judges that their mandatory death sentence should not be carried out. Pitt and Temple's concern was probably only partly motivated by humanitarian considerations: they wished to pin the blame firmly on to Newcastle and his associates, and did not want to see the Admiral used as a scapegoat. George II did not take kindly to their efforts. In a letter to the Duke of Newcastle, Baron Münchausen, the Hanoverian representative in London, reported that he was 'horrid angry' and resented personally any challenge to the court-martial's decision; from the outset he was determined to confirm it (Clark, p.324). Byng was duly executed on 14 March 1757. Three weeks later, the King demanded the resignations of Pitt and Temple, his anger against them having been reinforced by the refusal of his favourite son, the Duke of Cumberland, to take over command of the British forces in Germany so long as Pitt remained as a minister.

Pitt's dismissal broke the back of Devonshire's government, and both he and George II soon accepted that it could not continue much longer. George eventually asked Henry Fox to draw up an alternative list of ministers, which he attempted to do, but failed to persuade a sufficiently senior team to serve with him, especially as 'public opinion' loudly demanded the return of Pitt, who resolutely refused to serve under his rival. The King then invited Earl Waldegrave to form a government (see Chapter 9), but his efforts collapsed after three days, by which time a deal had finally been struck between Pitt and Newcastle. They agreed together to form a government, which took office on 29 June 1757, with Newcastle as First Lord of the Treasury, and Pitt resuming his earlier post as Secretary of State (South), and acknowledged as 'war minister'. Fox was bought off with the lucrative post of Paymaster-General and the award of a peerage for his wife. Devonshire was happy to make way, and joined the Pitt-Newcastle government as Lord Chamberlain, a post he held until 1762. He remained a highly respected figure, was regarded as the effective leader of the Whigs and a trusted counsellor of George II. Some indication of the influence he continued to wield is revealed in the fragmentary diary which he kept during the years between 1759 and 1762. This was published in a scholarly edition in 1982 (Brown and Schweizer). A valuable historical document which throws much light on the inner machinations of the Pitt-Newcastle government, it reveals Devonshire as a shrewd observer but not very active participant. It shows him as a man who was primarily concerned to serve the King's interest, even in ways not wholly appreciated by the monarch himself. Indeed, he quotes himself as saying to the King's mistress, Lady Yarmouth, 'I have no motive but the King's service'. The occasion was a determined attempt to persuade the King to make Lord Temple, Pitt's brother-in-law, a Knight of the Garter in order to deter him (and probably also Pitt) from resigning their ministerial posts at a critical time. The King loathed Temple, but eventually accepted the force of

Devonshire's unasked for advice, and the resignations were averted (Brown and Schweizer, pp.9, 24–38).

Devonshire's cosy relationship with the monarchy came to an abrupt end on 25 October 1760, with the death of George II. His grandson and successor, George III, had a deep-seated aversion to leading Whig politicians who had served his predecessor, and though Newcastle was the principal target of his ire, Devonshire was not far behind. He was never to enjoy the confidence of the new King, despite his earnest desire to serve him. The arrival of Lord Bute as the new King's closest adviser, followed by appointment as First Lord of the Treasury, in succession to Newcastle, in May 1762, convinced Devonshire that he no longer had a useful role to play, and he ceased attending cabinet meetings, though he did not resign his post. In October 1762, George III wanted him to attend a meeting of the Privy Council to discuss the final peace terms being negotiated with France. Devonshire declined, on the grounds that he was insufficiently informed on the subject. A few days later, the King's coach overtook Devonshire's on the way to London, and George mistakenly assumed that he was on his way to cabal with other Whig dignitaries against the government. When Devonshire came to the Court to take his leave of the King before travelling north to Chatsworth, the King refused to see him, and dismissed him from office. A few days later he personally erased Devonshire's name from the list of privy councillors.

Shortly afterwards, Bute, and Henry Fox, now again leader of the House of Commons, began the 'slaughter of the Pelhamite innocents', in which a large number of officials who had been appointed by Newcastle or his brother, Henry Pelham, were peremptorily dismissed from office (see Chapter 4). Among the victims were Newcastle himself, the Marquess of Rockingham and the Duke of Grafton, who were dismissed from their Lord Lieutenancies respectively of Middlesex and Nottinghamshire, the North and West Ridings of Yorkshire, and the county of Suffolk. In sympathy with them, Devonshire immediately resigned as Lord Lieutenant of Derbyshire, bringing to an end a half century in which this post had been held by three successive Dukes of Devonshire. This was effectively the end of his political career, though he did host a dinner party of senior Whigs opposed to the introduction in March 1763 of a Cider Tax by Bute's government (see Chapter 6). Bute got his Bill through, but its unpopularity was a major factor in his decision to resign a few days later. Devonshire's health then began to deteriorate. He suffered from dropsy, and the following year he travelled to Spa, in Germany, to take the waters, in the hope of a cure. He died there on 2 October 1764. The editors of his diary (Brown and Schweizer, p.18) speculated that 'his death at the age of 44 may have been hastened by the ingratitude of the young Sovereign whose family owed so much to the House of Cavendish'. He was a man of limited abilities, but a high sense of duty, who did his best to oil a system of government whose equilibrium was shaken by the machinations of coarser and more ambitious men.

Works consulted

Bigham, Clive (1924), *The Prime Ministers of Britain 1721–1924*, London, John Murray.

Brown, Peter D. and Schweizer, Karl W. eds. (1982), *The Devonshire Diary*, London, Royal Historical Society.

Brooke, John (1972), *King George III*, London, Constable.

Clark, J.C.D. (1982), *The Dynamics of Change: The Crisis of the 1750s and English Party Systems*, Cambridge University Press.

Howat, G.M.D. (1974), 'The Duke of Devonshire', in Herbert Van Thal, ed., *The Prime Ministers*, Volume I, London, Allen & Unwin.

Lawson, Philip (1998), 'William Cavendish, Fourth Duke of Devonshire', in Robert Eccleshall and Graham Walker, eds., *Biographical Dictionary of British Prime Ministers*, London, Routledge.

Schweizer, Karl Wolfgang (2004), 'Cavendish William, Fourth Duke of Devonshire', in *Oxford Dictionary of National Biography*, Oxford University Press.

6
John Stuart, Third Earl of Bute – the King's 'Dearest Friend'

John Stuart, third Earl of Bute, was the first Scotsman to become Prime Minister, the first Tory and the first, and perhaps the only one, to owe his appointment exclusively to his role as a royal favourite. He was the scion of a not particularly distinguished Scottish aristocratic family, his grandfather, the first Earl, serving as a Privy Councillor during the reign of Queen Anne. His father, the second Earl, lived only till the age of 33, and died, having risen no further than becoming the Lord Lieutenant of the County of Bute (an island abutting the Firth of Clyde), and for the last two years of his life a Lord of the Bedchamber to George I. The second Earl, however, made a rather grand marriage, to Lady Anne Campbell, daughter of the first Duke of Argyll, whose two brothers, the second Duke, and the Earl of Islay, were to become the most influential figures in Scotland, during the long premiership of Sir Robert Walpole. The young John Stuart was to inherit his father's title at the age of nine, and his two uncles were largely responsible for his upbringing, and Islay, in particular, greatly influenced him.

John was born in Edinburgh, on 11 May 1713, the eldest son and the second of eight children. He was one of the first Scottish nobles to attend Eton, where his contemporaries included two other future Prime Ministers, George Grenville and William Pitt, as well as Horace Walpole, the putative younger son of Robert Walpole. A scholarly figure, he went on to the University of Leyden, in the Netherlands, in 1728, graduating in Civil Law, four years later, at the age of 19. By 1732, accordingly to Professor McKelvey, 'Bute had become a stranger to Scotland, even his vacations from school having been spent at the English estate of his uncles. By education and inclination the young earl was a member of the English aristocracy' (McKelvey, p.4). A further break from his Scottish background was his marriage in 1736 to Mary Wortley Montagu, the only daughter of the famous and eccentric traveller and writer, Lady Mary Wortley Montagu, and 'her miserly husband Mr Wortley' (ibid.). Edward Wortley Montagu may have been a miser, but he was the owner of immense estates in Yorkshire, which his daughter was to inherit, and Bute's marriage provided him with the firmest of financial bases. After his graduation he had gone to live on the family estate at Mount Stuart, in Bute, where he was now able to make major improvements. Most of his time, however, was spent on pursuing his studies in a wide variety of fields, but particularly in botany, becoming in due course an acknowledged authority on British plants. His uncles, however, foresaw a political future for him, and in 1737, Lord Islay secured his election as a Scottish representative peer, when a vacancy arose from the death of the Earl of Orkney. He also obtained a lucrative sinecure as a commissioner of police for Scotland, and in 1738, he was made a Knight of the Thistle. 'As a personable and well connected young nobleman, Bute had every reason to assume that the future would provide still greater rewards' (McKelvey, p.5). The following year, however, his political career came to a juddering halt, when his two uncles found themselves on different sides on the question of whether Britain should go to war with Spain (see Chapter 1). Argyll was all for war, but Islay supported Robert Walpole's effort to avoid conflict by negotiating the Convention of Pardo with Spain. Argyll joined in the revolt against Walpole on the issue, and Bute supported him, but Walpole was able to win the critical parliamentary division and Argyll and Bute were forced into opposition, Bute losing his seat as a representative peer in the subsequent election, in 1741. It was 20 years before he was able to return to the House of Lords.

Bute retired for five years to live on his estate, where he began to raise a large family, consisting eventually of five sons and six daughters. Life in a Scottish backwater, however, eventually began to pall, and in 1746 he bought a half share in Kenwood House, adjoining Hampstead Heath, from his uncle, Lord Islay, who had now succeeded his elder brother, becoming the third Duke of Argyll. The following year a chance encounter totally changed the future course of his life. He had gone to a race meeting at Egham, which was attended by Frederick, Prince of Wales, the disaffected son and heir to George II. The two men were unacquainted, but when it started to rain the bored Prince retired to a tent, and called for a game of cards. 'There was no one of sufficient quality to take a hand with him until an equerry recollected that he had seen Lord Bute on the course. Bute was brought in, presented, and sat down at the table' (Bigham, 1924, p.119). They hit it off very well, and soon became inseparable companions, Bute becoming a fixture at Leicester House, the Prince's London residence, where opposition politicians met to plot and carouse. The Prince found him good company, but had no very elevated opinion of his talents, describing Bute to Lord Waldegrave as 'a fine showy man who would make an excellent ambassador in a court where there was no business' (ibid., p.120). Frederick's wife, Princess Augusta, however, was completely taken by this handsome and erudite Scottish noble, who became her principal adviser after the death of the Prince in 1751. A frightened woman, Augusta's fears centred on the risk of George II dying before her son, Prince George, came of age. This would necessitate the appointment of a regent, and though she herself was scheduled for this role, she feared that the Duke of Cumberland, George II's second son, would be substituted in the event. In her fanciful mind, it was then just a short step to her imagining Cumberland behaving like Richard III, who was regent to his young nephew, Edward V, and whom he murdered, together with Edward's younger brother, in the Tower of London, and had himself proclaimed King. Augusta communicated her fears to her son, who became physically afraid of his uncle. Cumberland was not a very nice man, as his reputation as the 'Butcher of Culloden' showed, but he was devoted to serving his nephew's interests, and none of his actions gave the slightest justification for his sister-in-law's paranoia. Bute should have firmly told Augusta that her fears were groundless, but he chose not to do so. A rumour, put about by Horace Walpole, that they were lovers, was given almost universal credence. It was, indeed, the basis of a devastating retort delivered to the princess by one of her maids of honour (later the notorious Duchess of Kingston) whom she had reproved for her promiscuity, asking her 'les raisons de cette conduite'. 'Ah, Madame', she replied, 'chacun a son but' – an obvious pun on Bute's name (Bigham, p.120). Modern scholars, however, have expressed doubts. John Brooke, for example, the author of a much admired biography of George III, wrote:

> Two persons less likely to engage in a love affair than Bute and the Princess could hardly be imagined. In 1755 Bute was forty-two, happily married to an attractive and devoted wife, and the father of a large family. He had never been suspected of gallantry. The Princess was thirty-six, the mother of nine children, and more famed for her discretion and good conduct than for her beauty or sexual charms. Everything we know of the character of either is evidence against a love affair. (Brooke, 1972, p.48)

Whatever the truth of the matter, there is no doubting the closeness of Bute's relationship to the Princess or the enormous confidence that she had in him. She used all her wiles on a reluctant George II to get him to appoint Bute as tutor, and later Groom of the Stole (effectively head of the Prince's household) to her son, the future George III, and his tutorship began in1755, when the still immature and impressionable prince was barely 17. In addition to his duties with the Prince, Bute became the acknowledged leader of the Leicester House faction, and represented its interests in his dealings with the Court and with other politicians, his greatest *coup* being to recruit William Pitt, in an alliance which led indirectly to the resignation of the Duke of Newcastle as Prime Minister in 1757. Pitt was fiercely opposed to the government's policy of paying subsidies to continental allies in the war against France and Austria, and this was a view shared by Bute and his Leicester House cohorts. Bute, Princess Augusta and the young Prince George all felt that Pitt was now unreservedly attached to their cause, and – when he later joined the governments of Devonshire and the second Newcastle administration – were aghast when he promptly reversed his earlier stance over the payment of subsidies, and failed to consult Bute over important government decisions. They came to regard him as a fair weather friend, and reacted hostilely to him.

Prince George had had several other tutors before Bute, and none of them had regarded him as a very satisfactory charge. Sullen and indolent (by his own later admission), he had failed to take advantage of the knowledge which a series of learned and distinguished men had done their best to impart. With the arrival of Bute, all that was to change. The lonely and refractory boy, who had largely been excluded from the company of his own generation, had seldom before encountered an adult to whom he was able to relate. His father, whom he adored, had died when he was 12, and he was desperately in need of a 'father figure' to whom he could look up as a role model. Bute fulfilled this part to perfection. Twenty-five years older than the prince, and a former associate of his father, he 'represented all the qualities in which the prince was so deficient – handsome, self-assured, well educated' (McKelvey, p.54). George immediately responded to him, and resolved to put his indolence behind him. The very close relationship which they soon built up is reflected in the series of letters which the prince wrote to his tutor, and which were published under the editorship of Romney Sedgwick in 1939 (*Letters from George III to Lord Bute, 1756–1766*). He invariably addressed Bute as 'My dearest Friend', and was to write 'I am young and unexperienc'd , and shall exactly follow your advice, without which I shall inevitably sink', adding 'I daily return Heaven thanks, for having met with such a friend as you' (ibid.). Later, in June 1756, when George II, and leading ministers (including Newcastle) resolutely opposed Bute's appointment as Groom of the Stole, and he himself suggested that 'the simplest solution might be for him to leave Leicester House', he wrote imploring him not to do so:

> It is true that the Ministers have done everything they can to provoke me, that they have call'd me a harmless boy, and have not even deign'd to give me an answer when I so earnestly wish to see my Friend about me…I know few things to be more thankfull for to the Great Power above, than for its having pleased Him to send you to help and advise me in these difficult times. I do hope that you will from this instant banish all thoughts of leaving me. (Ibid., p.41)

Eventually, the Duke of Newcastle, not wishing to alienate a young man who might ascend to the throne at any time, withdrew his opposition,

and persuaded George II to agree to Bute's appointment, and his closeness to, and influence over, the prince grew even greater.

As a tutor, Bute was nothing if not thorough. He gave George an
extensive grounding in history, constitutional law, finance, sciences
and the arts, setting him to write lengthy essays, sometimes more than
50 pages long, which are preserved in the Royal Archives in Windsor,
complete with Bute's often pedantic annotations. If he had left it at
that, this would have been an excellent preparation for the future king's
reign. But he also imbued his young charge with his own deep political beliefs and prejudices. These were largely based on the writings of
Lord Bolingbroke, the former Tory (and sometime Jacobite) politician
and philosopher, particularly his *chef d'oeuvre, The Idea of a Patriot King*.
A key theme, as interpreted by Bute, was that the two first Hanoverian
monarchs had been derelict in allowing many of their prerogatives, preserved under the Glorious Revolution settlement, to be expropriated by
a corrupt Whig oligarchy, which had governed in its own interest rather
than for the public good. They should now be reclaimed by a monarch,
whose moral authority would be such that nobody would doubt that
he was acting in the interest of the country as a whole rather than any
party or faction. This king would appoint as his ministers only men
of 'virtue' rather the general run of politicians, most of whom, Bute
implied, were knaves or worse. Bute proceeded insidiously to poison the
mind of the young Prince against all the leading Whig politicians of the
day, reserving much of his venom for Pitt, whose achievements as a war
leader, he consistently downplayed, emphasizing instead the 'enormous
debts' which his policies incurred. George showed how completely he
had absorbed Bute's lessons by composing an essay on the British political system, which is copiously quoted in Brooke's biography:

> Let the day come in which the banner of virtue, honour and liberty
> shall be displayed, that noble actions and generous sentiments shall
> lead to the royal favour, and prostitution of principle, venality and
> corruption meet their just reward, the honest citizen, the zealous
> patriot, will lift up their heads, all good men will unite in support
> of a government built on the firm foundations of liberty and virtue,
> and even the degenerate mercenary sons of slavery will suppress their
> thoughts, and worship outwardly the generous maxims of a prince,
> while they in secret detest his maxims and tremble at his virtues.
> Power, wealth, and honours still remain the favourite objects, but let
> the royal fiat change, the road revive, the long untrodden path, and
> crowds of all denominations will soon frequent it, and a generous

reformation will ensue…The prince once possessed of the nation's confidence, the people's love, will be feared and respected abroad, adored at home by mixing private economy with public magnificence. He will silence every clamour, be able to apply proper remedies to the heavy taxes that oppress the people, and lay a sure foundation for diminishing the enormous debt that weighs this country down and preys upon its vitals. (Brooke, p.65)

A thoroughly idealistic young man, George took seriously Bute's insistence on the necessity for a high moral character, and resolved to shape his life accordingly. In this, he was largely successful, being, for example, the only one of the five Hanoverian kings not to keep mistresses. A high-minded man, as Bute himself was, he was unable, also like Bute, to avoid becoming self-righteous. Bolingbroke had written that the Patriot King 'must begin to govern as soon as he begins to reign…His first care will be…to purge his court and call into the administration such men as he can assure himself will serve on the same principles on which he intends to govern' (quoted by Bigham, p.121). It seems to have been explicitly agreed between Bute and the Prince, long before the long-awaited day of George II's decease, that he should become the first Prime Minister of the new reign.

Yet, when on 25 October 1760, word came of the King's sudden death, Bute's nerve failed him. He sensed that to dismiss Newcastle and Pitt at a time when their popularity was soaring after an unprecedented series of victories in the Seven Years War would be tempting Providence, and he advised George to await a more opportune moment. Meanwhile, he was content to act and to be seen as the power behind the throne. When Newcastle went to see the new King, he was told: 'My Lord Bute is your very good friend. He will tell you my thoughts at large'. What George intended was that though – for the time being – Bute was not to become First Lord of the Treasury, he would be the dominant force in the administration, equal or superior to both Newcastle and Pitt. The former was relatively relaxed about this prospect, concluding that if he humoured the new King by accepting Bute's projected role with equanimity it would protect his own influence and position. Pitt, however, sensed from the outset that this new constellation would not work, and that the King would soon have to choose between him and his former tutor.

Initially, Bute did not become a minister, and – if he had his constitutional position would have been anomalous, as he was not a member of either House of Parliament. As it was, some eyebrows were raised when he apparently attended the first Privy Council of the new King's reign, on 25 October, and his name was left out of the list of those attending published the following day in the *London Gazette*. He was sworn in as a member on 27 October. It was he who had drafted the King's address to the Council, and Bute may well have influenced George when he inserted into his first speech to Parliament the famous words 'Born and educated in this country, I glory in the name of Britain.' This was meant to emphasize the difference between him and his two predecessors, who continued to be viewed as foreigners throughout their reigns. It was certainly Bute, a Scot, who suggested substituting 'Britain' for 'England' in George's original wording. After five months, during which he held only the Court post of Groom of the Stole, but was in daily contact with the King, who constantly sought his advice, Bute's position was 'regularised' by his appointment to the cabinet as Secretary of State (North) on 5 March 1761. A week later, Lady Bute was created Baroness Mount Stuart of Wortley in the peerage of Great Britain, while Bute himself was elected as a Scottish representative peer, in May, returning to the Upper House after an interval of 20 years. Bute's appointment was resented by most of the Whig members of the Cabinet, who rightly perceived him as a 'cuckoo in the nest', not least by Pitt, who had not been consulted, and who felt that Newcastle, who had, should have objected strongly, instead of quietly acquiescing in a move which was likely to undermine his own position, as well as Pitt's. Once in the Cabinet, Bute played a dominating role in all its discussions, though he did not attempt to question Pitt's direction of the war. In the summer of 1761, he played a leading part in formulating the British position in peace negotiations with France, which proved abortive. Instead, the French King, Louis XV, agreed to renew a 'family compact' with his first cousin, Charles III of Spain, which many saw as a prelude to Spanish entry into the war on the French side. Pitt was vehemently of this view, and proposed a pre-emptive strike against Spain, in the form of an attack on the annual 'treasure fleet' on its way from South America. Bute strongly opposed this in the Cabinet, and his arguments won round all the other members, with the exception of Pitt's brother-in-law, Lord Temple. Pitt, unwilling to be over-ruled on any issue concerning the war, immediately resigned, on 5 October 1761, declaring 'I will be responsible for nothing that I do not direct' (see Chapter 9).

With Pitt gone, there was no one to challenge Bute's dominance, and he took over running the war effort, scaling back Britain's participation in the war in Germany, and its subsidy to Prussia, in a bid to reduce the 'enormous debts' which so worried him and the King. This alienated Frederick the Great, who henceforth saw Britain as an unreliable ally, and sought instead an alliance with Russia, to the great consternation of Pitt, who accused Bute of leading Britain into isolation. Meanwhile, the evidence grew that Spain was preparing to intervene in support of France, and on 4 January 1762 Bute himself took the initiative of declaring war, despite his earlier stance. He was now to rival Pitt's earlier energy in prosecuting the war, at least in its maritime dimensions, and 1762 became another 'year of victories', with both Havana and Manila being seized from Spain, and Martinique, Grenada, St. Vincent, St. Lucia and Tobago from France. Meanwhile, in May 1762, Newcastle, feeling that he had become a mere cipher in his own government finally resigned, leaving the way open for Bute to become First Lord of the Treasury, and thus the nominal as well as the actual head of the administration. George Grenville, a younger brother of Earl Temple, and brother-in-law to Pitt, from whom he was estranged, succeeded him as Secretary of State (North), while Henry Fox, who remained as Paymaster-General, became Leader of the House of Commons, assuring by his none too scrupulous means that a solid majority was maintained for Bute's policies, despite his growing unpopularity. It was Fox who initiated the so-called 'massacre of the Pelhamite innocents', in October 1762, when George III wrongly suspected Newcastle and Devonshire of plotting a 'coup', and stripped them of their lord lieutenancies, while dismissing a wide range of their followers from more junior posts (see Chapter 5). Bute and the King were now determined to bring the war to an end as quickly as possible, in order to end the drain on Britain's finances, and the Duke of Bedford was despatched to France to negotiate the best terms he could get. This did not prove difficult, as both France and Spain, following their new round of defeats, were in no mood to extend the struggle, while France's allies – Russia, Austria and Sweden – had already signed separate peace agreements with Prussia, restoring the ante-bellum situation in Central Europe. On 10 February 1763, the Treaty of Paris was signed between Britain, France, Spain and Portugal. Its main provisions included the cession by France to Britain of Canada, Cape Breton Island and the Middle West as far as the Mississippi, but it retained the islands of St. Pierre and Miquelon and a share in the Newfoundland fisheries. In the West Indies, Britain also obtained the islands of Grenada, Dominica, St.Vincent and Tobago, while annexing Florida from Spain. In Africa it acquired Senegal, while its dominant position in India was assured by the defortification of all the remaining French enclaves. In Europe it recovered possession of Minorca, and France was compelled to evacuate and restore the territories it had conquered in Hanover, Hesse and Brunswick.

Most historians have concluded that this was an honourable peace which brought a fair reward for the achievements of British arms, but it was heavily criticized by Pitt who claimed that the French had been let off too lightly. Thanks to the efforts of Henry Fox, the peace treaty had little difficulty in winning parliamentary approval, but Pitt, who was widely regarded as a martyr, largely won the battle for public opinion, and Bute (whose nickname was 'Jack Boot') became wildly unpopular, being the target of many demonstrations where jackboots and petti-coats (an allusion to his rumoured affair with Princess Augusta) were burnt. Bute was also subjected to savage attacks in the press, John Wilkes founding his famous publication *The North Briton*, of which 45 issues appeared between June 1762 and April 1763, for the specific pur-pose of hounding Bute and the many Scottish associates whom he was believed to have brought into office. Altogether, at this period, Bute 'was lampooned in over 400 prints and broadsheets' (Schweizer, 2004). Bute became unnerved, fearing assassination. 'On 25 November [1762], on his way to the opening of Parliament, he was hissed and pelted by the mob, and if the Guards had not been summoned his life would have been in danger' (Brooke, p.100). Unfamiliar with the capricious ways of the London mob, Bute concluded that it must have been bribed to attack him by his political opponents, and told George III that he wished to resign as a minister, and revert to his previous status as a privileged courtier controlling the government from behind the scenes. George, not lacking courage himself when faced by a hostile mob, was disappointed, but sympathized with Bute and believed that his fears were justified. Bute agreed, however, to remain in office at least until the Treaty of Paris had been ratified. This happened in March 1763, by which time the government was involved in a heated controversy over a proposal by the Chancellor of the Exchequer, Sir Francis Dashwood, to impose a tax on cider. Its critics maintained that 'the collection and enforcement of [this tax] would have threatened personal liberty through the intrusion of inquisitorial officials into private dwellings', while 'the measure was portrayed by Bute's opponents as part of an odious scheme to introduce a "general excise" similar to that envisaged by Walpole in 1733' (Schweizer, 2004). The measure proved intensely unpopular, but Bute strongly defended the Bill in the House of Lords, and it received royal approval on 1 April 1763. The effort finally un-nerved Bute, and he resigned eight days later, recommending the King to appoint Henry Fox in his place. George III baulked at this, regarding

Fox as a man of insufficient 'virtue', whereupon Bute proposed his own protégé, George Grenville, in the belief that he would be happy to act as his puppet. He was to be grievously disappointed. Bute had been less than a year in office, 317 days, the first of a series of short-lived pre-miercies, reflecting the impatience and immaturity of the young monarch. Altogether, George III ran through six different Prime Ministers in the first ten years of his reign, before settling on Lord North, in 1770, who was to serve for twelve years.

Bute retained his position as Keeper of the Privy Purse, but otherwise was now a simple courtier. Nevertheless, both he and the King intended that he should still have the overall direction of the government, but this was to underestimate the determination of Grenville and his fellow ministers to be their own masters. As recounted in Chapter 7, Grenville consistently outmanoeuvred him, and the King was eventually obliged to dispense with Bute's services, and to promise not to meet him privately. After George III peremptorily dismissed Grenville, in July 1765, Bute and his close associates were much involved in the comings and goings which led to the formation of the governments of Lord Rockingham, and subsequently of William Pitt, now Lord Chatham, in July 1766. Bute and his friends were deeply disappointed at not being included in Chatham's government, and Bute wrote a letter of bitter complaint to the King. George, however, who had by now become thoroughly disillusioned about Bute's political judgment, returned a cold reply, and the friendship, which George had often said would continue for the rest of their days, was at an end. This breach, however, was not known to the public, and for several years afterwards Bute was widely believed to wield a secret and malign influence on the King. His reputation as a bogyman continued to haunt him up to and beyond his death, which did not occur until 1792, nearly 30 years after he had ceased to be Prime Minister.

The death of Bute's father-in-law, Edward Wortley Montagu, in 1761 had left Bute as one the richest men in the country. His family's wealth was further increased by the grand marriages which several of his children were to make. Bute acquired the magnificent estate of Luton Hoo, in Bedfordshire, and commissioned Robert Adam to build a grand London residence in Berkeley Square. This was to be known as Bute House, but before it was finished he sold it off to the Earl of Shelburne, and it was subsequently renamed Lansdowne House. He also built a villa at Highcliffe, in the Isle of Wight, where he was to spend his declining years. He also became a major patron of both the arts and the sciences, being a particularly generous benefactor of several Scottish universities.

He continued his interest in botany, publishing in 1785 a nine-volume work entitled *Botanical Tables Containing the Families of British Plants*, containing 654 hand-coloured plates, which won him the approbation of such international scholars as Linnaeus and Albrecht von Haller. He may have been pompous and narrow-minded, and was certainly pedantic, but there was no doubting the seriousness of his scholarship. His poor historical reputation is at least partly due to the fact that most history was written by Whigs, including such contemporaries of Bute's as Horace Walpole and the Earl of Waldegrave. Recently, there has been an attempt at least partially to rehabilitate him, led by Professor Karl Wolfgang Schweizer. Writing in the *Oxford Dictionary of National Biography*, he concluded:

> Ultimately, however, Bute is more than a symbol of the aberrations conventionally associated with George III's early reign. Though brief and turbulent, his tenure as secretary of state and as prime minister was not without success. While his plans for political reform remained unfulfilled, Bute showed himself generally capable of leading a ministry in time of domestic stress and international conflict. For all his limitations, he implemented a coherent political strategy, one that consolidated Britain's imperial achievement and projected a minimalist continental policy at a time of intensifying national concern over the financial consequences of war. Altogether, he was a responsible, cautious minister who maintained his concentration on the most important issues and had a clear sense of political priorities. (Schweizer, 2004)

There is something in this, but Bute's principal contribution was to act as a Svengali to a future monarch. He was largely responsible for moulding the man who came to the throne in 1760. A better man, and far more conscientious, than the other Hanoverian rulers, he was unfortunately to prove a worse king. Bute must bear much of the blame for this.

Works consulted

Bigham, Clive (1924), *The Prime Ministers of Britain 1721–1924*, London, John Murray.

Brooke, John (1972), *King George III*, London, Constable.

McKelvey, James Lee (1973), *George III and Lord Bute: The Leicester House Years*, Durham, North Carolina, Duke University Press.

Pares, Richard (1953), *George III and the Politicians*, Oxford, OUP.

Rudé, George (1962), *Wilkes and Liberty*, Oxford, Clarendon Press.
Schweizer, Karl W. ed. (1988), *Lord Bute: Essays in Re-Interpretation*, Leicester, Leicester University Press.
Schweizer, Karl (1998), 'John Stuart, Third Earl of Bute', in *Biographical Dictionary of British Prime Ministers*, London, Routledge.
Schweizer, Karl Wolfgang (2004), 'John Stuart, Third Earl of Bute' (1713–1792), in *Oxford Dictionary of National Biography*, Oxford, OUP.

7

George Grenville – Able Premier, Undermined by His Own Prolixity

The Right Honourable Treasurer of and One of His Majesty's George Grenville His Majesty's Most Honourable Privy Council

George Grenville was a reluctant politician, but once he had committed himself to a political career, he gave it his all, and mastered the details of both Parliament and administration more comprehensively than any of his contemporaries. Horace Walpole described him as 'the ablest man of business in the House of Commons, and, though not popular, of great authority there from his spirit, knowledge, and gravity of character'.

Although he rose to be Prime Minister, he did not enjoy the success which his talents deserved. Caught between his rivalry with his elder brother, Lord Temple, and his brother-in-law, William Pitt, and the impatience of the young George III, his ambitions were circumscribed, and he finished up by being more respected than influential. Born in London on 14 October 1712, the second of five sons and a daughter, his father, Richard Grenville, was descended from a Norman family who had been local landowners in Buckinghamshire since the twelfth century, with an estate at Wotton Underwood. Although he, and several of his ancestors, had been Members of Parliament for Buckinghamshire constituencies, they had never amounted to very much on the national political scene. The family's importance greatly increased, however, through inter-marriage with the much grander Temple family, their neighbours in Buckinghamshire, with their magnificent estate at Stowe. Richard Grenville had married Hester Temple, whose brother, Viscount Cobham, was immensely wealthy, and controlled a string of parliamentary constituencies. This meant that, in the course of time, all five of Richard Grenville's children were able to take up seats in the House of Commons.

Very little is known of George's childhood, as all the family papers were destroyed in a great fire at Wotton in 1820. All his biographer is able to say about it was:

> George enjoyed a happy childhood, with devoted parents and a closely knit family providing all the amusement and stimulus he required. At Eton and Christ Church, Oxford, he proved a conscientious, hard-working scholar; he did not gamble or drink heavily and left no hint of scandal behind him. (Lawson, 1984, p.3)

As a second son, George realized that he would have to earn his own living, and set his sights on a legal career, joining the Inner Temple in 1729, and being called to the bar in 1735, aged 23. During this period, he was dependent for financial support on his elder brother, Richard (later Lord Temple), and though he inherited £3000 from his father, in 1727, this too was administered by his brother. Philip Lawson comments: 'He endured this period of dependence with good grace but in his later years economy and thrift became the *modus vivendi* of George's family life. These restraints coloured his attitude to personal finances and eventually those of the nation too' (ibid., p.4).

George was doing well in the law, and had no thought of switching professions. But, in 1741, when he was 28, his uncle drafted him in to fill a vacancy in one of his 'pocket' boroughs – Buckingham – where the electoral role contained only 13 voters. Cobham had become a man with a mission. A strong Whig, and previously a loyal supporter of Sir Robert Walpole, he had fallen out with the Prime Minister in 1733, when he fiercely opposed his plans to introduce a general excise duty (see Chapter 1). Walpole responded by stripping Cobham of the colonelcy of his regiment, and Cobham planned to take his revenge, bringing into Parliament, in the 1734 general election, four relatives sworn to oppose Walpole, including George's elder brother, Richard, and William Pitt. This group, all of whom took an ultra-patriotic line, were mockingly referred to by Walpole as 'the boy patriots', but were otherwise known as 'Cobham's Cubs'. All four of them made a mark in the House by the virulence of their attacks on Walpole, and Pitt quickly won a reputation as a much-feared debater. By 1741, Walpole's position had weakened and he appeared vulnerable because of the lukewarm way in which he was prosecuting the 'War of Jenkins' Ear' (see Chapter 1). Cobham called for reinforcements, bringing into the House not only George Grenville, but his younger brother, James. Grenville's aunt, Christian Lyttelton, thought it a great pity that her nephew should abandon 'so promising a legal career' to become an opposition politician. 'A bold stroke for so young a lawyer to begin with being against the Crown', she told her son, the Bishop of Carlisle, and blamed his friends and relatives for 'putting him on so hazardous a point'.

George's election passed without incident – he was unopposed, and his expenses came to a modest £58 12s 7d. He hadn't sought to get into Parliament, but he made an instant mark. His maiden speech, on 21 January 1742, supporting a motion by William Pulteney to investigate Robert Walpole's conduct of the war caught the attention of Horace Walpole, who wrote in a letter: 'There were several glorious speeches on both sides; Mr. Pulteney's two, W. Pitt's and Grenville's...' (ibid., p.8). Grenville very soon went on to establish himself as a highly effective parliamentarian. He lacked Pitt's bravura as an orator, but his speeches were always well prepared and well informed, and he soon developed a mastery of parliamentary procedure unrivalled by any other MP. It was an extremely rare event for him to come off second best in a debate. It was not long before Grenville was recognized as the effective number two to Pitt among Cobham's group of opposition Whigs in the House of Commons. When, in 1744, the group was brought into the government of Henry Pelham, Grenville became a member of the Admiralty Board, and its chief spokesman in the House of Commons, the First Lord, the Duke of Bedford, being in the House of Lords. After three years, he was promoted to be a Lord of the Treasury, and became the secondary spokesman for Treasury affairs in the Commons, where Pelham himself combined the posts of First Lord of the Treasury and Chancellor of the Exchequer. He held this post for seven years, proving himself a first class administrator, as well as a highly effective parliamentarian. Temperamentally, he was ideally suited to these twin roles, his cousin, Thomas Pitt, recalling that he was:

> a man born to public business, which was his luxury and amusement. An Act of Parliament was in itself entertaining to him, as was proved when he stole a turnpike Bill out of somebody's pocket at a concert and read it in a corner in despite of the efforts of the finest singers to attract his attention. (Thomas, 1974, p.118)

Grenville's salary at the Admiralty Board was £1000 a year, which was increased to £1400 at the Treasury. This was sufficient for him to lead a decent but unostentatious life, but he was always very careful with money to avoid having to becoming over-dependent on his brother who had inherited large fortunes from their uncle, Lord Cobham, and his wife, who died respectively in 1749 and 1752. Lady Cobham had been a viscountess in her own right, and Richard Grenville inherited the title, becoming the second Viscount Temple. He also took over the family seat of the Cobhams at Stowe, vacating the Grenville estate at Wotton in George Grenville's favour. Grenville himself also received a series of (relatively small) legacies from his father, who died in 1727, his younger brother, Thomas, a naval captain who died in battle in 1747 and from Lord Cobham, in 1749. He scrupulously declined to make any money, other than his official salary, from his ministerial posts throughout his career, and he carried over into his administration of public finances the same frugality he showed in handling his own affairs.

In May 1749, at the age of 36, Grenville, was married to the 29-year old Elizabeth Wyndham, daughter of the former Tory leader, Sir William Wyndham, and grand-daughter of the snobbish sixth Duke of Somerset, who showed his disapproval of the forthcoming match, by bequeathing Elizabeth a humiliatingly small legacy of £100 a year. This was, Horace Walpole observed, 'Just such a legacy as you would give to a house keeper to prevent her going into service again' (Lawson, 1984, p.56). The bride was no great beauty, her looks having been blemished by a bout of smallpox, so much so that Lady Bolingbroke opined that 'she looked more like 49 than 29' (Thomas, p.117). Nevertheless, the marriage proved a triumphant success; they became a devoted couple, producing nine children, one of whom was himself to become Prime Minister (William Grenville), while Mrs. Grenville was a committed and astute supporter of her husband in all his activities. She was much later to be described by one of Grenville's friends as 'the first prize in the marriage lottery of our century' (Lawson, 1984, p.56). Grenville also gained by acquiring two brothers-in-law – Charles, Earl of Egremont, and Percy, later Earl of Thomond, who became important political supporters.

When Pelham unexpectedly died, in March 1754, it was a distinct set-back for the Cobham-Pitt faction. The new Prime Minister – Pelham's elder brother, the Duke of Newcastle – was much less well-disposed to them than Pelham had been. Newcastle became First Lord of the Treasury, but the Chancellorship of the Exchequer was reserved for a member of the House of Commons. George Grenville, who had by this time built up a formidable mastery of Treasury affairs, rightly believed that he was the best-qualified person to take over the position. Instead, it was given, in rapid succession over a period of 18 months, to Sir William Lee, Henry Bilson Legge and Sir George Lyttelton, Grenville having to make do with the non-cabinet post of Treasurer of the Navy, though he was appointed to the Privy Council, and his salary increased to £2000. He swallowed his disappointment, but began to wonder whether William Pitt, who was about to become his brother-in-law on his marriage to his sister, Hester, and his own elder brother, Richard, now Viscount Temple, might not have used their influence to press his claims more strongly. Whatever, his feelings, however, Grenville remained outwardly loyal to Pitt, who continued as Paymaster-General in Newcastle's government, but also began to establish links with the Leicester House faction, associated with the 'alternative court' of the young Prince George and his mother Princess Augusta (see Chapter 9). This brought Grenville into touch with the Earl of Bute, the leader of the faction, who formed a high opinion of his abilities and marked him down as a valuable potential ally.

In November 1755, Pitt, losing all patience with Newcastle, who had consistently refused to promote him to the leadership of the House of Commons, and was indeed preparing to give the post to his great rival, Henry Fox, launched a massive attack on the government in the debate on the King's speech. He focused on the policy of paying subsid-ies to Russia and the German state of Hesse in an attempt to draw them into the looming war against France. Pitt maintained that this policy was to the benefit of George II's electorate of Hanover rather than of

Britain, and saw no reason why the British Treasury should foot the bill. Grenville backed up Pitt in a well-argued speech, which was, however, a great deal less provocative in its tone. This did not save him from the ire of Newcastle, who – having assured himself of massive majorities in the two parliamentary divisions on the motions moved by Pitt – promptly dismissed the two men from their government posts. Pitt, according to Grenville's biographer, 'was not in the least dismayed at the prospect of opposition; indeed he felt more comfortable that his antagonism towards Newcastle could now have free rein' (Lawson, 1984, p.84). Grenville was less happy, feeling keenly the loss of his ministerial salary. Nevertheless, alongside their new Leicester House allies, he joined Pitt in mounting a sustained campaign against involving the country in 'continental entanglements', and in advocating that the war against France, which was formally declared in May 1756, should be fought on a maritime basis, and in particular in defence of the North American colonies, rather than on European soil.

Grenville continued to interest himself in naval matters and made a powerful speech in favour of abolishing the practice of 'press gangs' in the recruitment of sailors, which he described as 'inhumane and a most inefficient means of guaranteeing naval personnel in times of war' (Lawson, 1984, p.85). He spoke with authority as a former Admiralty minister, but his arguments fell on deaf ears. Nor did he and Pitt enjoy much success in rallying opinion against Newcastle, who kept a tight grip on his parliamentary following. Things began to change, however, with the outbreak of war, and the serious setbacks suffered by British forces, notably the loss of Minorca and of Fort Oswego in Canada, and the 'Black Hole of Calcutta' incident in India. Newcastle found it progressively harder to find spokesmen in the Commons to defend his policies, and when Henry Fox threw in his hand, and resigned as Leader of the House in October 1756, he realized the game was up, and a month later submitted his resignation to George II, advising that Pitt should be asked to form a new government (See Chapters 4 and 9). The King was not willing to accept Pitt as Premier, but agreed to the appointment of the Duke of Devonshire, with Pitt, who became Secretary of State (South), recognized as the dominant figure in the government. Grenville hoped to be appointed Paymaster-General, the post held earlier by Pitt, but was persuaded to resume his position as Treasurer of the Navy. He was disgruntled by his failure to win promotion, particularly as for most of the period of the Devonshire government he had to deputise for the often ill Pitt as Leader of the Commons.

Grenville's second term as Treasurer of the Navy lasted for only five months. As an Admiralty minister, he took it upon himself to advise the King to exercise clemency, after Admiral Byng had been sentenced to death for his alleged failure fully to exert himself in resisting the French invasion of Minorca (see Chapters 5 and 9). His brother, Lord Temple, who was First Lord of the Admiralty, also made representations on Byng's behalf, as did William Pitt, and an exasperated George II peremptorily dismissed both men on 6 April 1757. Three days later, in solidarity with them, Grenville submitted his own resignation. The King, however, had over-reached himself – and the outburst of public support for Pitt soon convinced him – and the majority of leading politicians – that Pitt's presence in the government was indispensable. It took another three months of wrangling and intrigue before a much-broadened government was installed, with the return of the Duke of Newcastle, as Prime Minister, and Pitt back in his former post of Secretary of State (South), and more dominant than ever. He was not able, however, to secure the post of Chancellor of the Exchequer for Grenville, in the face of determined resistance by the King, and in the end Grenville agreed to efface himself in order that the administration could be formed. So, for a third time, he became Treasurer of the Navy, and was to serve for five years. During this time, he won a high reputation for efficiency, and also as a reformer, his Bill to improve the pay and conditions of sailors passed into law, despite strong opposition in the House of Lords, at the second attempt, in 1758. He continued to deputise for Pitt in the Commons throughout this period, and in February 1761, was finally admitted to the cabinet, while continuing to serve as Treasurer of the Navy. During this period, however, his close relations with Pitt, and to some extent with Temple, began to deteriorate. He undoubtedly felt that they should have exerted themselves more strongly in support of his own promotion, and policy differences between them began to appear. These notably concerned finances, where the ever frugal Grenville was aghast at the insouciance with which Pitt allowed the national debt to soar upwards as a result of his ambitious military and naval operations. Grenville also stayed close to Lord Bute and the Leicester House faction, who had turned against Pitt, believing that he had used them as a lever to bring himself to power, and had subsequently neglected to consult or inform them on government policies.

The death of George II, October 1760, and the accession of George III, with Bute becoming the King's closest adviser, and later Prime Minister, proved to be a turning point in Grenville's career. When, in

February 1761, Arthur Onslow, decided to stand down, after 33 years as Speaker of the House of Commons, there was a great deal of support for Grenville, now widely recognized as a distinguished and assiduous parliamentarian, to succeed him. Feeling that he had reached his ceiling, as a minister, Grenville was happy to accept the post, but Lord Bute, and the King himself, dissuaded him, implying that they had higher plans in view. It did not take long for these to materialize. The following October Pitt, having been over-ruled by the Cabinet, egged on by Lord Bute, on the issue of declaring war on Spain, promptly resigned. He was joined by Lord Temple, now Lord Privy Seal, and Grenville's younger brother James, who held a junior ministerial post. Grenville conspicuously declined to follow them, and Bute sent for him, and proposed that he should take Pitt's place as Secretary of State of the Southern Department. Fearing a family split, and the risk of being attacked by his brother-in-law in parliamentary debates, Grenville declined, but recommended his wife's brother, the Earl of Egremont instead. Bute agreed, but ten days later offered Grenville the leadership of the House of Commons, which he accepted, causing an immediate breach with his family, the childless Temple cutting Grenville's sons out of his will and refusing all communication with him.

Grenville proved to be an able leader of the House, and a valuable ally of Bute's within the Cabinet. After attempts to appease Spain had broken down during the autumn of 1761, Bute, who had led the resistance to Pitt's proposal only three months earlier, declared war on 2 January 1762. Immediately the question arose, as to how great a priority should be given to pursuing operations against this new enemy. Bute, supported by Grenville, wanted to divert money raised to continue operations in Germany, to finance naval attacks on Spanish possessions in the Caribbean and the Far East. They therefore proposed to cut the £5 million subsidy promised to Prussia, a suggestion hotly contested by the Prime Minister, the Duke of Newcastle. At a series of Cabinet meetings, held in April 1762, Newcastle was outvoted on the issue, and the following month resigned, feeling that he had become a mere cipher within his own Cabinet. He was succeeded by Bute, who was now the nominal as well as the actual head of the government. His and Grenville's view seemed to have been triumphantly vindicated when British forces seized both Havana and Manila later in the year. This quickly led to the signing of a peace treaty with both France and Spain, in February 1763, bringing an end to the Seven Years War. On the other hand, the decision led to the ending of the alliance with

Frederick the Great's Prussia, which left Britain dangerously isolated on the European continent.

If Bute had expected Grenville to be a docile follower, he had an unpleasant surprise, when he came to form his government. He offered him the post of Chancellor of the Exchequer, which he had long hankered after, but Grenville's appetite for power had grown during his long years of waiting. He turned down the offer, and insisted on being appointed as a Secretary of State, assuming control of the Northern Department, which Bute himself was vacating on becoming Prime Minister. Both he and George III were taken aback by Grenville's demand, and did their best to argue him out of it. As his brother-in-law, Lord Egremont, was already Secretary of State (South), it was inappropriate, the King suggested, for Grenville to hold the parallel post. When Grenville still insisted, Bute proposed a compromise, moving Egremont to become Lord Lieutenant of Ireland. An enraged Grenville 'refused to take any part in this proposition, and said it was impossible for him to take the seals, to have a personal affront given at the same moment to Lord Egremont' (Lawson, 1984, p.133). At this, the King relented, and Grenville was sworn in as Secretary of State (North) on 28 May 1762, his brother-in-law remaining in charge of the Southern Department. Lawson cites the Grenville family biographer, L.M. Wiggin, enumerating the qualities which Grenville had used in reaching high office as 'hard work, ability, and at the last stubbornness' (Wiggin, 1958, p.264).

Grenville's term as Secretary of State was brief and unhappy. Almost from the outset, he found himself at odds with Bute and the King. Both of them were desperate to end the war as soon as possible, in order to reduce the heavy burden on public finances. Consequently, they gave private assurances to French peace negotiators, that they would make concessions beyond those already agreed by the Cabinet. In particular, they promised the return to France of the Caribbean island of St. Lucia, captured early in 1762. When word came from the French Foreign Minister, the Duc de Choiseul, that France was now ready to accept the British peace terms, Bute reported this to the Cabinet, expecting general acceptance. Grenville, however, no less eager for peace, believed that appeasing the French was not the right way to go about it. He strongly opposed the cession of St. Lucia, and rallied a majority of the Cabinet against the proposal. Nevertheless, Bute sent the Duke of Bedford to France with a mandate to complete the negotiations, to the horror of both Grenville and Egremont, who felt that he was too weak a figure to stand up to the wiles of French diplomacy. When Bedford's first dispatches arrived from France, Egremont forwarded them to

Grenville, who was in the country, with a covering note saying 'you will see that silly wretch has already given up two or three points in his conversation with Choiseul, and that his design was to have signed without any communication here' (Lawson, 1984, p.138). Grenville joined in the criticism of Bedford, and he and Egremont both insisted that the British terms should be stiffened after the news arrived on 29 September of the conquest of Havana. Bute was forced to concede the point, but began to wonder whether Grenville could be relied on to steer the anticipated peace treaty through the House of Commons, when he was so lukewarm about its terms. He sought out Henry Fox, an accomplished, and none too scrupulous, parliamentary performer, who agreed to resume the post of Leader of the House, which he had earlier held in 1755–56. There followed two unpleasant interviews between Grenville, and first, Bute, and then, George III, at which they spelled out their intentions for him. He was relieved of his post as Secretary of State, after less than five months, and instead was offered the First Lordship of the Admiralty, at a salary of £2500, less than a third of what he had been receiving.

It was a humiliation, but Grenville felt obliged to accept his fate. His breach with Temple meant that he had no alternative source of revenue, and desperately needed his ministerial salary, even if it was substantially reduced. Nor did he relish the prospect of again putting himself under William Pitt's leadership to campaign against the peace terms. So, writes Lawson, 'he took the admiralty, ate humble pie and nursed his grievances in the hope of settling the score at some future date' (ibid., p.141). George III was greatly disappointed in him, telling Bute, in March 1763, that Grenville 'had thrown away the game he had two years ago' (Beckett and Thomas, 2004). Yet, less than a month later, he invited Grenville to form a new government, replacing that of Bute, who resigned shortly after Parliament ratified the Treaty of Paris, bringing the Seven Years War to an end (see Chapter 6). Bute had been unnerved by the violent protests against him, and the calumnies which had been spread about his alleged affair with the King's mother, Princess Augusta, and was determined to relinquish the premiership. George III reluctantly accepted his resignation, but was resolved to keep him as his principal adviser, who would control the new government from behind the scenes. Bute advised him to appoint Henry Fox, a proposal which the King found highly distasteful, on account of his 'bad character' and corrupt ways. Nevertheless, he wrote to Bute, if this was the only solution that Bute could propose, he would accept it, adding 'but I own from the moment he comes in I shall not feel myself interested in public affairs and shall feel rejoiced whenever I can see a glimmering hope of getting quit of him' (Brooke, 1972, p.101).

Fox was duly offered the Treasury, but aware of his own unpopularity, and fearful of assuming the responsibility, he declined, preferring to hold on to his lucrative post as Paymaster-General, and finally securing his peerage, as the First Baron Holland, though he had hoped for an earldom. Fox suggested Grenville, and George III – concluding that he would otherwise be forced back on Newcastle or Pitt – agreed.

So Grenville became First Lord of the Treasury and Chancellor of the Exchequer on 6 April 1763. He was somewhat surprised at his sudden elevation, and it has been suggested that he accepted the post under the most humiliating conditions, with Bute handpicking his ministers, and the King making it clear that he held his new posts only on sufferance. He wrote to Bute about his new ministers in the most contemptuous terms, saying 'I care not one farthing for these men I have now to do with. [They] are mean in their manners of thinking as well as their actions. They forget what they owe me, but I shall not, therefore sooner or later they shall suffer for it' (ibid., p.102).

In further letters to Bute, he complained of Grenville's 'tiresome manner' and 'selfish disposition'. When the new Prime Minister made a trivial error, forgetting to make an appointment for Lord le Despenser (the former Sir Francis Dashwood) to kiss hands on his succession to a his peerage, he gave him a quite disproportionate dressing down. Nevertheless, Grenville was able to insist on a number of conditions – the retention of his brother-in-law, Lord Egremont, as a Secretary of State, appointments or sinecures for several of his supporters and relatives, and the promise of a pension of £3000 for when he left office. In their entry on Grenville, in *The Oxford Dictionary of National Biography*, J.V. Beckett and Peter D.G. Thomas comment that the 'Duke of Newcastle knew little of this, but shrewdly perceived that Bute had chosen the wrong man if he wanted a puppet minister'.

Initially, Grenville made his way carefully, and his government was widely seen as a 'triumvirate', in which he shared power almost equally with the two Secretaries of State, Egremont, and the Earl of Halifax, a highly experienced minister, whose earlier achievements included the foundation of a colony in Nova Scotia, whose capital, Halifax, was named after him. The three men worked well together, and were united in their resentment that the King insisted on continuing to consult with Bute on public business. Bute himself was hardly to blame for this, taking himself off to Harrogate to take the waters, and then retiring to his country seat at Luton Hoo, declaring that 'he was determined to be a private man for the rest of his days, never to intermeddle in Government' (Lawson, 1984, p.156). Yet the King refused to let him go, constantly writing to him, and insisting on receiving his advice. He also secretly authorized Bute to sound out opposition politicians with a view to replacing Grenville as Prime Minister, and lied to Grenville when he taxed the King about it.

Meanwhile, Grenville worked hard at consolidating his position in the House of Commons, where he attracted considerable support because of his efficiency and his ready responsiveness to Members' views and interests. On most occasions, he dominated the House, though he once fell victim to the ready wit of his brother-in-law, the Elder Pitt. Speaking on the cider tax, which was the final act of the Bute government, he admitted its unpopularity, but asked where else he could raise the money. 'Tell me where', he repeated several times, and Pitt who was sitting opposite, started to hum the opening lines of a well-known hymn, 'Gentle Shepherd tell me where.' The House dissolved in laughter, and the nickname 'Gentle Shepherd' stuck to Grenville for the rest of his life (Bigham, p.104). After four months, the ministry felt strong enough to deliver an ultimatum to the King. Either he must give the Cabinet his full support, and cease to depend on Bute or he must seek a new government. George III chose the latter alternative, and – despite his earlier hostility to Newcastle and Pitt – put out feelers to them. But Pitt, in particular, set his demands too high, in a two-hour interview with the King, and George III came scurrying back to Grenville, asking him to stay on, saying, according to an account written up in Mrs. Grenville's diary:

> that he wished to put his affairs into his hands; that he gave him the fullest assurances of every support and every strength that he could give him towards the carrying his business into execution; that he meant to take his advice, and his alone, in everything: that it was necessary the direction should be in one man's hands only, and he meant it should be his. (Lawson, 1984, p.169)

Had the King been sincere in making these declarations, and had Grenville believed in his sincerity, all might have been well, but, as Lawson put it, 'the basis of trust and mutual understanding...had crumbled away during the summer months' (ibid.). Grenville did not believe that Bute had finally been shown the door by the King, and was constantly on his guard, periodically lecturing the King (at consider-able length) on his duties during his audiences, which only reinforced the deep dislike that the King had for him. Nevertheless, an early gov-ernmental reshuffle was harmoniously agreed between the two men. It was occasioned by the deaths of two ministers – Lord Egremont, who quite unexpectedly succumbed to an apoplectic fit, and the Earl of Granville (formerly Lord Carteret), the veteran Lord President of the Council. Egremont's place at the Southern Department was filled by the Earl of Halifax, whose post as Northern Secretary was taken by the Earl of Sandwich, previously First Lord of the Admiralty. Granville's place was more difficult to fill, but it was eventually assumed by the Duke of Bedford, who commanded the support of around 20 MPs, and whose entry into the government sensibly increased its parliamentary major-ity. Bedford and Sandwich assumed that they would form a new 'tri-umvirate' with Grenville, but after his trial of strength with the King he was determined to be master of his own house, and, with the King's support, refused to agree to this.

Although, the principal mark he made during his premiership was in greatly improving the efficiency of the government machine and its financial structures, Grenville is chiefly remembered for two events – the early stages of the John Wilkes affair and the passage of the Stamp Act, widely blamed as the seminal cause for the rebellion of the North American colonies ten years later. John Wilkes was a radical MP, who had set up an opposition newspaper, *The North Briton*, partly financed by Lord Temple, for the express purpose of criticizing the government of the Earl of Bute, who was attacked in its pages with great venom. After Grenville became Prime Minister, it continued to attack the gov-ernment, though in less personal terms. Issue number 45 of the paper, published in April 1763, however, contained what ministers regarded as a serious libel, and the Earl of Halifax, whose department included powers and responsibilities held in modern times by the Home Office, issued a general arrest warrant for un-named persons associated with the publication. Some 48 persons were arrested, including Wilkes, who was thrown into the Tower of London, but a week later was released by order of the Lord Chief Justice, Charles Pratt, on the grounds that his arrest was a breach of parliamentary privilege. Wilkes and his associ-ates then launched a legal action against Halifax, which resulted in the award of damages to them, and a definitive ruling that the issue of 'general warrants' (that is those not naming individuals) was illegal. The government, however, was not prepared to let matters rest, and par-liamentary resolutions were passed declaring issue 45 a 'seditious libel' and a satirical work published by Wilkes, entitled *Essay on Woman*, an 'obscene and impious libel'. Then, on 20 January 1764, ministers carried a motion in the Commons expelling him from the House so that he could face trial on these charges. Wilkes fled to Paris, but was tried in his absence the following month, found guilty, and later was declared an outlaw for impeding justice. Grenville did not take the initiative in the moves against Wilkes, which were promoted by Halifax and Sandwich, and was content that the law courts had declared general warrants illegal (they were never again used), but he ably defended the government's conduct in the Commons, winning crucial votes of confidence against opposition motions strongly backed by Pitt. This might have seemed the end of the matter, so far as politics was concerned, but the issues raised by the Wilkes case, which had important consequences both for the freedom of the press and the rights of MPs, kept recurring over the next dozen years, involving the premierships of Rockingham, Chatham, Grafton and North.

Grenville was much more directly involved in the introduction of the Stamp Act of 1765. Determined to reduce the national debt, which had ballooned during the recently concluded Seven Years War, he was resolved that the North American colonists, on whose behalf the war had largely been waged, should make some contribution towards paying off the debt, and in particular to financing the large British garrison which was being maintained as a safeguard against possible French moves to regain the territorial losses they had suffered during the war. Grenville considered alternative methods of raising money, but concluded that the levying of stamp duties, which had been in force in Britain since 1671, would be the most efficacious. It would be 'the least exceptionable means of taxation', he told the Commons in his budget speech on 9 March 1764, 'because it requires few officers and even collects itself' (Lawson, 1984, p.200). Under the proposal, which met little opposition in the Commons, stamp duty would be imposed on all colonial commercial and legal papers, newspapers, pamphlets, cards, almanacs and dice. Grenville allowed for a year's delay in applying the Act, in order that the views of the colonists on the actual implementation could be heard, but he did not at all anticipate the barrage of complaints that soon materialized. Indeed, he believed that his Act was an extremely moderate measure, calculated to raise only one-third of the cost of the British garrison, whereas many MPs felt that the colonists should contribute the full amount. Grenville had lost office by the time that the effects of the American boycott of the Act were felt, and the new Rockingham administration hastened to repeal it (See Chapter 8). But the damage had been done, and the cry of 'No taxation without representation' was heard throughout the length and breadth of the 13 colonies. None of Grenville's four successors over the next decade were able or willing to accept the full consequences of the new American militancy, and it was probably only a matter of time before open conflict broke out between the colonists and their 'motherland'.

Grenville was supreme in the Commons, but his relations with the King continued to deteriorate, exacerbated by Grenville's stubborn insistence on controlling official appointments, even those – like Keeper of the Privy Purse – which had previously been regarded as personal appointments by the monarch. In this case, he proposed the appointment of the Earl of Guildford, father of the young Lord North MP, who was a member of Grenville's Treasury Board. The King held out for his own choice, Sir William Breton, a close friend of Lord Bute's, and Grenville gave way with very bad grace after a prolonged argument. There were also periodic conflicts about patronage in Scotland, which was controlled by Bute's brother, James Stuart Mackenzie, who was Lord Privy Seal for Scotland. Grenville endeavoured, with only moderate success, to win precedence for his own nominees. The King came to dread his audiences with his Prime Minister, complaining, 'When he has wearied me for two hours, he looks at his watch to see if he may not tire me for an hour more' (Brooke, p.108). George III was not the only person to be annoyed by Grenville's prolixity. His cousin and devoted political supporter, Thomas Pitt, described him as 'to a proverb tedious...he was diffuse and argumentative, and never had done with a subject after he had convinced your judgment', while Horace Walpole noted that his favourite occupation was talking, and 'brevity was not his failing' (ibid., pp.107–8).

In March 1765 the King, who had not quite reached his twenty-seventh birthday, fell ill with recurrent coughs and fevers, and fears were widely expressed that he might die within a year. He himself proposed a Regency Bill, to provide for that contingency, which would have resulted in the young Prince George, then aged nearly three, coming to the throne. The King declined to name the Regent in the draft Bill, apparently leaving himself the option of making a nomination after it became law, if his illness then took a more serious turn. This led to a widespread suspicion that he intended to choose his mother, the Princess Augusta, who was known to be very close to the Earl of Bute, and it was feared that this was a roundabout way of restoring the

King's former favourite to power. This was far from being the King's intention, but he failed to take Grenville into his confidence as to his reasons for not wanting to name the intended Regent in the Bill. After a parliamentary revolt, he was forced to agree to the naming of Queen Charlotte, which had always been his intention, but he had not wished to upset his own brother, Edward, Duke of York, who had strong nominal claims, but in whom George III had little confidence. The King's failure to consult his ministers over the affair did nothing to improve the existing poor relations between monarch and Prime Minister. The Bill was eventually passed, in May 1765, with Queen Charlotte's name added, but by then the King had recovered his health, and it became a dead letter.

On the very day the Regency Bill received the Royal Assent, fierce riots broke out in London, led by silk workers protesting at the Government's failure to control the importation of silk. The King blamed Grenville for the riots, and saw this as an opportunity to dismiss him, and summoned Pitt to form a new administration. But Pitt unexpectedly refused the offer unless his other brother-in-law, Lord Temple, would agree to serve with him. But Temple had recently had a highly emotional reconciliation with Grenville, and refused to be party to his ejection from office. So once again the King was thwarted, and had to come cap-in-hand back to Grenville to beg him to stay on. Sensing the weak position of the King, Grenville and his Cabinet then imposed humiliating conditions on him before they agreed to resume office. The King wriggled, tried to induce Newcastle and his friends to take office, but they refused to do so without Pitt, and then after two agonizing discussions with his Uncle, the Duke of Cumberland (who had by then effectively replaced Bute as his most intimate adviser) concluded that he had no choice but to submit. The terms imposed by Grenville and his colleagues were that the King should have no more contact with Bute or his brother, James Stuart Mackenzie, that they should have complete control over patronage, and that, in particular, the Marquess of Granby should be appointed as Commander-in-Chief, Lord Holland (the former Henry Fox) should be dismissed as Paymaster-General, and that a Lord Lieutenant of Ireland should be appointed 'by the full approbation and recommendation of the ministers'. After a long day of consultations, on 24 May 1765, George III summoned Grenville at 11 o'clock at night, and agreed to the conditions, seeking only to soften the blow to Mackenzie. He agreed to strip him of patronage powers in Scotland, 'but begged that he should be allowed to retain the sinecure office of Lord Privy Seal of Scotland which the King had promised him for life' (Brooke, 1972, p.119). But Grenville, completely insensitive to the King's personal feelings, was adamant: Mackenzie must go. The King replied, in words he repeated to the Earl of Egmont, who was First Lord of the Admiralty and his only unconditional supporter in the Cabinet, that:

> He saw evidently that they were not satisfied with his parting with his power, but that nothing would content him but his parting with his honour too – bid him take notice what he told him – and earnestly and in great anger take notice of this – more than once – that he had forced him to part with his honour – that as a King for the safety of his people he must submit – but that nothing induced him to this but the danger of the crisis. (Ibid.)

Grenville and his Cabinet were jubilant at their triumph at the King's expense, and fatally assumed that they were now assured of a prolonged spell in government. They could hardly have been more wrong. For as the King's biographer, John Brooke, put it: 'From 22 May 1765 to the day of Grenville's death on 13 November 1770 the King's politics revolved round two aims: first to get Grenville out of office, and next, to make sure he never came back... and he never did' (ibid.) So determined was George III to oust Grenville, that he turned to two men whom he had earlier utterly despised to do the dirty work for him. One was his uncle, the Duke of Cumberland, whom he and his mother had once feared would murder him, to become King himself (as the future King Richard III had done to his two nephews, 'the princes in the Tower'). The other was the Duke of Newcastle, the senior Whig whom he had blamed for the widespread corruption which he believed had infested Government and Parliament during the reign of his predecessor, George II. Less than a month after his humiliation on 22 May, the King commissioned Cumberland to recruit a government which would allow him to get rid of Grenville. Cumberland immediately sounded out Pitt, but he refused, sensing that Cumberland would be the real head of the government, and that he would be only a figurehead. Cumberland then approached Newcastle, who – aged 72 and with 40 years of senior ministerial office behind him – now felt unable to bear the burden of supreme responsibility. He therefore suggested his young protégé, the Marquess of Rockingham, who was highly congenial to Cumberland, who shared his passion for horse-racing. Newcastle accepted the post of Lord Privy Seal, but otherwise the Rockingham government, which took office on 13 July 1765, was an inexperienced and untested team, largely manned from the ranks of the Jockey Club. It looked even more light-weight when, a few months later, Cumberland unexpectedly died, at the age of 44. George III was not worried; he had got rid of his *bête noire*, having told a friend of Horace Walpole that he 'would rather see the Devil in his closet than Mr. Grenville' (Brooke, p.119).

Grenville emerged from his premiership a much bigger figure than when he had entered, and now led a large and loyal band of parliamentary followers. He was the outstanding opposition figure during the largely unsuccessful ministries of Rockingham, Chatham (the elder Pitt) and the Duke of Grafton, which governed for the next five years, but the King resolutely refused to employ him again as a minister (let alone as Premier), and over-looked him again, in January 1770, when he despairingly turned to Lord North. A few months later his health began to decline, and he died of a blood disorder on 13 November 1770, at the age of 58.

He was Prime Minister for 2 years and 85 days, but if he had known to keep his mouth shut and show a minimum of tact in the presence of the King, he might well have had a much longer and more successful tenure. As it was, he set a new – and much higher – standard of ministerial efficiency than any of his predecessors and most of his successors, and he won the grudging admiration of Edmund Burke, who had been a political opponent, but who was to say of him after his death:

> Undoubtedly Mr. Grenville was a first-rate figure in this country. With a masculine understanding; and a stout and resolute heart, he had an application undissipated and unwearied...If he was ambitious, I will say this for him, his ambition was of a noble and generous strain. It was to raise himself, not by the low, pimping politics of a court, but to win his way to power, through the laborious gradations of public service, and to secure to himself the well-earned rank in parliament, by a thorough knowledge of its constitution and a perfect practice in all its business...this country owes [him] very great obligations. (Lawson, 1984, p.1)

Works consulted

Beckett, J.V. and Peter D.G. Thomas (2004), 'George Grenville (1712–1770)', in *Oxford Dictionary of National Biography*, Oxford University Press.

Bigham, Clive (1924), *The Prime Ministers of Britain 1721–1924*, London, John Murray.

Brooke, John (1972), *King George III*, London, Constable.

Lawson, Philip (1984), *George Grenville: A Political Life*, Oxford, Clarendon Press.

Lawson, Philip (1998), 'George Grenville', in Robert Eccleshall and Graham E. Walker, eds., *Biographical Dictionary of British Prime Ministers*, London, Routledge.

Rudé, George (1962), *Wilkes and Liberty*, Oxford, Clarendon Press.

Thomas, Peter D.G. (1973), 'George Grenville', in Herbert Van Thal, ed., *The Prime Ministers*, Volume 2, London, Allen & Unwin.

Wiggin, L.M. (1958), *A Faction of Cousins: A Political Account of the Grenvilles 1733–1763*, Newhaven, Yale University Press.

8
Charles Watson-Wentworth, Second Marquess of Rockingham – the Conscience of the Whigs

If George Grenville is blamed for first having provoked the rebellion of the North American colonists, and Lord North condemned for waging an unsuccessful war against them, the second Marquess of Rockingham may fairly be remembered as the man whose wise counsels, had they been heeded, might well have prevented the War of Independence from taking place. Yet his two periods in office were extremely brief – only 1 year and 113 days in all – and during the interim period of 16 years, during which he led a principled and consistent opposition, his warnings were just as consistently ignored.

A descendant of Thomas Wentworth, Earl of Strafford, chief adviser to Charles I, who was executed by order of Parliament, in 1641, Charles Watson-Wentworth was born on 13 May 1730, the fifth son and eighth child in a family of ten. His four elder brothers died in infancy or childhood, leaving him the heir to his immensely wealthy parents. His father, Thomas, the largest landowner in Yorkshire with extensive holdings also in Northamptonshire and County Wicklow, was an MP and a leading supporter of Sir Robert Walpole, which enabled him to make spectacular advances in the peerage, after being successively created a knight, a baron, a viscount and an earl, the Earl of Malton. At this stage, Walpole was reported to have remarked 'I suppose we shall soon see our friend Malton in opposition, for he has had no promotion in the peerage for the last fortnight' (Bigham, 1924, p.139). It was left to a later Premier, Henry Pelham, to go one step further, in 1746, when Malton was created a Marquess, the first and for a long time, the only one in the English peerage. Charles's mother, Lady Mary Finch, also came from a great Whig family, her father being the second Earl of Nottingham. To emphasize his eminence as a great territorial and political magnate, the first Marquess transformed his ancestral residence of Wentworth Woodhouse, near Rotherham, into a vast palace, with 240 rooms, and the longest country house façade in Europe (185 metres). It is still standing over 250 years later, and remains by far the largest privately owned residence in the United Kingdom.

Fears were expressed that Charles would not long survive his elder brothers, and he was much coddled as a young child. Yet by the age of 13, he had survived a number of serious aliments, and according to his uncle, Lord Winchelsea, 'the young man is of a pretty healthy strong constitution' (Hoffman, 1973, p.3). Known by the courtesy title of Viscount Higham, he attended Westminster School as a day pupil, living with his family at number 4 Grosvenor Square, his father's London residence, bought in 1741. At Westminster, from which he later transferred briefly to Eton, he was known particularly for his participation in adventurous pranks and in amateur theatricals. In 1745, when the Jacobite rebellion took place, the family seat at Wentworth Woodhouse was threatened by Prince Charles Edward's troops on their way south to Derby, and Lord Malton raised three regiments of militia, to one of which he appointed the 15-year-old Lord Higham as Colonel. By December 1745, the danger had passed, as the Young Pretender's forces were in full retreat in Cumberland. The militia was discharged, but the young Colonel, quietly slipped away, and under an assumed name rode to Carlisle, where he put himself at the disposal of the army of the Duke of Cumberland, who was in hot pursuit of the rebels. The Duke received him kindly, and was impressed by his youthful ardour, but having been forewarned by letters from Higham's anxious father, sent him back home, where he greatly feared the reaction of his parents. He need not have worried:

> Charles' devoted sister Mary tried to shelter him from parental wrath; but the need was probably slight. As his safety was assured, the more becoming did his adventure appear in the heir to a great name. Charles' spirit and courage won general applause; his ingenuity brought more guarded admiration; and his family feared only lest his 'military eagerness' should persist. The army was not the place for an only son. (Guttridge, 1952, p.4)

In the aftermath of the final defeat of the Pretender, at Culloden, in April 1746, Higham's father finally received his marquessate, and the young Charles became known as the Earl of Malton. To complete his education, Charles was despatched to Geneva, under the charge of George Quarme, who had been a captain in his militia regiment, where he applied himself to learning both French and Italian, as well as more traditional subjects, such as Greek and Latin. He was at one stage mildly rebuked by his father for his extravagance, and for accepting a gift of £100 from a dubious source. He wrote back full of remorse, and promised to reform his conduct, while Mr Quarme wrote that he was now applying himself diligently to his studies. He returned to England early in 1748, and preparations were then made for his departure on a 'grand tour', beginning in the summer, shortly after his eighteenth birthday. Few young noblemen could have embarked on a grander tour than the Earl of Malton. First of all, he made a round of visits to all 'the most considerable places in England', and then embarked, together with a new tutor, Major James Forrester, who had been released from his military duties on the express leave of the King and the Duke of Cumberland, for a two year stay, mostly in Italy, but also taking in visits to several of the principal royal courts of Europe. Everywhere he went, despite his shyness and modesty, he proved to be a great social success, a later visitor, Lord Stormont, reporting that 'never was any visitor so loved and esteemed in Florence, where every lady made frequent enquiries after him' (Guttridge, p.6). This, however, hardly had a beneficial effect on his health. According to S.M. Farrell:

> Although he had had several childhood illnesses, it may also have been in Italy, through at least one sexual liaison, that he contracted what was probably a persistent problem in his urogenital system. His 'old complaint', as he called it, caused him frequently recurring bouts of debilitating sickness and may have made him impotent, though some contemporaries regarded him as a hypochondriac. (Farrell, 2004a)

In many places he visited, he purchased works of art to be sent back to Wentworth Woodhouse. One acquisition was a fine harpsichord intended for the use of a Miss Mary Bright, to whom he was already apparently unofficially engaged, even though she was still barely 14. Malton concluded his grand tour with visits to four royal courts – those of Austria, Prussia, Brunswick and Hanover.

At Vienna, he was royally received, being seated next to the Emperor at dinner, and came away, he wrote to his father, 'violently fond of our allies the Emperor and Empress from conviction of it's being thoroughly the interest of England to keep up that alliance'. It was a different matter at Berlin, Britain and Austria's opponent during the recently concluded War of Austrian Succession. Here Frederick the Great declined to speak to Malton 'but talked ostentatiously to an unknown visitor from Denmark'. The rebuff in Berlin was compensated by 'ten delightful days at the court of Brunswick', but the highlight of the tour was undoubtedly Hanover, where George II was holding court as the Elector. His reception, he told his father, was 'not only extremely courteous but had an air of satisfaction at seeing a person of whose loyalty and fidelity his Majesty had a very good opinion...I constantly went to court both in the morning and evening and his Majesty did me the honour of speaking to me more or less every day. In short, my lord, you could not have wished a more gracious reception for your son'. The good impression he had made was confirmed by George II himself, who on his return to London told Malton's uncle, Henry Finch 'that he had never seen a finer and more promising youth than Lord Malton' (Guttridge, pp.8–9). Moreover, the Duke of Newcastle, the Prime Minister's brother and eventual successor, had also been in attendance at the court, and insisted on dining and supping with him each day. Malton was now indeed seen as a 'gilded youth', enjoying the good opinion of both the Monarch and the most senior of the Whig leaders. He was also well regarded by the King's favourite son, the Duke of Cumberland, with whom he shared a passionate interest in horse-racing.

Charles was never to see his father again. From Hanover, he had proceeded to Paris, when word came that the Marquess had died, at the age of 57, on 14 December 1750. Malton, still only 20, succeeded to the title and became one of the richest men in England. He came of age on 13 May 1751, and immediately received a letter from Newcastle informing him that he had been appointed to the offices held by his father, as Lord Lieutenant of the West and North Ridings of Yorkshire and *custos rotulorum* (or chief magistrate) of the North. A week later he took his seat in the House of Lords, 'and became assiduous in his attendance, especially when matters of interest to Yorkshire were being discussed' (Guttridge, p.11). Like his father before him, he immediately attached himself to the 'Old Whigs', under Newcastle, and was seen from the outset as their major ally in Yorkshire, where he controlled a string of parliamentary seats. His dominance in the county was further enhanced by his marriage, on 26 February 1752, to the now 16-year-old Mary Bright. She had inherited a fortune of £60,000, including two substantial estates near Sheffield, from her late father, Thomas Bright MP, and these were added to her husband's already large holdings in the county. Rockingham took his responsibilities as a landowner very seriously. He constantly sought to improve his estates, and was a pioneer of new agricultural techniques, being elected a Fellow of the Royal Society for his services in agriculture. His estimated annual income in rents at the time of his inheritance was £20,000: this had at least doubled by the time of his death 30 years later.

Soon after taking his seat in the House of Lords, Rockingham was appointed as a Lord of the Bedchamber to George II, which gave him a position of dignity in the court. In the House, Rockingham was seen as a nervous and hesitant speaker, but so greatly was he esteemed by the Whig leadership that he was invited to move the Loyal Address at the opening of Parliament in 1753. He declined, being – at least at that stage – unambitious for high office, preferring to concentrate on his responsibilities in Yorkshire. Here he made a false start, when he attempted to terminate a long-standing 'gentleman's agreement' between Yorkshire landowners that the two county MPs should be equally divided between the two parties. Rockingham proposed his friend Sir George Savile as a rival candidate to the sitting Tory MP in the 1754 general election. This went down badly with his fellow Whig landowners, who were desperate to avoid what would certainly prove a highly expensive election campaign, due to the very large electorate in Yorkshire. Savile might well have been elected had he run, but Rockingham bowed to the wishes of his fellow grandees, and withdrew Savile's candidature, offering him instead one of his own 'pocket boroughs'. But Savile yearned for the much greater prestige of being a county Member, and preferred to wait until the next general election, when the sitting Whig MP was expected to retire. (He, in fact, died in 1758, and Savile was returned unopposed in a by-election) Rockingham's reputation was damaged both by his rashness in proposing Savile, but also for his pusillanimity in withdrawing him when he met with resistance. He was reproved, in no uncertain terms, by his uncle, the highly influential Solicitor-General, William Murray (later the famous Lord Chief Justice, Lord Mansfield), who was his political mentor. Subsequently, he showed much more tact and better judgment in his electoral management of England's largest and most populous county, and succeeded, over the years, in turning it into a predominantly Whig preserve. By 1768, 26 of the 30 seats in the county were held by Whigs.

When the Seven Years War broke out in 1756, with British arms facing a series of setbacks, there was lively fear of a French invasion. As Lord Lieutenant of Yorkshire, Rockingham distinguished himself by raising record numbers of recruits both for the regular army, and for local militias, of which he formed three regiments within the county, one of which was commanded by Sir George Savile. Newcastle, who was now Prime Minister, following the death of his brother, Henry Pelham, in 1754, was delighted, and his already good opinion of the young Marquess soared. Alongside his public duties, Rockingham played a major role in the development and control of horse-racing, both in Yorkshire and nationally. He was a founder member, and one of the leading spirits, of the Jockey Club, and built imposing new stables at Wentworth Woodhouse, which produced a string of winners of classic races, notably the famous horse Whistlejacket, immortalized in one of George Stubbs's greatest paintings, acquired by the National Gallery in 1997. Rockingham was a regular visitor to race meetings at York, Doncaster and Pontefract, as well as at Newmarket. These meetings were frequented by many of the leading

Whig aristocrats, as well as by the Duke of Cumberland (a fellow steward of the Jockey Club), and much political wheeler-dealing undoubtedly took place in the intervals between races. Rockingham was supported in all his activities, by his wife, who acted as his political secretary, and often gave him shrewd advice. More activist in her approach than her somewhat languorous husband, she took charge of his correspondence, and often herself replied to letters which he had neglected to acknowledge. 'An intelligent, quick-witted, and musical woman, Lady Rockingham had eccentric habits and an engaging sense of humour – which some found too frivolous – and enjoyed a happy married life, despite having no children' (Farrell, 2004b).

Rockingham remained staunchly loyal to the old Whigs, and to George II personally, and in 1756 turned down an offer from Frederick, Prince of Wales, then at odds with his father, to become his Master of the Horse. He became very close to Newcastle and to the fourth Duke of Devonshire, the other leading Whig grandee, who was briefly Prime Minister in 1756–57. He was duly rewarded, in May 1760, being made a Knight of the Garter (a sure sign of the monarch's approval) six days before his thirtieth birthday. The accession of George III, five months later, and his promotion of the Tory, Lord Bute, represented the greatest challenge to the Whig supremacy in over 40 years, and Rockingham was determined to stand shoulder-to-shoulder with his political associates. When George III peremptorily dismissed Devonshire as a privy councillor, in November 1762, (see Chapter 5), he went straight to the King to resign his place at court, recounting their meeting in a letter to his wife, written the same day:

> I had an audience this morning of the King in which I acquainted him, with how much uneasiness & regret I had seen the tendency of all the late domestic measures, that I looked upon the last event of the Duke of Devonshire, as a further explanation & illustration of all the foregoing, that I was grieved to see that all persons, who had long been steadily attached to his Majesty's family etc, were now the mere objects of his Majesty's displeasure than of his favour, that the pursuit of such counsels had given much alarm, & that as I felt the whole so strongly in my mind I beg'd leave not to continue a Lord of the Bedchamber, lest my continuance should carry with it the appearance of approbation. (Hoffman, pp.42–3)

It was typical of Rockingham's high-mindedness and the sense of independence which his wealth and high social position gave him that he was prepared to speak to the King with such frankness. It had little effect on the monarch, who, according to Hoffman, heard him out 'with cold indifference'. But he set an example, which a number of followers of the Duke of Newcastle who held official appointments tried to emulate, by beginning a wave of 'rolling resignations', which they hoped would force Bute's removal from power. But there were too few of them to carry weight, and Bute found no difficulty in finding willing candidates to take their place. Aided and abetted by Henry Fox, then the Leader of the House of Commons, he struck back with the famous 'Massacre of the Pelhamite innocents', in which large numbers of supporters of the Duke, and of his late brother Henry Pelham, who had preceded him in the premiership, were systematically rooted out of their public appointments, both honorific and material. Rockingham was not spared: his Lord-lieutenancies of the West and North Ridings and other important posts he held in Yorkshire were taken from him. At the same time, both Newcastle and the young Duke of Grafton, a rising star in the Whig firmament, lost their own Lord-lieutenancies, though Devonshire was kept in place as the Lord Lieutenant of Derbyshire. He promptly resigned in sympathy with his fellows.

During the next two to three years, under the governments of Bute and George Grenville, Rockingham emerged as a major opposition politician, rarely speaking, but working energetically to marshal the forces of the Whigs, in both Houses of Parliaments. He was to be dubbed 'the Whip of Whiggery' (Hoffman, p.31). Then, in July 1765, the hand of destiny fell on him. George III, having become totally exasperated by Grenville, who he felt had failed to treat him with due respect, decided to get rid of him, come what may (See Chapter 7). Having failed to reach an accommodation with William Pitt, he turned in desperation to his uncle, the Duke of Cumberland and asked him to form a government. Cumberland was willing, but felt it inappropriate, as a Royal Duke, to assume the post of First Lord of the Treasury, so he turned to the Newcastle Whigs to provide a suitable candidate. Newcastle was now 72, and though anxious to play a leading role in the new government, was hesitant to push himself forward. Devonshire, having died some months earlier at the age of 44, was no longer available, while the Dukes of Grafton and Portland, not yet 30, were considered too young. This left Rockingham as the only major Whig grandee available. There was, nevertheless, considerable surprise that the choice should fall on a man who had no previous ministerial experience (in fact he remains only one of four Prime Ministers of whom this was true – the others being two Labour premiers of the twentieth century – James Ramsay MacDonald and Tony Blair, and most recently, David Cameron in 2010). Rockingham himself wrote to a colleague in Ireland:

> It must surprize you to hear that I am at the head of the Treasury ... but indeed the necessity here made it necessary that some thing should be done, & therefore howsoever unsuitable I might be for that office

from my health and inexperience in the sort of business, yet I thought it incumbent on me to acquiesce in the attempting it, rather than throw any fresh confusion into the negotiation. (Hoffman, pp.78–9)

The truth is that Rockingham did not see himself as becoming the head of the government, rather to act as chief lieutenant to Cumberland. The Duke was generally seen as being the 'real' prime minister, and it was in his houses – Cumberland Lodge in Windsor Great Park, and in Upper Grosvenor Street, Mayfair – that the cabinet meetings were held. It was during a meeting in his London residence on 31 October 1765 that he had a sudden seizure, and died at the age of 44. Rockingham, who had expected to be a mere deputy, found himself less than four months later carrying the ultimate responsibility. Not only was he inexperienced himself, but the same was true of most of his Cabinet, of whom only the Duke of Newcastle had a long period of ministerial service behind him. Newcastle thought that he should be running the show, but found himself shunted into the mainly honorific post of Lord Privy Seal. Most of the other ministers were chosen among the personal friends of Cumberland and Rockingham, mostly from among the racing fraternity. The principal members of the government were the young Duke of Grafton and General Sir Henry Conway, a nephew of Sir Robert Walpole, as the two Secretaries of State, and William Dowdeswell as Chancellor of the Exchequer. Dowdeswell was an expert on taxation, but as a former Tory was still feeling his way in what was a very self-consciously Whig government. Perhaps as significant, in the long run, as any of the ministerial appointments was Rockingham's choice of Edmund Burke to act as his private secretary. For the rest of the Marquess's life, he was to remain his right-hand man, giving him shrewd advice, and using his elegant pen to refine and project the political principles which motivated his master. Like the preceding Grenville government, at least in its early days, Rockingham's administration was effectively led by a triumvirate, consisting of himself, Grafton and Conway. John Brooke, the biographer of George III, is withering in his criticism of the government, describing it as: 'a constitutional anomaly. It is the strangest cabinet in British history…. It is the only one formed round the principal members of the Jockey Club' (Brooke, 1972, p.122).

At the outset, the government received warm support from the King, only too happy to have got shot of George Grenville. Yet its parliamentary position was weak, and it was in sore need of finding reinforcements. There were two possible alternative sources – the friends respectively of Lord Bute, and of William Pitt, either of whom would have assured Rockingham of a stable majority. The King was especially keen on an agreement being reached with Bute and his followers, in particular to secure the return of Bute's brother – James Stuart Mackenzie – as Lord Privy Seal for Scotland. He was nursing a bad conscience about having reluctantly agreed with Grenville on Mackenzie's dismissal, despite having previously given him an assurance that he could keep his post for life (see Chapter 7). But Rockingham and his colleagues refused point-blank to agree to this, and insisted on treating Bute and all his faction as pariahs. Their attitude to Pitt was quite different, but the government was badly split on how to deal with him. All the ministers would have welcomed Pitt's parliamentary support, but there were differing opinions about recruiting him, and/or some of his followers, into the government. On the one hand there were those, such as the Duke of Grafton, who were unreserved admirers of the 'Great Commoner' and who wished him not just to join the government, but to take over its leadership from Rockingham. Others remembered how dictatorial he had been as the dominant force in Newcastle's second government during the Seven Years War, and feared for their own authority if he were to become a colleague. There were also great reservations about Pitt's associates, particularly his two brothers-in-law – Lord Temple and George Grenville – whom Pitt might well insist on bringing into the government with him, were he to join. The King was horrified at the prospect of 'the family' as he called them, being brought back to power, and made it clear that Pitt would only be acceptable, if at all, without them. Ministers never reached agreement on how to deal with Pitt, and their continuing split on the issue progressively weakened the government.

Rockingham's government remained in office for barely a year, during most of which time it was chiefly involved in undoing some of the work of the two preceding governments. Most significantly, it repealed the Stamp Act of 1765 (see Chapter 7), which had imposed direct taxation on the American colonists for the first time. It had – quite unexpectedly – led to massive protests, only some of which were peaceful, such as the 'Stamp Act Congress' convened in New York in October 1765, and attended by representatives of nine colonies. They agreed on resolutions of 'rights and grievances' and agreed to petition both King and Parliament to repeal the Act and other objectionable measures. Meanwhile, there were widespread riots, stamp burning and intimidation of colonial stamp distributors, as well as an outright refusal to use the stamps, accompanied by a highly organized boycott of British imports. British manufactures and exporters took fright and lobbied the government to repeal the Act, which Rockingham – who was keen to conciliate the colonists – was readily persuaded to do. It took some time, however, to convince his fellow ministers, and even longer, the King, who at first argued for modification rather than outright repeal of the Act. He eventually agreed, however, and Rockingham felt aggrieved when the repeal was opposed in Parliament, not only by George Grenville and his followers, but by many self-proclaimed 'friends of the King' (Lord Bute's followers), leading Rockingham to believe that they were being privately encouraged by the King. He had it out with the monarch, and the obstuctionism ceased, but the basis of mutual trust between King and Prime Minister was badly shaken. In order to get the repeal through Parliament, however, Rockingham was forced to accompany it with a so-called 'Declaratory Act', based on earlier legislation concerning Ireland. This Act specifically spelled out the superiority of the British Parliament over the various legislative bodies in the colonies, and asserted its authority to pass binding laws on the colonies 'in all cases whatsoever'. The effect of this was to replace the Americans' current concerns over the Stamp Act with a permanent grievance that their interests could be arbitrarily over-ruled by a distant Parliament in which they were unrepresented. Rockingham did not intend that the Declaratory Act should actually be applied: he was in favour of a 'sleeping sovereignty' or 'salutary neglect', under which the colonies should largely be left to their own devices. Unfortunately, his successors had other ideas.

Two other noteworthy legislative measures were carried by Rockingham's government. One was to repeal the unpopular Cider tax, the last measure enacted by Lord Bute, and to replace it by a Window tax. The second was a resolution by the House of Commons declaring general warrants (that is arrest warrants not naming specific individuals) illegal. They had been used, under the Grenville government, for the arrest of John Wilkes and some 47 of his associates in the production of the dissident newspaper, *The North Briton* (see Chapter 7).

Pitt had supported the repeal of the Stamp Act, but was not ready to give consistent backing to the government, though he expected them to consult him before taking important initiatives. In April 1766, after receiving petitions from various mercantile interests, the cabinet considered introducing a Free Port Bill for the West Indies, as part of Rockingham's policy to foster free trade in the colonies. Rockingham suddenly remembered that no word of this had been made to Pitt, and he despatched Burke to see him and to acquaint him with the government's plans. He reported that he found the Great Commoner in a 'peevish and perverse mood', and he reacted unfavourably to a maladroit attempt by Burke to get him to spell out the 'conditions on which he would come into the King's service' (Hoffman, p.116). The haughty Pitt maintained that only the King himself should put such questions to him. A few days later, he 'appeared in the House and captiously seized on a routine motion touching the militia to declare open hostility toward the administration' (op. cit.). In so doing, he lit a fuse which rapidly led to the disintegration, and then the dismissal, of the government. The Duke of Grafton felt that he could not remain in an administration to which Pitt was hostile. He urged Rockingham that ministers should collectively give advice to the King to invite Pitt to form an administration. Rockingham refused and according to a letter written by Grafton to Conway, added that 'he saw no reason why the present Administration (if they received assurances from the king that people in office were to hold their posts at the good will of the ministers) should not carry on very well and with honour to themselves the King's business' (Grafton, 1898, pp.71–2).

But the ever impatient King was becoming increasingly disillusioned with Rockingham, whose capacity he had never rated very highly, once having remarked, according to Horace Walpole, that 'I thought I had not two men in my bedchamber of less parts than Lord Rockingham' (Bigham, p.141). When Grafton resigned, the King left to his ministers the choice of his successor, but was then aggrieved that they chose the Duke of Richmond, like Grafton an illegitimate descendant of Charles II. The King had a low opinion of Richmond, and only very grumpily acquiesced in his appointment. The last straw, so far as George III was concerned, was when Rockingham failed to bring forward proposals to Parliament to make financial provision for three of the King's younger brothers, who had recently come of age. The King intended that the money previously paid to the Duke of Cumberland, under the Civil List, should be applied to this purpose. Several ministers objected to the proposal being put to Parliament at the tail end of the session, when many MPs had retired to the country and it could not be properly debated, and Rockingham decided that it should be held over until the new session began much later in the year. The King, who had noted with approval a speech made by Pitt, on 24 April 1766, in which he had indicated that his own views on the proper role of government more or less coincided with his own, summoned 'the Great Commoner' to an audience on 12 July, at which they agreed that Pitt should form a government on 'as broad a basis as possible'. This meant that some of Lord Bute's followers would be included, and though several of Rockingham's ministers would be retained, neither he nor Newcastle should continue. The

King also insisted that no place should be found for Pitt's brother-in-law, George Grenville. On 30 July 1766, Rockingham's first government came to an end, after one year and 17 days. His successor became the first Earl of Chatham, and unwisely chose to lead his government from the House of Lords, assuming the post of Lord Privy Seal rather than First Lord of the Treasury, another fateful decision (see Chapter 9).

Rockingham had been blithely unaware of the extent to which he had annoyed the King, and had naively assumed that he was in no imminent danger. As his biographer comments:

> If Rockingham was so deluded... his delusion was honourable. He had carried all his measures and served his King well, restoring stability to empire (or so it appeared) and prosperity to commerce. There was abundant evidence of public satisfaction with what had been done. Why should Majesty withdraw support from so successful an administration? (Hoffman, p.23)

The answer was surely that Rockingham was more interested in being a good Whig, and sticking to his principles, than being Prime Minister. The jibe made against many Liberal American presidential aspirants that 'He'd rather be right than President' was never more apt than in his case. He consistently refused to bend his views to suit the King's prejudices, to indulge in empty flattery or to consider for a moment agreeing to the appointment of any of Lord Bute's friends, which would have mollified the King and made his own task of governing easier. He paid the price.

Rockingham had been the youngest ever Prime Minister, and now became an ex-Premier at the age of 36. For the next 16 years, he was, effectively, to act, albeit somewhat spasmodically, as Leader of the Opposition, though no such post existed at the time. During most of this period – between 1770 and 1782 – a Tory government, led by Lord North MP was in power. Rockingham did not lead a united Whig opposition, but his faction was the largest and much the most coherent. The 'Rockingham Whigs', as they became known, have some claim to be regarded as the first modern political party. The other factions were largely made up of the personal followers of leading politicians. A strong group of supporters of George Grenville, largely disintegrated after his death in 1770, while Pitt's (Chatham's) followers mostly transferred their allegiance to the Earl of Shelburne when he died in 1778. The Rockingham Whigs were strongly represented in the House of Lords, while in the Commons the oratory of Edmund Burke, and later of Charles James Fox, a brilliant younger son of Henry Fox, the first Baron Holland, made them a force to be reckoned with. The publication, in 1770, of Burke's pamphlet, *Thoughts on the Cause of the Present Discontent*, provided intellectual justification for the positions taken up by the Rockingham Whigs. The pamphlet argued that George III's attempts to create a more active role for the monarchy were not only against the letter but also the spirit of the constitution, which derived from the 'Glorious Revolution' of 1688–89. This pamphlet was also notable for Burke's justification of the role of 'party', which he defined as 'a body of men united on public principle, which could act as a constitutional link between king and Parliament, providing consistency and strength in administration, or principled criticism in opposition'.

A nervous, and initially ineffective speaker, Rockingham gradually overcame his inhibitions and spoke more frequently in the Lords, where he was listened to with some respect because of his status as a great grandee, his geniality and his apparently spotless character. It was regarded as noteworthy, and more than a shade eccentric, that he appeared more interested in pursuing a consistent line than on gaining office. On more than one occasion he declined invitations to join subsequent governments because he disagreed with their policies. Issues on which he felt strongly and opposed the government of the day included the repeated exclusion of John Wilkes from the House of Commons despite his being returned by his loyal electors in Middlesex, (see Chapters 9, 10 and 11), the use of secret service money to influence elections, attempts to restrict the freedom of the press, and the Royal Marriages Act of 1772, personally promoted by George III to give himself control over the marriages of his descendants and siblings. He proved an advocate of religious toleration, a very moderate supporter of electoral reform and sympathetic to the aspirations of Irish Catholics. Like Burke, he was convinced that George III was exceeding his constitutional powers in intervening so actively in government and in manipulating Parliament, and he also believed that the King was still under the active influence of the Earl of Bute, though there had been no contact between the two men for many years. In 1780, John Dunning, a leading Rockinghamite MP, caused a stir by carrying a parliamentary resolution stating that 'The influence of the crown has increased, is increasing and ought to be diminished'. Most notably, Rockingham was a firm and consistent advocate of conciliation towards the American colonists, strongly opposed Lord North's prosecution of the war against them, and as early as 1778 called for the immediate granting of American independence. In this, he went further than either Chatham or Shelburne, both of whom were highly critical of government policy but still believed it would be possible and desirable to reconcile the 'rebels' to continued British rule. His voice was not heard, and he and his friends were widely attacked as 'unpatriotic'. It was only after the news of General Cornwallis's defeat and surrender at Yorktown reached England, in November 1781, that the bulk of both parliamentary and public opinion began to swing to his side. Lord North realized that the game was up, and sought to resign, but it was only four months later, in March 1782 that George III reluctantly let him go, and – on North's advice – invited Rockingham to form his second government.

George III was initially averse to taking this step, and first approached the Earl of Shelburne, the leader of the Chathamites. But Shelburne declined, aware that he was unlikely to be able to command majority support in the Commons. The King, however, not wishing to deal directly with Rockingham, insisted on using Shelburne as a go-between, and also demanded that he should hold a senior post in the government. This was the only concession which Rockingham was to make – all the other important offices went to Whigs, mostly of the Rockinghamite connection. The only survivor from the previous government of Lord North was the Lord Chancellor, Lord Thurlow, a 'Vicar of Bray' character who succeeded in retaining office in several governments of highly different political complexions. Rockingham intended that his government would be a reforming administration, putting into practice all the policies which he had advocated while in opposition – a novel concept for eighteenth century politicians. One change which he implemented was to alter the designations of the two Secretaries of State, who, apart from their other responsibilities, had been in charge of foreign policy, being respectively heads of the Northern and Southern Departments. Rockingham proceeded to appoint Charles James Fox as Foreign Secretary, and Shelburne as Home Secretary, the first two men to hold these specific posts. Unfortunately, this did not have the intended effect of putting one person unequivocally in charge of foreign policy, as the Home Department was responsible for the colonies, which had great relevance, in particular, to the peace negotiations which were pending with the American colonists. Fox assumed that he would be responsible and was horrified when Shelburne, who was a great deal less sympathetic to the American cause, insisted on interfering. The other main ministers included Lord John Cavendish, as Chancellor of the Exchequer, the Duke of Grafton, as Lord Privy Seal, the Duke of Richmond as Master-General of the Ordnance and Edmund Burke, as Paymaster-General. John Dunning, now Lord Ashburton, became Chancellor of the Duchy of Lancaster.

Rockingham did not prove to be a strong leader of his government. His health was poor, his energy not over-abundant and he was hindered by the fact that the King insisted on treating Shelburne as at least his co-equal, and even taking clandestine steps to assure him the eventual succession to what he evidently hoped would be only a short-lived premiership. Nevertheless, he was determined to implement the policies which he and his followers had fervently preached for many years past. Foremost of these was the determination to curb the King's ability to control Parliament through the use of patronage and bribery, notably by the creation of 'placemen' among MPs. Three Acts of Parliament were rushed through to help bring this about. Two of these ('Clerke's Act' and 'Crewe's Act') had repeatedly been introduced by Rockinghamite MPs, during Lord North's long premiership, and had been voted down. Now produced as government measures, they at last reached the Statute book. The first disfranchised revenue officers, and the second excluded government contractors from the House of Commons. The third act, introduced by Burke, the Civil Establishment Act, imposed strict controls over government expenditure, to prevent it from being used for electoral purposes. The combined effect of these three measures was markedly to reduce the role of corruption in British politics, but – due to disagreement among the leading ministers – the government did not attempt any electoral reform measures which the more radical of them would have liked to push forward. These had to wait until the Younger Pitt briefly but unsuccessfully took up the challenge (see Chapter 14) a few years later, and were not, in fact, enacted until the passage of the 'Great Reform Bill' in 1832.

Rockingham, who was an absentee, but nevertheless enlightened Irish landlord, who kept himself well informed about Irish grievances, also acted to free the Dublin Parliament from its subordination to the Parliament in Westminster. His government repealed parts of the famous 'Poynings Act' of 1494, as well as the Irish Declaratory Act of 1720, ushering in a period of almost two decades during which Ireland became substantially self-governing. The Wolfe Tone rebellion of 1798, followed by the Irish Act of Union in 1800, brought this happy state of affairs to an end (see Chapter 14). Yet it was the peace negotiations to end the War of Independence which dominated the short life of the second Rockingham government. It declared an immediate end to hostilities in North America, and embarked on two parallel sets of negotiations, one with the American colonists and the other with the governments of France, Spain and the Netherlands which had intervened on the

American side. Fox proposed to concede recognition of independence from the outset, while Shelburne, encouraged by the King, wished to hold it back as a bargaining chip during the talks. At a Cabinet meeting on 26 June 1782, held in the absence of Rockingham, who was away ill at his home in Wimbledon, Fox was outvoted, and – threatening to his friends to resign – left the meeting in high dudgeon. After a further meeting, on 30 June, when he was again outvoted he declared that he would in fact resign, as soon as Rockingham was well enough to deal with the matter. The following morning, 1 July, news arrived that Rockingham was dead – his second ministry having lasted a mere 96 days, and was already on the verge of collapse. Rockingham's death, at the age of 52, was attributed to influenza, though the underlying cause was most probably the long-term effects of the urogenitary disease he had contracted over 30 years earlier. The King lost no time in appointing Shelburne as his successor, but his government was weakened from the outset by the refusal of Fox and the majority of the Rockinghamites to take part (See Chapter 12).

Rockingham was a man of only modest abilities, but of great wisdom and integrity. He saw his mission as being to maintain and rejuvenate Whig traditions derived from the 'Glorious Revolution' at a time when they were threatened by rampant opportunism and unremitting pressure from the Throne. Historically, he can be seen as having been on the 'progressive' side on most of the issues of his day, though he was certainly no advanced democrat, believing that government should be the business of an enlightened aristocracy. His immediate legacy was a strong parliamentary party, led by Charles James Fox, which was however condemned to long frustrating years in opposition as it was outmanoeuvred by the King and the Younger Pitt, and then fatally split by its response to the French Revolution (see Chapter 14). It was not until half a century after his death that a new generation of Whigs, led by Earl Grey and Lord John Russell, were able to take over the baton and lead governments inspired by his own principles. They revered Rockingham as a great precursor, but most historians have tended to neglect Rockingham and under-estimate his importance.

Works consulted

Bigham, Clive (1924), *The Prime Ministers of Britain 1721–1924*, London, John Murray.

Bloy, Marjorie (1998), 'Charles Watson-Wentworth, Second Marquess of Rockingham', in Robert Eccleshall and Graham Walker, eds., *Biographical Dictionary of British Prime Ministers*, London, Routledge.

Brooke, John (1972), *King George III*, London, Constable.

Farrell, S.M. (2004a), 'Wentworth, Charles Watson-, second Marquess of Rockingham', in *Oxford Dictionary of National Biography*, Oxford, OUP.

Farrell, S.M. (2004b), 'Wentworth, Mary Watson-, Marchioness of Rockingham', in *Oxford Dictionary of National Biography*, Oxford, OUP.

Henry Augustus, Third Duke of Grafton, (1898), *Autobiography and Political Correspondence*, edited by Sir William R. Anson, London, John Murray.

Hoffman, Ross J.S. (1973), *The Marquis: A Study of Lord Rockingham, 1730–1782*, New York, Fordham University Press.

Langford, Paul (1973), *The First Rockingham Administration, 1765–1766*, Oxford, OUP.

Langford, Paul (1974), 'The Marquis of Rockingham', in Herbert Van Thal, ed., *The Prime Ministers*, Volume I, London, Allen & Unwin.

Norris, John (1963), *Shelburne and Reform*, London, Macmillan.

9

William Pitt, the Elder, First Earl of Chatham – 'I am Sure That I Can Save This Country, and That Nobody Else Can'

For 250 years, the Elder Pitt has been revered as an exemplary, and highly successful, war leader – the forerunner and inspiration of Winston Churchill, whose life and career resembled his in a number of ways. He was, without doubt, a remarkable man, but recent scholarship, (and particularly the writings of the New Zealand academic Marie Peters), has confirmed that he was an erratic and deeply flawed character, whose achievements were a great deal more mixed than his reputation would suggest.

Pitt's family were minor gentry from Dorset, whose status was transformed by his grandfather, Thomas Pitt, who made a fortune as a trader in India, rising to the position of Governor of Madras, under the East India Company. He held this post from 1688 to 1709, returning to England, with an abnormally large diamond, which he sold at a considerable profit, earning himself the nickname of 'Diamond' Pitt. He purchased several West Country estates, the largest being at Boconnoc, in Cornwall. He also succeeded in marrying off all his five surviving children into titled families. His eldest, rather undistinguished son, Robert Pitt, was married to Harriet Villiers, granddaughter of the fourth Viscount Grandison. Thomas Pitt's estates gave him a commanding influence in three parliamentary constituencies, and Robert Pitt was to represent each of these in turn, during a parliamentary career of 22 years, culminating in his appointment as Clerk to the Household of the Prince of Wales (later George II).

William was the fourth child, and second son, of the seven children born to Robert and Harriet. Together with his chronically bad health, his position as a younger son was to prove a handicap to him, financially and psychologically, and was a contributory factor in his late arrival as a politician of the first rank. Like 10 of the first 26 Prime Ministers (Black, 1992, p.2), he was educated at Eton, an experience he detested, and was later to say to his ministerial colleague, the Earl of Shelburne, that 'he scarce observed a boy who was not cowed for life at Eton'. Jeremy Black comments:

> The public schools of the period were certainly violent, characterised by bullying, buggery and the bottle. It is unclear whether the strain of life at Eton was responsible for the onset of Pitt's ill-health. He suffered there from gout, but as that illness in his case had definite psychosomatic aspects, it may well have reflected his response to the school. (Black, p.3)

Pitt was determined not to subject his own children to similar treatment, and had them all educated at home by private tutors. Consequently, the Younger Pitt is probably the only one of Britain's 53 Prime Ministers (to date) not to have been to school. The elder William may not have enjoyed Eton, but seems to have done quite well there, unlike his elder brother, Thomas. His teacher, William Burchett, wrote to his father: 'Your younger son has made a great progress since his coming hither, indeed I never was concerned with a young gentleman of so good abilities, and at the same time of so good a disposition, and there is no question to be made that he will answer your hopes' (Ibid. p.3).

William proceeded to Trinity College, Oxford, where he remained only for a year, during which time he experienced difficulty keeping up with the conspicuous expenditure of his fellow students, most of whom came from wealthier families. His father originally intended him for the Church, where he could have provided one of the several livings on his estates, but changed his mind, shortly before his unexpected death in May 1727. The following year, William, then aged 19, transferred to the University of Utrecht, at that time probably a more distinguished seat of learning, though there is no information about the content of his studies there. In 1730, unsure of what to do with his life, he returned disconsolately to Boconnoc, now inherited by his brother Thomas, where time hung heavily on his hands, writing to a friend: 'I grow more and more out of temper with the remoteness of this cursed hiding place' (ibid., p.5). His only income was a legacy of £100 a year from his father, and he resented being otherwise dependent on his elder brother, to whom he was not close.

In 1731, he was rescued by an old school-friend, George Lyttelton, who introduced him to his uncle, the influential peer, Richard, first Viscount Cobham. Cobham was the commander of the King's Own Regiment of Horse, generally known as Cobham's Own. He offered Pitt a cornetcy in the regiment, which cost £1000, a sum which the family found difficult to raise. The Prime Minister, Sir Robert Walpole, is believed to have come to the rescue, and provided the money in the expectation of parliamentary support from Thomas Pitt and the MPs representing the pocket boroughs he controlled (Peters, 2004). In the event, Walpole was to be grievously disappointed (see below).

William departed with enthusiasm for what was soon to become, despite his best intentions, a tedious life in a series of dreary garrison towns. Evidently more intelligent and serious-minded than most of his fellow officers, it is clear from his letters to his favourite sister, Ann, that he soon fell in with their favourite pastimes of heavy drinking and whoring. This evidently exacerbated his gout, and possibly, Jeremy Black speculates on the basis of a letter which Pitt wrote to a nephew 20 years later, led to his being infected by a venereal disease. If so, he writes, 'that may have played a role in his late marriage, though other factors, principally his relative poverty, may have been responsible' (ibid., p.8). His brother, Thomas, was to marry at the age of 26; William remained a bachelor until he was 46.

After two years of this life, he took time out to depart on what was an abbreviated version of the Grand Tour, taking in only a brief visit to Paris, before proceeding to more lengthy stays in Besançon and Luneville, and shorter visits to Marseilles, Montpellier, Lyons, Geneva and Strasbourg, not being able to spare the time, or the money, to go on to Italy, usually the high point of such tours. In Besançon, he briefly fell in love with the beautiful younger daughter of a local squire, about whom he wrote to his sister Ann. He seems to have considered marriage to her, but rejected the idea because of her lowly background. Not long after his return to England, William's life abruptly changed, with his election to Parliament for the quintessential 'rotten borough' of Old Sarum (5 voters). This was one of the three seats now controlled by his brother Thomas, who had previously sat for it himself, before trans-ferring to the somewhat larger borough of Okehampton (300 voters), also under his control. Thomas had hesitated about bringing William in, flirting with the idea of selling the seat to somebody else, a move which William strongly opposed. Eventually Thomas gave way, and on 18 February 1735 William was elected unopposed in a by-election, at the age of 26.

At this time, Pitt seems to have had no fixed political opinions, and it is possible that, initially, he saw his election primarily as a means of furthering his military career. He regarded himself as a Whig, but chose to align himself not with Walpole, but with the dissident Whigs who formed the liveliest element of the Opposition, the Tories being some-what dormant. Even so, the Opposition Whigs were divided among themselves, the largest faction being led by William Pulteney in the Commons, and by Lord Carteret in the Lords. Pitt, however, joined a smaller group, mostly of younger MPs with family or personal connec-tions with Lord Cobham, who came to be known as 'Cobham's Cubs'. Cobham was fiercely opposed to Walpole, and – taking his cue from him – Pitt made a number of trenchant speeches criticizing the Prime Minister and his policies. Walpole, aghast at the temerity of one whom he had benefited, promptly responded by cancelling Pitt's commission, and in April 1736 his soldiering days came to an abrupt end after five years, without his having seen any action.

There were compensations. Pitt became a frequent visitor to Stowe, the magnificent country seat of Lord Cobham (now the site of a fam-ous 'public' school). Here he consolidated his friendship with George Lyttelton, now also an MP, and various members of the Grenville family, including four brothers, all of whom were to sit in Parliament. The eldest, Richard Grenville (later Earl Temple) was Cobham's heir, and the second, George Grenville, was to precede Pitt as Prime Minister, in 1763–65 (see Chapter 7). The brothers had a younger sister, Hester, whom, much later, in 1754, Pitt was eventually to marry. Meanwhile, Cobham had transferred the loyalty of his group to Frederick, Prince of Wales, now openly opposed to his father, George II, and running an 'alternative' court from his residence at Leicester House (the site of the present Leicester Square). The Prince appointed Pitt as Groom to his Bedchamber, at a salary of £400 a year, which was a welcome addition to the £300 a year, from successive legacies from his father, mother and grandfather, which made up his sole income.

Over the next few years, Pitt emerged as the most effective opposition critic of Walpole and his government, his speeches, invariably trenchant, and sometimes recklessly offensive, became parliamentary occasions not to be missed. He acquired numerous admirers, but also implacable enemies, who later obstructed his passage to power. Pitt carried his party identification lightly, presenting himself primarily as a 'patriot', whose over-riding objective was to increase national power and prestige. He strongly opposed Walpole's pacific attitude to Spain, and his attempt to avoid war by negotiating the Convention of Pardo, in January 1739. In a coruscating speech, he described the Convention as a 'national ignominy ... odious throughout the kingdom', and condemned the proposed payment of financial reparations to Spain as 'a public infamy' (Peters, 1998, p.22). The virulence of his intervention appalled Walpole's supporters, but won him a public kiss from the Prince of Wales, still vehemently opposed to his father and his ministers. When the Convention broke down, and Walpole was forced against his will to launch the 'War of Jenkins' Ear' (see Chapter 1), Pitt transferred his attack to the government's ineffectual prosecution of the struggle. This soon merged into the wider War of Austrian Succession, pitching Britain and Austria against France, Spain, Prussia, Saxony and Bavaria.

After the resignation of Walpole, in February 1742, Pitt played a leading role in efforts to hold him to account for his alleged corruption and misuse of power, making two powerful parliamentary speeches in support of the appointment of a committee of enquiry into his conduct as Prime Minister. Pitt was appointed to the committee, which met in secret, but skilful manoeuvring by Henry Pelham, now leader of the Commons, under Lord Wilmington, prevented it from pursuing its work to a conclusion (see Chapter 1). Meanwhile, Pitt stepped up his criticism of the war effort, focusing on Lord Carteret's forward policy in Germany, which he argued was much more in the interest of George II's electorate of Hanover than of Britain. He railed against the agreement to take 16,000 Hanoverian soldiers into British pay, saying that this was yet another example of the way in which 'this great, this powerful, this formidable kingdom is considered only as a province to a despicable electorate' (Peters, 2004). George II was deeply upset, and resolved never to employ Pitt as one of his ministers. Though critical of Carteret's policy, Pitt enthusiastically backed the war, but argued for a 'maritime strategy', asserting that the powerful British navy was more than a match for France and Spain, from both of whom it could expect 'easy pickings', in the Caribbean and North America, whereas there was, he believed, little to gain from engaging the formidable French forces on the Continent. Though alienating the King, Pitt's position, and his eloquent advocacy, brought him great popularity 'out of doors' (that is outside Parliament, in eighteenth century parlance), and increasingly with Tories and Opposition Whigs in the House of Commons.

Meanwhile, the death of Lord Wilmington, in July 1743, exacerbated divisions in the government, and precipitated a power struggle between the King's favourite, Lord Carteret, Secretary of State (North), and the trio of 'Old Corps Whigs', who regarded themselves as the political heirs to Robert Walpole. They were Henry Pelham, who became First Lord of the Treasury, his brother, the Duke of Newcastle, who was Secretary of State (South) and the Earl of Hardwicke, the Lord Chancellor. Pitt, now 36 years old and anxious to achieve ministerial office himself, sought to throw in his lot with the Pelhamites, and began to modify his criticisms of the government, focusing them almost exclusively on Carteret. In October 1744, he received a welcome financial boost, with the death of Sarah, Duchess of Marlborough, the widow of the great General. Herself a doughty opponent of Walpole, she had been charmed by Pitt's attacks on the former Prime Minister and his corrupt ways. In her will she left Pitt £10,000 'upon account of his merit in the noble defence he has made for the support of the laws of England, and to prevent the ruin of his country' (Black, p.58). A month later, however, Pitt was to suffer a considerable disappointment. Pelham and his associates succeeded in forcing the resignation of Carteret, and proceeded to bring into the government a number of former opposition Whigs. Yet, as Black remarks, 'Pitt was the sole leading opposition Whig who did not gain office' (Black, p.58). Pelham was anxious to include him, but Pitt probably pitched his demands too high, seeking the post of Secretary at War, which George II adamantly refused to grant him. Pelham privately assured Pitt that he would work on the King in the hope that he might later relent his implacable aversion to one who had made such bitter attacks on his beloved electorate of Hanover. Meanwhile Pitt went out of his way to support Pelham's government in his parliamentary speeches, even endorsing their decision to increase British military involvement in Germany. This disappointed some of his 'patriot' supporters who felt, that he was trimming his views in the hope of achieving office. It paid dividends, however, in 1746, when the Pelham government, by threatening resignation, successfully forced the King to cease his private consultations with Carteret (now the Earl of Granville) and secured the dismissal of almost all of his followers from their posts. One of the conditions, which Pelham and his colleagues imposed on the King, was 'That he will be graciously pleased to perfect the Scheme lately humbly propos'd to Him for bringing Mr. Pitt into some honourable Employment' (See Chapter 3).

George II reluctantly complied, appointing him to the very junior post of Joint Vice-Treasurer of Ireland, but three months later, in May 1746, he became Paymaster-General, a post he retained for over nine years, until November 1755. This was outside the Cabinet, but a highly sought position, as the holder traditionally was able to profit from the use of the very large sums of money which passed through his hands. Henry Pelham, who was Paymaster-General between 1730 and 1743, was one of very few eighteenth century holders of this office not to enrich himself in this way, but Pitt, despite his relative poverty, followed his example rather than that of most of his other predecessors. This certainly helped to foster his reputation as an incorruptible politician. Throughout his period as Paymaster-General, Pitt was seen, and saw himself, as something of an 'outsider' within the administration. He was not there because of great wealth or family connection, but had forced his way in because of his power as a parliamentary orator, and his rising popularity 'out of doors'. His ministerial colleagues wanted him in the government so that his debating powers could be exercised on their behalf in the House of Commons, rather than hammering them from the opposition benches. In the typically inelegant words which President Lyndon Baines Johnson used about FBI chief J. Edgar Hoover, two centuries later: 'Better to have him inside the tent pissing out, than outside pissing in.'

Pelham formed the highest opinion of Pitt's character and abilities, writing to his brother that he was 'The most able and useful man we have amongst us; truly honourable and strictly honest. He is as firm a friend to us, as we can wish for, and a more useful one does not exist' (Peters, 1998, p.57). He made no attempt, however, to promote him to the Cabinet, and Pitt was to continue as Paymaster-General for the remainder of Pelham's Premiership. He soon won a reputation as an energetic and efficient administrator, despite his periodic bouts of ill-health, and an able defender of the government's policies in Parliament. These included the compromise peace of Aix-la-Chapelle, which brought an end to the War of Austrian Succession, without achieving many of Britain's announced war aims. The previously highly belligerent Pitt admitted to the House of Commons that he had changed his views, saying: 'I have upon some former occasions, by the heat of youth and the warmth of a debate, been hurried into expressions, which upon cool reflection, I have heartily regretted' (Peters, 2004).

An additional reason for Pitt to feel obliged to conform to government policies, which he might earlier have hastened to condemn, was that he had become dependent on the patronage of the Duke of Newcastle. The Duke had provided him with pocket boroughs of his own at the 1747 and 1754 general elections, when Pitt's elder brother Thomas had withdrawn support from him at Old Sarum. When Pelham died in March 1754, to be succeeded by his brother, Newcastle, Pitt felt that the time had come for him to be promoted to a more senior position, having in mind the Secretary of State (North) post which Newcastle vacated on becoming Premier. He was to be grievously disappointed: Newcastle instead chose the ineffectual Earl of Holderness, while as Secretary of State (South), combined with the leadership of the House of Commons, he appointed the even more mediocre Sir Thomas Robinson. When Robinson proved totally inadequate, Newcastle still did not turn to Pitt, but to his great rival, Henry Fox, who succeeded Robinson in November 1755 (see Chapter 4). Well before this, Pitt began to loosen his ties with the administration, renewing contact with the 'alternative court' of Frederick Prince of Wales, only to be thwarted by the Prince's sudden death in March 1751. Pitt proceeded once again to alienate George II, by paying extravagant tribute to the Prince (who had been deeply estranged from his father), and began again to attack government policies in increasingly vehement Commons speeches, despite the fact that he remained a government minister. Fox, no mean parliamentarian himself, was to comment on Pitt's somewhat wayward conduct, 'He is a better speaker than I am, but thank God! I have more judgment' (Peters, 2004). The rivalry between the two men foreshadowed the more famous, and much more prolonged, struggle between their respective sons, the Younger Pitt and Charles James Fox (See Chapter 14).

In November 1754, Pitt finally got married, at the age of 46. His bride was the 36-year-old Lady Hester Grenville, the younger sister of the three Grenville brothers – Richard (now Earl Temple), George and James – who had been his fellow 'Cobham cubs' and were now his parliamentary allies. He had known her since she was in her teens, but the two had met again two months earlier during Pitt's annual visit to Stowe, where he began a whirlwind courtship. It was a love-match, on both sides, and the marriage brought continuing solace to Pitt among all his later disappointments, and provided him with a family life, with their three sons and two daughters, which he found deeply satisfying. In the judgment of his latest biographer, Marie Peters, 'Certainly, without Hester's unstinting devotion and skills of family management, Pitt's chronic ill health, financial irresponsibility and personal arrogance might well have wrecked, rather than merely hampered, his later career' (Peters, 2004). As it turned out, the marriage was the immediate prelude to the most productive, and constructive, seven years of his life, during which he rose to the peak of his fame and acclaim.

A year into his marriage, Pitt took the decisive step of breaking with the Newcastle government. He had already been highly critical of Newcastle's failure to take energetic action to oppose French encroachments on territory claimed by Britain in North America, and his negotiation of subsidy agreements with Hesse-Cassel and Russia, which Pitt believed was more in the interests of Hanover than of Britain. In November 1755, his impatience and indignation boiled over during an all-night debate on the annual Queen's Speech, reported on admiringly by the normally caustic Horace Walpole, in a letter to a friend (General Henry Conway): 'He spoke at past one, for an hour and thirty-five minutes: there was more humour, wit, vivacity, finer language, more boldness, in short, more astonishing perfections than even you, who are used to him, can conceive...'

Pitt concluded by calling for a war to be fought for the 'long forgotten people of America', a war to be fought by 'our proper force', the navy (Peters, 2004). This speech earned Pitt, as he must have foreseen, instant dismissal from the government, which released him to mount from the opposition benches a hail of attacks as Britain slid unprepared into the Seven Years War, and a series of disasters, of which the loss of Minorca, in June 1756, was only the most conspicuous. Pitt now totally dominated the House of Commons, where his only rival as an orator, the Attorney-General, William Murray, was removed to the House of Lords in 1756, on his appointment as Lord Chief Justice (he became Lord Mansfield). Unable to mount an effective response to Pitt, Henry Fox threw in his hand, and resigned, in October 1756, and Newcastle, despairing of finding an adequate substitute to lead the House of

Commons, followed a month later. George II then summoned Fox and invited him to form an administration, which, over a four-day period of complex negotiations with rival political figures, he attempted to do. Fox was determined that Pitt should join his government, which he adamantly refused to do. It was open to Fox to proceed without 'the great commoner', as Pitt was now known, on board, but he was loath to do so, fearing that his administration would not long survive. His ambition, also, was not so great that he was willing to risk everything for the highest post. He decided instead to set his sights on the Paymaster-Generalship, which he rightly believed would enable him to amass a large fortune. He achieved this objective a few months later, and served for eight years before retiring, with great pomp, but very little honour, as the First Baron Holland.

Newcastle's resignation, and Fox's failure of nerve, had demonstrated to George II that it was impossible at that time to proceed without Pitt's support. The King was still unwilling to have him as his chief minister, but Pitt indicated that he was ready to serve under the fourth Duke of Devonshire, provided that he played a decisive role in the government and that places were found for his own leading supporters, notably his brother-in-law, Earl Temple, who became First Lord of the Admiralty. (See Chapter 4). The new government was formed on 16 November 1756. Devonshire, who had only succeeded to his title a few months earlier, came from one of the most powerful Whig families, and was highly popular in both Court and political circles largely because of his apparent lack of personal ambition. He accepted the post of First Lord of the Treasury with some reluctance, making it clear from the outset that he did not expect to continue in office for very long. This was just as well, for the government lacked a parliamentary majority. The previous general election, in 1754, had been a triumph for Lord Newcastle, and the majority of MPs still looked to him for leadership, even though he was now in opposition. Only a minority of Whigs regarded themselves as supporters of the Devonshire-Pitt administration, though it did attract support from the Tories and the supporters of the 'Leicester House' faction, who looked to the 'alternative court' of the King's grandson and heir apparent, George, Prince of Wales. The Prince was still a minor, but his tutor, the Earl of Bute, was a highly influential figure on his behalf (see Chapters 4, 5 and 6).

Pitt's office was Secretary of State (South), coupled with the leadership of the House of Commons. It was understood from the outset that he would have overall direction of the war effort, which could not have been going more badly. There is no doubt that, at this juncture, Pitt saw himself as a 'man of destiny', saying to Devonshire, 'My Lord, I am sure that I can save this country, and that nobody else can' (Macaulay, 2004, p.317). Despite being heavily afflicted with gout, Pitt entered into his new responsibilities with great vigour, planning substantial reinforcements for America and naval support for the East India Company, which was locked in conflict with France. Despite his earlier opposition to the Treaty of Westminster, signed with Prussia in January 1756, he insisted on the payment of a large subsidy to Frederick the Great, Britain's only ally on the Continent, whose forces were facing the formidable combination of France, Austria and Russia. He also made preparations for the deployment of a large military force in northern Germany to aid the Prussian king. The two men soon formed something of a mutual admiration society, with Frederick saying of Pitt: 'England has been a long time in labour, but she has at last brought forth a man'.

The early months of the Devonshire administration were, however, dominated by the controversy over Admiral Byng and his alleged responsibility for the loss of Minorca to the French (see Chapters 4 and 5). Newcastle, anxious to divert from his own responsibility, had insisted that he be court-martialled, and the trial duly opened on 27 December 1756, ending a month later, with a verdict of guilty on the charge of 'not doing his utmost' to engage the French fleet during the siege of Minorca. The court imposed a mandatory death sentence, but coupled this with a unanimous plea for mercy. Public opinion was howling for Byng's blood, but many MPs felt that both the verdict and the sentence were unjust. Pitt was strongly of this opinion, and (together with Temple) urged the King to exercise the prerogative of mercy. George, however, was determined that the sentence should be carried out, and on 14 March 1757 the admiral faced a firing squad on the deck of HMS *Monarch* in Portsmouth Harbour. A few weeks later, on 6 April, both Pitt and Temple were peremptorily dismissed from office. It was not just the King's anger at Pitt's pleading for Byng that caused his demise. He had also deeply offended the King's younger and favourite son, the Duke of Cumberland ('The butcher of Culloden'), who was refusing to take over command of the armed forces so long as Pitt remained a minister. It was also the case that Pitt had been effectively out of action for around a month, with one of his periodic attacks of gout, and had been almost *incommunicado* at Bath.

Whatever motivated George II, he was totally taken aback by the public reaction. The City of London was up in arms, and 13 other cities in a 'golden rain', in Horace Walpole's words, showered the dismissed Secretary of State with the their freedoms and compliments. No doubt there was an element of manipulation by Pitt's followers, but it certainly appeared to be a rare example of spontaneous support by 'out of doors' opinion for a politician denied royal favour. Not only that, the entire government machine ground to a halt, with Devonshire anxious to throw in the sponge, and a ceaseless round of negotiation and intrigue began, as George II tried in vain to secure a stable government without calling on the services of Pitt. Among other intermediaries he employed, was the pleasure-loving second Earl of Waldegrave, whom he actually appointed as First Lord of the Treasury, on 8 June 1757. After three days, the Earl concluded that his task was hopeless, and he advised the King to send for Pitt. (By some reckonings, Waldegrave qualifies as the second shortest serving Prime Minister, after William Pulteney, Lord Bath, who unsuccessfully tried to form a government in February 1742, but gave up the attempt after two days. Neither man however, has been credited by historians as having actually been in power, and both have been excluded from most roll calls of British Premiers).

If Pitt was now seen as indispensable, so was the Duke of Newcastle, who still commanded majority support in the Commons. Henry Fox, who was Cumberland's leading supporter, was also seen as somebody who needed to be accommodated if a new government was to prove viable. After performing a seemingly endless series of minuets around each other, these three men finally agreed to come together, with Newcastle becoming First Lord of the Treasury, and nominal head of the government, Pitt resuming his post as Secretary of State, but acknowledged as the War Minister and dominant figure in the government, and Fox securing his coveted role of Paymaster-General.

The new government took office on 29 June 1757, almost three months after Pitt's dismissal. The general course of events during the so-called Pitt-Newcastle government, which lasted for nearly five years (the final eight months without Pitt), is described in Chapter 4. Although the two men had their differences, they got on surprisingly well, with Pitt allowed an increasingly free hand in running the war, and Newcastle assuring consistent parliamentary support and raising prodigious amounts in taxation and loans to pay for his ambitious strategy. The war that Pitt waged was the first to be conducted on something approaching a world-wide scale, involving campaigns in North America, the Caribbean, West Africa, Germany, the French coast and India. Pitt was not in a position to plan all these campaigns down to the closest detail, though the instructions to commanding officers, written in his own hand, left little room for their own initiatives. The vast distances involved, and the slowness of communication meant that things seldom worked out precisely in the way that Pitt intended. Nor was his military judgment invariably sound. The series of raids on the French coast which he insisted on, in an effort to relieve pressure on the allied forces in Germany, had very little effect and the resources committed to them could almost certainly have been employed with greater profit elsewhere. What Pitt contributed was his aggressive spirit, his overwhelming commitment to victory, his energy (despite his ill-health) and his ability to impose his dynamic will on all his colleagues and subordinates.

It did not take long for Pitt to turn the war round, and for the setbacks of 1756 and 1757 to be followed by a run of successes in 1758, including the capture of two great French fortresses in North America – Louisbourg on Cape Breton (the 'gateway to Canada') and Fort Duquesne in Pennsylvania, which the victorious British general, John Forbes, promptly renamed Pittsburgh. But it was in 1759, the so-called 'Year of Victories' and still regarded as the most successful year in the whole of British military history, that Pitt's renown as a great war leader reached its apex. In May a prize French possession, the sugar island of Guadeloupe, was captured, followed by Fort Niagara in June. In August, the French army was heavily defeated at Minden by a largely Anglo-Hanoverian force commanded by the Prussian General, Prince Ferdinand of Brunswick, while Admiral Edward Boscowen overwhelmed the French fleet in the Battle of Lagos Bay. In September, Quebec was taken after a titanic struggle in which both the British and French commanders, General James Wolfe and the Marquis de Montcalm, were killed. The year, which also saw the complete expulsion of the French from their West African territories in Senegal and Gorée Island, was rounded off by yet another naval victory, by Admiral Edward Hawke, in the Battle of Quiberon Bay. The following year, 1760, saw the surrender of Montreal to the British and the effective end of French rule in Canada. Meanwhile in India, the defeat at Wandiwash of the Comte de Lally (who finally surrendered his forces at Pondicherry in January 1761) marked the triumphant end of a campaign, in which the turning point had been Robert Clive's famous victory at Plessey, in June 1757. The French dream of becoming the dominant force in India was well and truly over.

During these years church bells were constantly ringing to celebrate the news – often belated – of one success after another. So much so that the ever caustic Horace Walpole was to write that 'we are forced to ask every morning what victory there has been for fear of missing one'

(Turberville, 1929, p.255). Pitt's reputation and popularity soared, and it seemed that there was no limit to the scope and span of his power. Then, on 25 October, 1760, George II died, a week short of his seventy-seventh birthday. Long resistant to Pitt, and forever wary of Newcastle, he had warmed to both men as the flow of victories continued, and was more than content that they should remain indefinitely in office. Not so, with his grandson and successor, George III. The new King, barely 22 years old, headstrong and impatient, was determined to govern in his own way and not subordinate himself to a Whig oligarchy, as he believed the first two Georges had done. Influenced by the writings of Lord Bolingbroke, particularly *The Idea of a Patriot King*, he saw it as his duty to rise above political factions and represent the nation as a whole. He therefore despised Newcastle, whom he saw as the epitome of factional government, and had also formed a low opinion of Pitt, who he believed had joined the Leicester House circle for opportunist reasons and drifted away when it no longer appeared to be a useful vehicle for his own ambitions. George wanted to displace the Pitt-Newcastle government and install his former tutor, the Earl of Bute, but realized that he could hardly do this in the midst of a war the course of which was bringing the government great popularity. Instead, he resolved to insert Bute into the administration, with special and direct access to himself, in a manner which he must have known would undermine the position of both of his most senior ministers (see Chapters 4 and 6). Initially, Bute held no higher formal office than Groom to the Stole, but in March 1761 he was appointed Secretary of State for the Northern Department, in succession to the Earl of Holderness. This put him, in formal terms, in a position of equality to Pitt, and he began increasingly to challenge Pitt's previous ascendancy within the Cabinet. One point at issue was the continuation of the war against France. Pitt was in favour of carrying it on until Britain's traditional enemy had been brought to its knees, but others felt that sufficient territorial gains had already been made to secure a favourable peace settlement, and bring an end to the heavy financial sacrifices of which the country was beginning to weary. In France, too, pressure was building up for a negotiated peace, and Pitt was forced to agree to the opening of negotiations in May 1761. Pitt was not alone in taking a fairly hard line, particularly in seeking to exclude France, which had in any event lost Canada, from the lucrative Atlantic fisheries waters off Newfoundland, but he argued his case more petulantly, which upset many, including the French Foreign Minister, the Duc de Choiseul. This was not, however, the reason that the negotiations failed, the Duc becoming convinced that he could secure a better deal if the hitherto neutral Spain could be induced to enter the war on the French side.

When the two Bourbon monarchs, Louis XV and Charles III, who were first cousins, renewed the 'Family Compact' between their kingdoms in August 1761, this appeared to be an imminent possibility, and Pitt argued strongly for a preemptive attack on Spain, and the seizure of the annual treasure fleet which sailed from South America. When he put this to the Cabinet, only his brother-in-law, Earl Temple, the Lord Privy Seal, supported him. An angry Pitt, flounced out of the government, on 5 October 1761, declaring: 'I will be responsible for nothing that I do not direct'. His self-removal from power left Bute the effective leader of the government, and within eight months, Newcastle, feeling that he had become a mere cipher, also resigned, enabling the King to appoint Bute as First Lord of the Treasury and the head of a reconstructed government. Although Bute had led the opposition to war with Spain, he himself was to announce the declaration of war only three months later (see Chapter 5). Few of Pitt's fellow ministers were sad to see him go, having grown tired of his arrogance and dictatorial ways. Bute, however, wanted to soften the blow for him, and with George III's blessing offered Pitt the governor-generalship of Canada or the largely sinecure appointment of Chancellor of the Duchy of Lancaster. Pitt declined, but accepted a pension of £3,000 a year for his own lifetime and that of his wife Hester and eldest son, John. He refused a peerage for himself, but Hester was created Baroness Chatham. These actions disappointed some of Pitt's own supporters, and – for a time at least – he lost some of his popularity, while his wife was lampooned as 'Lady Cheat'em'.

Despite Pitt's withdrawal from office, the war continued to go well for Britain, with sensational victories over Spain, notably the conquest of both Havana and Manila during 1762. On the continent, however, Frederick the Great was almost overwhelmed by a combination of his Russian, Austrian and Swedish adversaries, but was saved by the fortuitous death of the Tsarina Elizabeth, in January 1762. Her successor, Tsar Peter III, promptly halted all operations, enabling Frederick to negotiate peace treaties which preserved his territories, including Silesia, which he had annexed from Austria in the earlier War of Austrian Succession. With both Britain and France being abandoned by their allies, the two countries, together with Spain, met in Paris early in 1763, and agreed peace terms, under which Britain gained Canada, Cape Breton, the Mid-West as far as the Mississippi, four West Indian islands and Senegal from France, while confirming its dominant position in India. From Spain it gained Florida, while regaining possession of Minorca, which had been occupied by France.

Out of office, Pitt retired to the country, saying he 'hoped never to become a public man again', and determined to devote himself primarily to his young family, in which he took great delight. However, he was drawn back by the parliamentary debate on the preliminary terms of the peace treaties with France and Spain. Although very ill, swathed in white flannel, hobbling on a crutch and supported in the arms of his servants, he spoke for 3 hours and 25 minutes, denouncing the terms as 'inadequate, dishonourable and dangerous'. They were also, he said, 'insecure because they restored the enemy to her former greatness'. Pitt was particularly critical of the restoration of Guadeloupe and Martinique to France, and her retention of the islands of St. Pierre and Miquelon, off the Newfoundland coast, which enabled her to retain her share of fishing rights in the North Atlantic. It was not one of Pitt's finest speeches, and it was poorly delivered and had little effect on the Commons, which voted by 319 to 65 in favour of the government's proposals. But it helped to sustain Pitt's reputation as a patriot, and in later years when France was able to offer crucial support to the American revolutionaries, his judgment seemed to be retrospectively vindicated. For the next five years, Pitt led a restless existence, seemingly unable to decide whether to live a quiet life of contemplation or to plunge back into political controversy. He was not an easy person to cooperate with. As a young man, he had been congenial, if not gregarious. But years of ill-health and frustrated ambitions had coarsened his character, and he became increasingly irritable, self-centred and, at times, paranoid. He quarrelled with two of his brothers-in-law, George Grenville (who became Prime Minister in 1763) and Earl Temple, something he could ill afford to do, as his personal following among leading politicians was very small. A true manic depressive, he alternated between brief spurts of enthusiasm, and long periods of inactivity, during which he became reclusive. Only marriage and his young family – two daughters and three sons born between 1755 and 1761 – seemed to give him lasting satisfaction: he spent long hours with them, especially with his second son, William, whom he coached in oratory from a very young age, and whom he appeared to be consciously grooming for a political career which would surpass his own. In 1765, Sir William Pynsent, an admirer whom he had never met, left him his splendid estate at Burton Pynsent, in Somerset, and Pitt was henceforth able to play the role of country gentleman which he did with great panache, building a new wing to the house and a range of classical farm buildings, where he personally but not very successfully supervised the dairy herd, and erected a column in memory of his benefactor (Black, 1992, pp.20–1). He acquired other properties, both in town and country, and adopted a style of life, complete with liveried servants, he could ill afford, falling grievously into debt, and often having to resort to mortgages and loans from wealthy friends.

Between May 1762 and July 1766, George III went through three Prime Ministers – Bute, Grenville and Rockingham – none of whom was able to serve him for long to his satisfaction (See Chapters 6–8). Pitt remained in opposition, though his appearances on the political scene were spasmodic, due largely to his fluctuating health and frequent bouts of depression. Among his more notable parliamentary interventions was his fierce opposition to the imposition of the Stamp Act on the American colonies and support for John Wilkes' campaign for civil liberties (see Chapter 8). On several occasions he was approached to join one or other government, or to form one of his own, but the demands he made proved unacceptable either to the Prime Minister or the King. His own stance fluctuated wildly – sometimes he took an anti-party line like the King, deprecating all factions, and 'connexions', and at other times claimed to be a true Whig who could only work with those who adhered most strictly to the precepts of the 'Glorious Revolution'. By July 1766, however, when Rockingham's government appeared to be breaking up, Pitt's appetite for power had returned, and he had fewer scruples in accepting an invitation from George III to form an administration of his own.

George's action had been prompted by a speech which Pitt had made on 24 April 1766, in which he had indicated that his own views on the proper role of government more or less coincided with those of the King. On 12 July the two men met, and agreed on the formation of a government on 'as broad a basis as possible', but both men had firm views on those individuals they wished to exclude (Black, p.261). George III wished particularly to do without the services of George Grenville, whom he had peremptorily sacked as Prime Minister one year earlier, and was pleased to hear that Pitt had decisively broken with his brother-in-law. For his part, Pitt did not wish to have as colleagues anyone who had previously served as Prime Minister, in order that his own pre-eminence would not be challenged, which meant that no place could be found for either Newcastle or Rockingham, who had succeeded the Duke as the effective leader of the 'Old Corps' Whigs.

In forming his administration, Pitt made two decisions which, with the benefit of hindsight, could be seen as virtually guaranteeing its failure. He decided not to take the post of First Lord of the Treasury, or as one of the Secretaries of State, but the non-executive position of Lord Privy Seal. Harry Harris MP, a protégé of Henry Fox (who was not included in the ministry) shrewdly commented: 'Pitt, having by this arrangement a cabinet place void of business, interferes in measures just as far as he pleases, while both the responsibility of office and the drudgery of it fall totally upon others' (Black, p.262).

Pitt's other – more fatal – error was to abandon the House of Commons, and to accept the title of Earl of Chatham. In doing so, he gave up one of his trump cards – his total mastery of debates in the lower House, which was by no means balanced by his entry into the House of Lords, where the atmosphere was less amenable to his style of oratory. In fact, Chatham was to speak in the Lords on only two occasions during the more than two years of his premiership. It was not just the facility of speaking in the Commons that Chatham lost – his reputation as 'the great commoner' went with it, and he lost much of his popularity by his apparent eagerness to take a peerage. The example of Walpole and Pelham, his two most effective and long-serving predecessors – both of whom insisted on governing from the Commons – seem to have been lost on Pitt. As Black points out, 'Before the time of Lord Liverpool [1812–27] there was not to be a single Lords-led Hanoverian ministry that endured any time' (Ibid., p.264). Lord North, who joined Chatham's government as a junior minister, and who later took care to remain in the Commons throughout the whole 12 years of his own premiership, wrote to his father, the Earl of Guildford, already on 31 July 1766, describing Chatham's move as foolish, and commenting: 'I should have thought administration more steady with him in the House of Commons' (ibid., p.263).

The government which Chatham formed, on 30 July 1766, was hardly a cohesive team, but rather an *ad hoc* collection of individuals, some more talented than others. The key post of First Lord of the Treasury, went to the youthful Duke of Grafton, an illegitimate descendant of Charles II, whose good intentions hardly made up for his inexperience. The two secretaries of state were General Henry Conway and the Earl of Shelburne, both close political associates of Chatham. The Chancellor of the Exchequer was Charles Townshend, probably the best speaker in the House of Commons, but notably unreliable and willful. He was to die suddenly, in October 1767, when he was succeeded by Lord North.

Pitt had taken the peerage, and chosen to be Lord Privy Seal, because of concerns about his health and whether it would stand up to the strain of leading the Commons and shouldering the most demanding office in the government. In doing so, however, he surrendered much of his authority, and he had great difficulty in controlling the administration which he headed. During the Pitt-Newcastle government, he had been able to call on the sense of national unity, which the war with France engendered, and his lack of skill in man management was less apparent as he had the Duke to smooth over differences with colleagues. Now he was on his own, and – as Black comments – 'His strong will had become increasingly imperious as a consequence of his successful role in the Seven Years War, while his subsequent political isolation had made him more aloof'. He quotes the opinion of John Pringle MP, written as early as December 1766:

> Nothing can prevent the system being effectual but the risk there is of the ministers disagreeing amongst themselves, which may possibly happen as it is said Lord Chatham is very absolute and [has] little communication with the best of them. I will have this done, is the language used; no reply, not one iota shall be altered. These are the answers said to be made to some of the ministers on their remonstrating against some measures proposed, and, mortifying to tell, they were obliged to support them in the House though some of them did it very awkwardly. (Ibid., p.266)

Unlike during the Pitt-Newcastle government, when his energies had been exclusively focused on the war effort, Chatham had no over-arching objective during his own administration, and took a very uneven interest in the main issues which confronted it. His attention was principally directed to foreign affairs, and in particular to renewing the alliance with Frederick the Great's Prussia, which he blamed Lord Bute for allowing to lapse during his premiership in 1762. Frederick had turned instead to Russia, with whom he had forged an alliance in 1764. Chatham, then in opposition, had urged in vain that Britain should propose turning this into a 'triple alliance' linking all three countries. As soon as he came to power, he commanded the British ambassador in Berlin, Sir Andrew Mitchell, to make a formal approach to Frederick along these lines. Mitchell, a veteran on the Berlin diplomatic circuit, and well informed about Frederick's intentions and the detailed nature of his relationship with Russia (now ruled by Catherine the Great, after the murder of her husband, Peter III, in 1762), was highly sceptical, but carried out Chatham's instructions, and reported back that the Prussian King was not interested. The British Prime Minister was dissatisfied, and ordered Mitchell to make a second approach two months later.

This, he did, on 1 December 1766, with no greater success. The Duke of Grafton, effectively the number two figure in the government, was later to comment in his *Autobiography* 'Mr. Pitt's plan was Utopian, and I will venture to add, that he lived too much out of the world to have a right knowledge of mankind' (Grafton, 1898, p.91).

Chatham had no greater success in his plans for dealing with India and the American colonies in the aftermath of the Seven Years War, when he was outmanouvred by his Chancellor of the Exchequer, who favoured quite different policies. Chatham was opposed to the East India Company enjoying revenues from the territories acquired during the war, which he wished to utilize to finance the defence of India. He therefore proposed a parliamentary enquiry into the affairs of the company accompanied by a declaration that the revenues should revert to the British government. Chatham was over-ruled by the Cabinet in favour of Townshend's proposal that an amicable agreement, under which an annual grant would be paid to the government, should be sought with the company. Chatham's health broke down in early 1767, and he retired for long intervals to Bath or to Burton Pynsent, where he was unable to attend to public business for long periods. In his absence a Revenue Act, was drawn up by Townshend, imposing customs duties on a number of goods, including tea, which was exported from India by the East India Company. The imposition of this Act led to continuing difficulties with the American colonists, culminating in the 'Boston Tea Party' in 1773 (see Chapter 11).

Had Chatham been in good health, it is just possible that, despite his largely self-imposed difficulties, he could have made a success of his government. George III was now extremely well disposed to him, and was ready to give him a great deal of support. But in January 1767, he suffered what can charitably be described as a prolonged nervous breakdown, though some observers felt that he was actually going mad. He lost all control of the government, and failed to give a lead on policy issues, saying that they should be left to the 'wisdom' of the House of Commons. Insofar as there was an effective leader of the government, it was the Duke of Grafton, but he lacked natural authority and was also isolated in the House of Lords, so other ministers and the Commons itself were largely left to go their own ways. Chatham's last meeting with the King was in March 1767, though he continued in office for another 18 months. The King for long refused to believe that Chatham had become incapable of directing his government, and sent Grafton down to see him in Somerset in July 1767, even though Chatham had refused a visit from him the previous month. Grafton reported that

Chatham was able to discuss politics, but 'his nerves and spirits were affected to a dreadful degree...his great mind bowed down, and thus weakened by disorder'. The following month he legally signed over the care of his private affairs to his wife, while his old friend, George Lyttelton was reported as telling James Harris MP:

> Pitt disabled by dejection of spirits almost approaching to insane melancholy...[London Lord Mayor] Beckford offered him a Letter of Business, which threw him into agitation on the sight of it, and he would not open it...scarce any one sees him but Lady Chatham...criminal to ask how he does – servants turned off for inquiring. (Black, p.274)

Chatham's doctor, Anthony Addington, the father of a later Prime Minister (Henry Addington, Lord Sidmouth), a specialist in mental health, was confident that he would recover, and prescribed alcohol, plenty of meat and little exercise. Chatham appears to have offered his resignation, in January 1768, but the King refused to consider it, writing to him that 'your name has been sufficient to enable my administration to proceed' (ibid., p.275). Nevertheless, in February 1768, his office of Privy Seal was placed into commission, and in the following October, Lady Chatham was to write that 'the very weak and broken state' of her husband's health had 'reduced him to the necessity of asking the King for permission to resign' (ibid., p.275). By now, even George III was forced to admit that Chatham's government had been a fiasco, and he resolved never to employ him as a minister again. The government was reconstructed, with Grafton, who continued as First Lord of the Treasury, now confirmed as Prime Minister (see Chapter 10).

In the months following his resignation Chatham slowly recovered from his mental illness, and he returned to court, in July 1769, reinvigorated, and apparently anxious to regain office. He made common cause with the Rockinghamite Whig opposition, setting himself up as an arch-defender of civil liberties and of constitutional reform (including many issues arising out of the Wilkes affair – see Chapters 6 and 7) and a powerful advocate of concessions to the American colonists, who were chafing against the imposition of 'taxation without representation'. When Grafton's government fell, in January 1770, their hopes of taking power were disappointed, when the King turned instead to Lord North, whom he found the most tractable of his Prime Ministers, and one of the best at keeping control of the House of Commons. (He was to serve for 12 years, and George III was most upset when he finally insisted on resigning in 1782, after the defeat of the British forces in the American War of Independence.)

Chatham celebrated his sixtieth birthday a month after leaving office, and he was to live for another nine and half years. They were largely years of political frustration to him, but much private happiness, as he luxuriated in his young family, at Burton Pynsent, and indulged himself in a passion for landscape gardening. He lived well beyond his means, and was constantly having to mortgage his properties or seek loans from wealthy friends, and his health remained precarious. There was no recurrence of his mental illness, but he continued to suffer periodically from gout. His alliance with the Rockinghamites broke down after two years, and henceforth he was a rather isolated figure, withdrawing for long periods from parliamentary activity, and keeping close touch with only one other senior figure, the Earl of Shelburne. Shelburne had been a Secretary of State in Chatham's government, and remained a devoted supporter. Even John Wilkes, whose cause he had earlier backed with passion, turned against him, when Chatham failed to support his more radical claims.

After 1774, the only issue which aroused him was the dispute with the American colonists. He combined a strong sympathy with their demands with a conviction that the British Parliament should remain the sovereign authority over the colonies. Thus, he consistently called for concessions to be made to them in the period before hostilities broke out at Lexington in April 1776. Thereafter, he just as consistently advocated a generous peace settlement, which would allow the Americans effectively to be responsible for their own affairs, subject only to their recognizing the ultimate authority of the British crown and Parliament. On 33 May 1777, he rose from his sickbed, and hobbled into the House of Lords, resting on a crutch, to make an impassioned appeal for peace. 'You cannot conquer the Americans', he said, 'I might as well talk of driving them before me with this crutch'. As the war went increasingly badly, with the news, in December 1777, of the surrender of General Burgoyne and his army to the Americans at Saratoga, demands began to be made that the former great war leader should be recalled to office. Lord North repeatedly asked to resign, and in March 1778 implored the King to appoint Chatham in his place.

George III very reluctantly agreed that an approach should be made, but refused to meet with him. The proud Chatham replied that he was willing to form his own ministry, but would only negotiate this directly with the King, who, however, declined to take the matter further, and insisted that North should continue in office. He was reported as declaring that he 'would rather lose his throne than submit to [Chatham] as minister' (Peters, 1998, p.238). Meanwhile, the French recognized American independence, and prepared to send both naval and military support to the rebels. Fearing that the war was effectively lost, the Rockingham Whigs now urged that peace negotiations should be sought on the basis of recognition of American independence. This was too much for Chatham, who despite his long-standing sympathy for the American cause, was too much of an imperialist to contemplate a complete cession of British rule over the 13 North American colonies. His last visit to the House of Lords was on 7 April 1778, when, swathed in flannel and clearly in a weak physical condition, he rose to make a dramatic but largely incoherent speech opposing a resolution by the third Duke of Richmond to let the colonies go their own way. The man who had once said 'If I were an American, as I am an Englishman, while a foreign troop was landed in my country, I never would lay down my arms – never! never! never!', now declared: 'If the Americans defend independence they will find me in their way.' When Richmond replied to his arguments, he intervened a second time, but collapsed in a sudden fit, and was carried out of a shocked Chamber by his two grief-stricken sons and a son-in-law. A famous painting recording the scene, by John Singleton Copley, and sometimes misleadingly entitled *The Death of the Earl of Chatham*, hangs in the National Portrait Gallery. In fact, he lingered on for just over a month, dying on 11 May, at Hayes Place, his suburban home near Bromley.

The House of Commons voted on the day of his death that there should be an official funeral and that a memorial to him should be erected in Westminster Abbey. It also agreed to pay off all his debts. George III King was surprised, and not best pleased, but acquiesced in their decision, and modern visitors to the Abbey may read the following words:

Erected by the King and Parliament
As a Testimony to
The Virtues and Ability
of
WILLIAM PITT EARL OF CHATHAM
During whose Administration
In the Reigns of George II and George III
Divine Providence
Exalted Great Britain
To an Height of Prosperity and Glory
Unknown to any Former Age
Born November 15, 1708; Died May 11, 1778

Together with Robert Walpole, the Elder Pitt has been seen as one of the two outstanding British political leaders of the eighteenth century. They came from a similar social background; both were Etonians and both Whigs, but otherwise they were very different men, and their political careers could hardly have been more dissimilar. What they undoubtedly shared was an exceptional appetite for power. Walpole was able to satisfy this for the unprecedentedly long span of almost 21 years during which he was Prime Minister. Pitt, however, was only able to get his hands near the levers of power for two relatively brief periods: in 1756–61 (when he was at least nominally junior to the Dukes of Devonshire and Newcastle), and in 1766–68, for most of which time he was an impotent 'passenger' in his own administration, which was ineffectively led by a third duke, the Duke of Grafton. For one of his remarkable talents, the remainder of his career can only be seen as a sad story of relative failure. This is partly attributable to bad health, but also to his character and temperament. In truth, the Elder Pitt was a very indifferent politician, compared not only to Walpole, and his own younger son, William, but also to much more mundane figures such as the Duke of Newcastle. He was notably deficient in man management, and greatly blighted his own prospects by the gratuitous offence he caused to the successive monarchs under whom he served, George II and George III. Pitt unfortunately combined the greatest obsequiousness in the royal presence, where it was said that 'he used to bow so low, you could see the tip of his hooked nose between his legs' (Peters, 1998, p.237), with unthinking public attacks on policies and causes the kings were known to favour. Pitt also upset many ministerial colleagues by the dictatorial way in which he imposed his will, without any pretence of discussing the pros and cons. He was too much of a loner to bother to build up any considerable band of personal supporters, and foolishly quarrelled with his influential brothers-in-law, George Grenville and Earl Temple. In the political arena, at least, Pitt seemed incapable of friendship. The most damning testimony in this respect came from the Earl of Shelburne, his closest political associate, who wrote that he was 'never natural...constantly on the watch, and never unbent...I was in the most intimate political habits with him for ten years...without drinking a glass of water in his house or company, or five minutes conversation out of the way of business' (ibid., p.243).

As an orator, and more especially in the House of Commons, Pitt far exceeded any of his contemporaries, who came to regard him as a modern Demosthenes. Few verbatim texts of his speeches have survived, as parliamentary reporting was not permitted, so it is difficult to judge the quality of his argumentation. It is evident that his style was very different from that of his son, William Pitt the Younger, who was to impress by the logical, step-by-step way in which he built up his case. The Elder Pitt appears to have been a much more emotional speaker, who depended more on the striking phrase, the use of paradox, his flashing eyes and dramatic and theatrical gestures. Horace Walpole favourably compared him to David Garrick, the leading actor of the day. The fear and admiration which his speeches provoked were eventually to carry him to high office, despite the manifold and partly self-inflicted handicaps which he bore. It was not enough however, to sustain him at the pinnacle for long, particularly after he had abandoned his favoured arena, the House of Commons. He was often accused of hypocrisy because of the aplomb with which he trimmed his views in the hope of achieving office. Yet there is no doubt that his consistent advocacy of 'patriotic' policies was absolutely genuine and sincere. This lay behind his implacable conduct of the Seven Years War, when, in Horace Walpole's words, he seemed determined 'that his administration should decide which alone should exist as a nation, Britain or France' (ibid., p.246). Walpole bracketed his personal ambitions with his aspiration for his country, concluding, he 'aspired to redeem the honour of his country, and to place it in a point of giving law to nations. His ambition was to be the most illustrious man of the first country in Europe' (ibid., p.246). For a time at least, he succeeded in his objectives, but he was to die a disappointed – if not despairing – man.

Works consulted

Bigham, Clive (1924), *The Prime Ministers of Britain 1721–1924*, London, John Murray.

Black, Jeremy (1992), *Pitt the Elder*, Cambridge, CUP.

Brooke, John (1972), *King George III*, London, Constable.

Clark, J.C.D. (1982), *The Dynamics of Change: The Crisis of the 1750s and English Party Systems*, Cambridge, CUP.

Henry, Augustus Third Duke of Grafton (1898), edited by Sir William R. Anson, *Autobiography and Political Correspondence*, London, John Murray.

Lord Macaulay (1904), *Critical and Historical Essays, Vol. 3*, London, Methuen.

Pares, Richard (1953), *King George III and the Politicians*, Oxford, OUP.

Peters, Marie (1998), *The Elder Pitt*, London, Longman.

Peters, Marie (2004), 'Pitt, William, first earl of Chatham [Pitt the elder] (1708–1778), *Oxford Dictionary of National Biography*, Oxford, OUP.

10

Augustus Henry Fitzroy, Third Duke of Grafton – Well-Intentioned Dilettante

Augustus Henry Duke of Grafton

Augustus Henry Fitzroy was the great-great grandson of Charles II, to whom he bore a certain physical resemblance, and of one of his more long-term mistresses, Barbara Villiers, Duchess of Cleveland. Born on 28 September 1735, he was the elder surviving son of Lord Augustus

Fitzroy and of Elizabeth Cosby, daughter of Colonel Cosby, a former governor of New York. His father, a naval officer, died of fever in Jamaica, aged 25, when Augustus was five years old. The death of his uncle, Lord Euston, in 1747, left him as the heir to his grandfather, the second Duke. Augustus's mother remarried in 1747, and he and his younger brother Charles were largely brought up by the Duke. From 1747, Augustus himself bore the courtesy title of the Earl of Euston.

The young Lord Euston was educated, first at Hackney School, in East London, then at Westminster, and finally at Peterhouse, Cambridge. Meanwhile, 'as a boy he met the famous William Pitt at Lord Cobham's seat at Stowe, and conceived a strong admiration for him' (Bigham, 1924, p.58). It would be more accurate to say that, from that moment onwards, he hero-worshipped the 'Great Commoner', and this was the key to his own political career. After leaving Cambridge, he embarked on the 'grand tour', accompanied by a Swiss tutor, a Monsieur Alléon, of Geneva, whom he described as 'a real gentleman, and a man of great honor, with much knowledge of the world; but who was more fitted to form the polite man than to assist, or encourage any progress in literary pursuits' (Grafton, 1898, p.3). M. Alleon's deficiency in that respect was more than compensated by Lord Albemarle, the British ambassador in France, in whose house he stayed for a lengthy period, giving him 'the opportunity of seeing the best company in Paris, which I cultivated much to my satisfaction.' In Albemarle's library, he was able to pursue his love for history, and

> to study those principles of government which were ever present to my mind from the time I first read the sound system of Mr. [John] Locke. I lost no opportunity of improving myself in that science, on which the most essential interests of mankind in this world depend. (Grafton, p.4)

Not long after his return, Euston married Anne Liddell, the daughter and heir of a wealthy Northumberland coal owner, Baron Ravensworth, in January 1756. He was 20, and she 18. The following December, he was elected unopposed to Parliament in two by-elections, one in a pocket borough controlled by the Duke of Newcastle, the leader of the Whigs and currently Prime Minister, and a week or two later for his family's borough of Bury St. Edmunds, which he chose to represent. In the meantime, he had been appointed as a Gentleman of the Bedchamber to the young Prince George (the future George III). Euston remained an MP for less than five months, as the death, on 6 May 1757, of his grandfather, left him as the 3rd Duke of Grafton. The second Duke had been a great favourite of George II: he was, according to the *Memoirs* of the Earl of Waldegrave:

> a few days older than the King; had been Lord Chamberlain during the whole reign and had a particular manner of talking to his master on all subjects, and of touching upon the most tender points, which no other person ever ventured to imitate. He usually turned politics into ridicule; had never applied himself to business; and as to books was totally illiterate; yet from long observation, and great natural sagacity, he became the ablest courtier of his time; had the most perfect knowledge both of King and ministers; and had more opportunities than any man of doling good or bad offices. (Bigham, p.59)

The new duke thus started off on a good footing with the monarch, recalling in his *Autobiography:*

> When I waited on His Majesty at Kensington, and was admitted into the closet, in order to deliver the ensigns of the Order of the Garter of my late grandfather, the King, after a few common questions, said, and with tears evidently rising his eyes, 'Duke of Grafton, I always honoured and loved your grandfather, and lament his loss. I wish you may be like him; I hear that you are a very good boy.' (Grafton, pp.10–11)

Grafton played little part in politics or in the House of Lords over the next few years, though he counted himself as a strong supporter of the Pitt-Newcastle government, which took office in June 1757. He spent the bulk of his time at his country estates, at Euston Hall, Suffolk and Wakefield Lodge, in Northamptonshire. His great passions were hunting and the turf (he bred racehorses which three times won the Derby and twice the Oaks). but he also took much interest in farming, and in collecting and talking about books. His marriage to Anne Liddell was not a happy one, and they quarrelled incessantly. Four children, of whom only two survived – a boy and a girl – were born during the first five years of their marriage, but in 1761 they left on a prolonged continental tour, ostensibly because of Anne's ill health, but perhaps in an attempt to patch up the marriage. They returned a year later in no better humour with each other, and though another son was born in 1764, their union was effectively over. In 1763, Grafton had met the famous courtesan, Nancy Parsons, whose outstanding beauty was immortalized in a portrait by Joshua Reynolds (now in the Metropolitan Museum of Art, in New York), and began a passionate affair with her, openly disporting her as his mistress at the Ascot races and installing her in a secluded property on his estate at Euston Hall. He was formally separated from Anne in 1765, and – in the evident hope of exchanging one duke for another – she began what seemed to be a promising affair with the young Duke of Portland (another future Prime Minister), who then humiliated her by unexpectedly announcing his engagement to a daughter of the fourth Duke of Devonshire. Anne then lowered her sights and eloped with a mere Irish peer, eight years her junior – John Fitzpatrick, the Earl of Upper Ossory. They had a child in 1768, but were only able to marry after she and Grafton were divorced by an Act of Parliament in 1769.

On his return to England in 1762, Grafton became active in politics, as the leader of a group of 'young friends' of the former Prime Minister, the Duke of Newcastle. He made a strong speech in the House of Lords against the peace proposals which the new Prime Minister, George III's favourite, Lord Bute, was proposing to end the Seven Years War. Regarded as an effective parliamentary debater, he was marked down as a likely candidate for office if Newcastle or Pitt were to return to power. When Bute, and his ally Henry Fox, launched their purge of Whig notables in December 1762 (see Chapter 5), he was stripped of his Lord-lieutenancy of the county of Suffolk. The resignation of Lord Bute, in April 1763, led to the appointment of George Grenville as his successor, and Grafton remained in opposition, working closely with Lord Temple and with William Pitt – Grenville's brother and brother-in-law respectively – who were estranged from him. At Temple's urging, Grafton visited John Wilkes who had been committed to prison in the Tower of London, under a controversial 'general warrant', for alleged seditious libel (see Chapter 7). Grenville's ministry lasted just over two years, by which time he had so exasperated George III (see Chapter 7) that the monarch arbitrarily dismissed him, and invited his uncle, the Duke of Cumberland, to form a new administration. Cumberland did not want formally to head the government, but persuaded the Marquess of Rockingham to take the post of First Lord of the Treasury, and – as recounted in Chapter 8 – selected the remaining ministers primarily from his friends in the Jockey Club, of which Grafton was a leading member. With few exceptions, the new Cabinet was thus made up of very inexperienced politicians, including the 29-year-old

Grafton, who assumed the post of Secretary of State for the Northern Department – one of the three key posts in the government – without any previous ministerial record. Grafton was far from pushing himself forward, and only accepted office on the basis that every effort would be subsequently made to bring the Elder Pitt into the government in a leading role.

The government took office in July 1765, but the sudden death of Cumberland four months later, left it under the direction of a trio of neophyte politicians – Rockingham, as First Lord of the Treasury, Grafton and General Sir Harry Conway, who was Secretary of State of the Southern Department. In practice, Grafton's main contribution was to act as *de facto* leader of the House of Lords, given Rockingham's poor qualities as an orator and his reluctance to speak in the House. Grafton's performances were generally regarded as satisfactory. Rockingham's premiership, which lasted for just over a year, was punctuated by periodic negotiations with Pitt to determine whether, and on what terms, he would join the government, or to lend his parliamentary support. Pitt proved a difficult interlocutor, sometimes being unwilling to commit himself and at other times putting forward unrealistic demands. Grafton, who strongly believed that Rockingham should make way for Pitt, became increasingly frustrated, and when, in May 1766, Rockingham refused point blank to do this, and Pitt responded by attacking the government, felt he could no longer remain as a minister (see Chapter 8). His resignation destabilized the government, and led indirectly to its fall two months later. His replacement was his remote cousin, the Duke of Richmond, another descendant of Charles II, through Louise de Kéroüalle, Duchess of Portsmouth, and the last *maitresse en titre* of his reign. George III only reluctantly agreed to Richmond's appointment, and when – shortly afterwards – Rockingham angered him by delaying the submission to Parliament of a proposal to make financial provision for three royal princes – abruptly withdrew his support and, in July 1766 invited Pitt to form a government 'on as broad a basis as possible'.

Pitt retained many of Rockingham's minsters and, to please the King, included several former supporters of the Earl of Bute. Unwisely, however, he declined to become First Lord of the Treasury, preferring the non-departmental post of Lord Privy Seal, and to go to the House of Lords as the Earl of Chatham. He offered the post of First Lord to his brother-in-law, Richard Grenville, Earl Temple, but Temple refused when Pitt made it clear to him that he would not exercise the full powers previously associated with that post. Pitt then approached Grafton, who, doubting his own capacity and almost entirely lacking in ambition, also refused. At this, according to his *Autobiography*:

> Mr. Pitt, shewing strong marks of disappointment, rose from his chair, and declared that he must fairly tell me that his whole attempt to relieve the country and His Majesty was at an end; and that he must acquaint the king, that he was once more frustrated in his endeavors to serve him; and that he should recommend to His Majesty to employ others; for that he could do nothing if he had not my assistance at the Treasury. (Grafton, p.90)

Chatham clearly wanted to have somebody who was his unconditional supporter, and who would do what he was told, in this key post. With the greatest of reluctance, and deeply regretting that he could not get back to his horses and hounds, and his ravishing mistress, Grafton allowed himself to be persuaded, little realizing what he was letting himself in for.

For the first seven months or so of the government, Grafton found himself virtually playing the part of errand-boy to Chatham, receiving precise instructions on what to do and whom to appoint, and not daring to undertake anything under his own initiative. Then, from March 1767 onwards, there was an almost total change in his situation, with Chatham retiring to Bath or to his country estate, breaking off all communications with his ministers and leaving them effectively to their own devices (see Chapter 9). He was suffering from a severe nervous breakdown, or even incipient madness. As First Lord of the Treasury, Grafton was expected to act as Prime Minister, but lacked the authority and self-confidence to do so, and made only feeble attempts to coordinate the activities of his fellow ministers. Nor did his 'private life' add to the respect in which he was held. Marital fidelity was by no means regarded as *de rigueur* for Whig grandees of the eighteenth century, but Grafton showed altogether too little respect for public sensibilities by entertaining at his London house in the company of Nancy Parsons, and taking her to an opera performance in the presence of the Queen. He was also widely criticized for neglecting his duties, Horace Walpole described him as 'an apprentice, thinking the world should be postponed to a whore and a horse race', while former Premier George Grenville wrote in a letter: 'The account of the Cabinet Council meeting being put off, first for a match at Newmarket, and secondly because the Duke of Grafton had company in his house, exhibits a lively picture of the present administration' (Bigham, p.62).

Periodically, Grafton wrote rather pathetic letters to Lady Chatham, begging to be allowed to visit her husband to discuss government business with him, to no avail. However, the King gave him warm encouragement to carry on, and to seek to bolster the government's parliamentary position by opening it out to other factions. The death of the mercurial Charles Townshend, in October 1767, led to the appointment of Lord North, as Chancellor of the Exchequer, in October 1767. North also assumed the role of leader of the House of Commons, where he was to show consummate skills as a parliamentary manager. Less satisfactory was the recruitment of two prominent supporters of the Duke of Bedford, in January 1768, Viscount Weymouth replacing General Conway as Secretary of State of the Northern Department, and the Earl of Hillsborough becoming a third Secretary of State, with responsibility for the colonies. Finally, in October 1768, Chatham resigned, and Grafton became Prime Minister in his own right, though he refused to use the title, and forbade his family from referring to him as such.

His cabinet was virtually unchanged, except that the Earl of Bristol replaced Chatham as Lord Privy Seal, while Lord North, having proved himself an effective leader of the Commons, was now more clearly seen as the number two figure in the government. Grafton was far from being a dominant figure, seldom giving a clear lead over divisive issues. More 'liberal' than most of his colleagues, he was on several occasions out-voted within the Cabinet, and calmly accepted defeat without any thought of resigning or fighting to reverse the decision. The most difficult issue with which he had to contend was how to deal with the re-emergence of John Wilkes, who had been living as an outlaw in France since his expulsion from the House of Commons in January 1764, and his conviction for publishing 'seditious, obscene and impious' libels (See Chapter 7). Wilkes had returned to England in February 1768, and offered himself as a candidate for London in the general election the following month, coming bottom of the poll. Unperturbed, he immediately transferred his candidacy to Middlesex, where he fought a rousing campaign, under the slogan 'Wilkes and Liberty' against the two sitting Members, and horrified 'respectable opinion' by coming top of the poll in a constituency which had a much wider electorate than usual. He then surrendered himself to the Court of King's Bench to answer the charges on which he had been convicted four years earlier, and was fined £1000 and sentenced to 22 months' imprisonment, from which he sought a royal pardon. Ministers were divided about how to react, with Grafton himself being highly reluctant to take any action against Wilkes. But more hard-line ministers, strongly pressed by the King, insisted on proposing his renewed expulsion from the House of Common, which was carried on 3 February 1769. The irrepressible Wilkes stood, and was elected unopposed, in the subsequent by-election, on 16 February, and again on 16 March, after a further expulsion, despite a Commons resolution that he was 'incapable of being elected to serve in the present Parliament'. Finally, and in despair, the ministry found a candidate to oppose him in a third by-election, on 13 April. On this occasion, Wilkes secured 1143 votes, and his opponent, Colonel Henry Luttrell, only 296, but the Commons declared Lutrell duly elected. Nobody was particularly proud of this outcome, but it settled the issue for the time being, though Wilkes later staged a comeback, being elected Lord Mayor of London, and when he was again elected for Middlesex in the 1774 general election, he was allowed to take his seat.

Like Rockingham, Grafton was a consistent believer in seeking conciliation with the American colonists, and had opposed the imposition of tea and other duties by Charles Townshend, as Chancellor of the Exchequer, in 1767. When, in 1769, harsh measures were proposed by the Colonial Secretary, Lord Hillsborough, in response to widespread disturbances following the imposition of the Townshend duties, Grafton opposed them, but was outvoted in the Cabinet by five votes to four. Grafton also wanted to repeal the duties on tea, but was overruled. On Irish issues, he had more success in promoting a more liberal line. He passed the Octennial Act, requiring elections every eight years, whereas previously there had been general elections in Ireland only on the death of the monarch. He also laid down that the Lord Lieutenant should be resident in Dublin, whereas previously – like most of Ireland's Protestant landlords – he had spent most, if not all, of his time in England.

Meanwhile, there were significant changes in Grafton's private life. In 1769, following the birth of a son to his estranged wife Anne, by her lover, the Earl of Upper Ossory, he sued her for divorcé, which required an Act of Parliament, passed on 23 March. Three days later, Anne married Upper Ossory, and there was much speculation that Grafton would now wed Nancy Parsons. But she had recently started a passionate affair with the handsome 24-year-old Duke of Dorset, and Grafton abruptly terminated his own liaison with her. Within three months, now aged 33, he married Elizabeth Wrottesley, the highly respectable 23-year-old daughter of Sir Richard Wrottesley, a clergyman and former MP, who was the Dean of Worcester. Described as 'not handsome, but quiet and reasonable, having a very amiable character', her marriage to Grafton appears to have been a happy one. They had 13 children, and Grafton – who some 30 years later wrote his *Autobiography* in the form of a series of letters to his eldest son – said of Elizabeth that her 'merit as a wife, tenderness and affection as mother of a numerous family, and exemplary conduct thro' life, need not be related to you' (Grafton, p.235). As for Parsons, she remained with Dorset for seven years, and then left him for another young aristocrat, the second Viscount Maynard, whom she married, and then began an 'odd *ménage à trois*' with him and the 19-year-old fifth Duke of Bedford (Hanham, 2004). As Viscountess Maynard, she lived till the age of 80, being buried in Paris in the winter of 1814–15, having devoted her old age 'to pious good works'.

Grafton continued to be subjected to criticism for not applying himself whole-heartedly to his duties, and spending altogether too much time on the hunting field and the race track. Some of the most ferocious assaults on him were penned by the anonymous writer, 'Junius', whose cutting and witty letters in the leading London newspaper, *The Public Advertiser*, between 1768 and 1773, became required reading for all who had any serious interest in politics. Some 60 individuals were suspected at one time or another as being the author, but modern scholarship, based on textual analysis, points a finger pretty conclusively at Sir Philip Francis, a leading civil servant (Cordasco, 2004). Francis had no known motive for the extraordinary venom he showed towards Grafton, but it is possible he might have been put up to it by Lord Temple, who never forgave Grafton for accepting the First Lordship of the Treasury in 1768, after he had turned it down (see above). A sensitive man, Grafton was on more than one occasion tempted to resign in the face of such provocation, but worse was to come with the recovery from mental illness of his erstwhile hero, Lord Chatham. He returned to court on 7 July 1769, 'when his manner towards Grafton was particularly cold and ungracious' (Durrant, 2004). It soon became apparent that he was working to discredit the government in the hope of being recalled to office by the King. In Parliament he cooperated with the Rockinghamite opposition, and the government's majority fell dangerously low in several divisions. In January 1770, Chatham's two strongest supporters within the government, the Lord chancellor, Lord Camden (formerly Charles Pratt), and the Master of the Ordnance, the Marquis of Granby, both tendered their resignations. In an effort to bolster his tottering administration, Grafton, with the King's strong backing, appealed to Charles Yorke, son of the former Lord Chancellor, Lord Hardwicke, to take Camden's place. This had always been Yorke's ambition, but as a Rockinghamite he felt cross-pressured and hesitated to take the post. The outcome of his indecision is poignantly described by George III's biographer, John Brooke:

> The King had no patience with hesitation at such a moment, and told Yorke that if he refused this time he should never again have the offer. What with the King's threats, his brother's warning, and Rockingham's reproaches, poor Yorke hardly knew which way to turn. After three days' agony of mind and body he kissed hands, went home and took to his bed. On 20 January he died. Rumour had it that he had committed suicide in an agony of remorse; but contemporary accounts by his wife and brother indicate that he died a natural death, probably from the bursting of a blood vessel. (Brooke, 1972, p.157)

Grafton, who believed the suicide rumour, was deeply shocked, and tried to get the Attorney-General, William de Grey, to take the post. When he declined, he submitted his own resignation. George III always referred to this subsequently as a 'desertion', but his personal relations with Grafton remained good. Nor did he find it difficult to find a satisfactory successor. He lost no time in approaching Lord North, who suited him very well – remaining in office for 12 years, whereas the previous six premiers during the reign had only managed 10 years between them.

Grafton had served as Prime Minister for 1 year and 106 days. He remains to this day the second youngest Premier, after the Younger Pitt, having succeeded his father, Lord Chatham, at the age of 33. He was to live another 45 years, serving on two occasions as Lord Privy Seal, first under Lord North, from whose government he resigned in 1775 in protest against its hard-line policy against the American colonists, and again in the governments of Lords Rockingham and Shelburne, in 1782–83. In none of these governments did he play a very active role. When the younger Pitt became Premier in December 1783, he was again offered the same post, but chose instead to retire to his country pursuits, and never held office again, though he retained his somewhat dilettante interest in politics. When he was still Prime Minister, he had been appointed as Chancellor of Cambridge University, and he played an active part in university affairs, associating himself particularly with a group of liberal churchmen in Cambridge. He himself took an increasing interest in theological matters, writing two books, and becoming an active adherent of the Unitarian church. He lived on until 1811, dying at the age of 75. In 1804, he was to write a series of letters to his son, which were put together by Sir William Anson, the Warden of All Souls College, Oxford, in 1898, and published, with a commentary, as his *Autobiography*. It was notable both for the brevity of the references to his personal life, and the magnanimity which he showed to his opponents and critics. Apart from this volume, no other biography has yet appeared, which makes him almost unique among British Prime Ministers. To the best of my knowledge, only the Earl of Wilmington has suffered comparable neglect by later authors. The best assessment of his political career was written as long ago as 1924, by Clive Bigham, later the second Viscount Mersey. His summing up appears eminently judicious:

> Grafton was a fair example of a Stuart; well-intentioned loyal and honourable, not without capacity and taste, but bored by business, lacking in industry and determination, and overmuch given to sport and pleasure. His high rank and early promise brought him great place, but want of endurance and the misfortunes of the times made him fail in it. A competent colleague in ordinary circumstances, he was called upon to act as a leader in days of difficulty and for this he had neither the character, the energy nor the courage. (Bigham, p.66)

He does not lack geographical memorials. In London NW1, Grafton Street, Fitzroy Square and Euston Road and Station are all named after Grafton or members of his family, while in the United States, there is a Grafton, Vermont and a Grafton town and county in New Hampshire.

Works consulted

Bigham, Clive (1924), *The Prime Ministers of Britain 1721–1924*, London, John Murray.

Black, Jeremy (1992), *Pitt the Elder*, Cambridge, CUP.

Bloy, Marjorie (1998), 'Augustus Henry Fitzroy, Third Duke of Grafton', in *Biographical Dictionary of British Prime Ministers*, London, Routledge.

Brooke, John (1972), *King George III*, London, Constable.

Cordasco, Francesco (2004), 'Junius (fl. 1768–1773)', in *Oxford Dictionary of National Biography*, Oxford, OUP.

Durrant, Peter (1974), 'The Duke of Grafton (1768–70)', in Herbert Van Thal, ed., *The Prime Ministers*, Volume I, London, Allen & Unwin.

Durrant, Peter (2004), 'Fitzroy, Augustus Herbert, third duke of Grafton', in *Oxford Dictionary of National Biography*, Oxford, OUP.

Henry, Augustus Third Duke of Grafton (1898), *Autobiography*, ed. by Sir William Anson, London, John Murray.

Hanham, A.A. (2004), 'Parsons, Anne [Nancy] married name Anne Maynard, Viscountess Maynard', in *Oxford Dictionary of National Biography*, Oxford, OUP.

Kilburn, Matthew (2004), 'Anne, Countess of Upper Ossory [other married name Anne FitzRoy, duchess of Grafton]', in *Oxford Dictionary of National Biography*, Oxford, OUP.

Rudé, George (1962), *Wilkes and Liberty*, Oxford, Clarendon Press.

11

Frederick North, Styled Lord North – Outstanding Parliamentarian, Pity about the Colonies. ...

In British political folklore, Lord North has long held the distinction of being regarded as the worst Prime Minister the country has ever had. It would be a bold person who tried to reverse this verdict as it was undeniably during his premiership that the 13 British colonies in North America were lost. Yet this should not obscure the fact that North was one of the abler men to hold the top office, and possessed many good qualities.

Frederick North was born on 13 April 1732 in Albemarle Street, off Piccadilly, in London. He was the first child of Francis North, (third Baron, and later first Earl of Guilford) and his first wife, Lady Lucy Montagu, daughter of the Earl of Halifax. Guilford, who was descended from a long line of 'courtiers, lawyers, politicians and writers' (Whiteley, 1996, p.1) had been appointed a Gentleman of the Bedchamber to Frederick Louis, Prince of Wales, the estranged son of George II, two years earlier. The Prince of Wales became the godfather of the infant Frederick, who was named after him, and it was not long before he started good-humouredly to tease Guilford with how similar to him was his godson. If the prince had indeed cuckolded Guilford, he apparently did not suspect this at the time, but his later treatment of his daughter, Lucy, who was born two years after Frederick, was peculiar, to say the least. Her mother died in child-birth, aged 25, and Guilford packed their daughter off to his late wife's family, and put it about that she also had died. (In fact, she lived until 1790, marrying a tradesman, Thomas Bradley, and living in Preston). That Prince Frederick Louis was a renowned libertine, who fathered several illegitimate children, makes his paternity of both children appear more probable.

In 1736, the Prince married Princess Augusta of Saxe-Gotha, and the following year she gave birth to their first son, George, the future George III, a putative half-brother to Frederick North, who was five years his senior. There was never a public scandal involving the Prince, who died in 1751, when Frederick North was 19 and the future King 14, but many years later, when North was Prime Minister, there were a number of innuendoes in the press and even occasionally in parliamentary interventions. In the absence of any DNA evidence, the question is never likely to be definitively resolved, but the pictorial evidence points strongly to the prince being North's real father. It was presented in 1979 in a profusely illustrated book (Smith, 1979, pp.25–67). Most significantly, the book contains portraits from respectively, the National Portrait Gallery and the Courtauld Institute, of Prince Frederick Louis and Frederick North, both painted when young men in their 20s, which show an extraordinary resemblance. By contrast, a portrait of the Earl of Guilford, again from the Courtauld Institute, shows absolutely no similarity at all to that of his supposed son. The book also includes portraits of Frederick North and George III, in their mature years, again taken from the National Portrait Gallery and the Courtauld Institute (ibid., pp.107–8), which also show a marked resemblance.

Whatever suspicions he may have had – and despite his rejection of his daughter, Lucy – Guilford brought up the young Frederick himself, and integrated him into the largish family which he accumulated during his two subsequent marriages. The first of these, to Elizabeth Legge, the Dowager Viscountess Lewisham, in 1736, produced a son and three daughters, while she brought three step-children from her previous marriage into the family. Her marriage to Guilford was a happy one, but she – too – died in childbirth, in 1745. Six years later, Guilford was to marry a third time – to Katherine, Dowager Countess of Rockingham. This marriage brought no further children, but a great deal of money to the previously cash-strapped Guilford. He proved an affectionate if somewhat strict father to all his brood, and Frederick grew up in a happy family atmosphere, and was to remain on good terms with his 'father' throughout his long life (he was to die only two years before Frederick, in 1790). The only thing that marred the relationship was the tight-fistedness of Guilford, who kept him on a very short rein, leaving him to get deeply into debt.

Frederick's step-brother, William Legge (later the second Earl of Dartmouth), who was only one year older than him, became his inseparable friend and companion throughout their lives. They, however, were to attend different schools, William going to Westminster, and Frederick to Eton, where he proved a highly competent if rather slovenly student, very popular with both boys and teachers and much remarked upon for his high moral standards. When he left Eton, at 17, Guilford, who had received glowing reports from his teachers, wrote him a letter, saying, 'My dear Man, or rather Boy: It gives me great pleasure to find you have left a very good name behind you, & I hope you will preserve it at Oxford….Believe me my Dear, Your Very Affectionate Father' (Whiteley, 1996, p.8)

At Oxford, he enrolled at Trinity College, where his step-brother had already been since the previous year. Both boys replicated the high reputations they had gained at their schools, excelling in their studies and setting a high moral example to their fellow students. When they left, in 1751, the President of Trinity wrote to Guilford, referring to them as those 'most amiable young gentlemen whose residence was a very great advantage as well as an ornament to the College (ibid.). Peter Whiteley, North's most recent biographer, comments:

> North's time at school and university can clearly be considered well-spent, but there is something lacking. There is never any hint of rebellion or wish for independence, a trait that appears at least briefly

in most adolescents. He seldom found it easy to challenge authority whether represented by his father or the King. His precocious virtue, however, never turned stale or tiresome as he grew older; it was fortunately leavened with a ready wit. He had an unpompous ability to accept jokes at his own expense and to respond to humour in others. (Ibid., p.9)

The year 1751 proved to be a most significant one in the life of Frederick and his family. Guilford had continued to work in the service of the Prince of Wales, and since 1749 had acted as Governor to his eldest son, Prince George. But then, on 20 March 1751, Frederick Louis, who had been nursing a cold, died quite unexpectedly, and Guilford was out of a job. King George II took over responsibility for his grandson, and appointed Lord Harcourt in Guilford's place. Guilford had suddenly lost his salary, and – whether or not in consequence of this – married a very wealthy widow, Katherine, the Dowager Countess of Rockingham, less than three months later. Thus newly endowed, he was in a position to send Frederick North and William Legge off on a very extensive grand tour, mostly in Germany and Italy, which kept them occupied for almost three years. In 1752, Guilford was compensated for the loss of his court appointments by being promoted to an earldom. Frederick consequently assumed the courtesy title of Lord North, by which he was known for almost the whole of his adult life. William Legge had meanwhile become the second Earl of Dartmouth, on the death of his grandfather. The two young milords were accompanied on their grand tour by a Mr. Golding, their chaperon/tutor, but rarely can such an appointment have proved so unnecessary, given the notorious piety and serious-mindedness of his two charges. Their time was mostly spent sight-seeing, and in the social round, but they did not neglect the educational opportunities available to them, in particular acquiring fluency in German, Italian and, especially French. 'This acquirement', North's youngest daughter, Lady Charlotte Lindsay, was later to write 'together with the observations he had made upon the men and manners of the countries he had visited, gave him what Madame de Stael called *l'esprit européen*, and enabled him to be as agreeable a man in Paris, Naples and Vienna, as he was in London' (Whiteley, pp.14–15). Whiteley himself comments:

Agreeable is a term well justified in describing North. He returned from his Grand Tour a man of the world, cultivated, unobtrusively amusing and at ease in the best circles. Though not profound or given to original or abstract thought, he possessed a good, clear mind that was frequently underrated by his opponents. His confidence in his social position never made him arrogant or quick to take offence and he remained throughout his life a very enjoyable companion. (Ibid., p.15).

Very soon after their return to England both young men took their seats in Parliament, Dartmouth in the House of Lords, and North in the Commons. He was elected unopposed for the Banbury constituency, on 15 April 1754, two days after his twenty-second birthday. Banbury was unusual in being a single-member constituency, the vast majority of English seats returning two members. It was not exactly a 'pocket' borough of Lord Guilford's – the electors being the 18 members of the borough corporation – but he was the main landlord in the area, and they usually did his bidding. North was to represent Banbury for 36 years until he entered the House of Lords, only two years before his death, when he inherited the earldom of Guilford. He was elected, altogether, on 11 occasions, never facing any opposition. Largely for conventional reasons, North stood unofficially as a Whig, but Whiteley quotes one of his descendants as saying that 'his tendencies were Tory; he came from a Tory family and he never attached himself to the interests of any of the Whig houses'. He also pointed out that Horace Walpole, in his *Memoirs of the Reign of George III*, 'stated flatly that he was a Tory, underlying the words for emphasis' (ibid., p.24). Later historians have followed Walpole's lead, North's government invariably being described as Tory. Despite this, it was a very leading Whig, the Duke of Newcastle, who gave North his first leg up in politics. A distant cousin, he invited his kinsman to second the address in reply to the King's speech, in December 1757, apparently his maiden speech, though he had already been in the House for over three years. He was warmly commended by Lord Guilford, and wrote back:

> I am extremely obliged to your Lordship for your repeated congratulations to me & to my Friends for all the kind things they have written on my behalf. I possessed myself & spoke I believe with a loud voice & a tolerable manner & to that much more than my matter I owe my reputation. (Smith, p.71)

In fact, the 25-year-old North was being over-modest. His speech was widely acclaimed as an outstanding success, and he was immediately seen as a likely candidate for ministerial office. His uncle the Earl of

Halifax, who was President of the Board of Trade, wrote to him that he 'could now conscientiously regard him as having first claim to a vacancy on the Board of Trade' (ibid., p.72). A month later, he received an offer from Lord Newcastle to head the Embassy in Turin, the capital of the Kingdom of Sardinia. North consulted Guilford before rejecting the offer, writing 'I have observed that most men who have passed their youth in foreign employments make no great figure in Parliament at their return (ibid., p.72). Meanwhile, on 20 May 1756, he had got married to the 16-year-old Anne Speke, daughter of a West country landowner. It was widely observed that Anne was far from good-looking, but as North was no oil painting himself it could be judged that they were well matched. (Horace Walpole was to describe the corpulent North in the following terms: 'two large prominent eyes that rolled about to no purpose, for he was utterly short-sighted, a wide mouth, thick lips and an inflated visage gave him the air of a blind trumpeter') It was generally believed that Anne was a considerable heiress, but in fact she brought with her only a modest estate, Dillington House, Ilminster, in Somerset, and her expectations of being left a far more considerable property by her uncle, Sir William Pynsent, were to be dashed (see below). The marriage, which was to produce four sons and three daughters, seems to have given great satisfaction to both partners. Their youngest daughter, Lady Charlotte Lindsay, in her own old age, wrote about her mother in a letter to Lord Brougham, saying that she:

> was plain in her person, but had excellent good sense, and was blessed with singular mildness and placidity of temper. She was also not deficient in humour, and her conversational powers were by no means contemptible; but she, like the rest of the world, delighted in her husband's conversation, and being by nature shy and indolent, was contented to be a happy listener... Whether they had been in love when they married I don't know, but I am sure there never was a more happy union than theirs during the thirty-six years that it lasted. I never saw an unkind look, or heard an unkind word pass between them; his affectionate attachment to her was as unabated as her love and admiration of him. (Whiteley, p.17)

In June 1759, North was appointed as the Lord of the Treasury, with a salary of £1400 a year, a welcome addition to his income of around £2000, on which was finding it increasingly difficult to live. This may have been a reason why he clung to office, in May 1762, when Newcastle and his closest associates resigned, leaving the Earl of Bute in charge of the government. North did not get on with Bute, and his first inclination was also to resign, but he was dissuaded by Lord Guilford and by his uncle, Lord Halifax, who became a Secretary of State. North was probably highly relieved when Bute left office less than a year later, and was succeeded by George Grenville, a man he respected though he was never personally close to him. Grenville increasingly used North to present government policies in the House of Commons, where he spoke on some 50 occasions in the next two parliamentary sessions. In particular, North took the lead in presenting the case against John Wilkes (see Chapter 7), including moving the motion, in January 1764, to expel him from the House of Commons. The same month, however, found him speaking against government policy, when he opposed the repeal of the unpopular cider tax, introduced under Lord Bute. This was to cost him dear, as the cider tax was particularly abominated by West country landowners, including Sir William Pynsent, his wife's uncle. Pynsent apparently had never met William Pitt, but admired him greatly (see Chapter 9), and as North phlegmatically wrote in a letter to Lord Guilford: 'Our neighbour Sir Wm Pynsent has left all his estate to Mr. Pitt. It is reported, and from pretty good authority that he left it all to me but alter'd his will in consequence of the Cider Tax' (ibid., p.17).

When Grenville's government was peremptorily dismissed, in July 1765, North was the only member of the Treasury Board not turned out, and the new Rockingham government would have liked him to stay, but he insisted on resigning out of loyalty to Grenville, even though he had no personal attachment to him, and also perhaps because of his anger that his uncle, the Earl of Halifax, had been dismissed along with Grenville. Several Cabinet members were particularly anxious, however, to recruit him, not least for his debating power in the Commons, when the new Prime Minister was in the Lords. Charles Townshend, for example the Paymaster-General, wrote to Lord Newcastle that 'there is no one belonging to the late administration whose talents would be more use to the present' (Thomas, 1976, p.16). Eventually, the Earl of Dartmouth, who was President of the Board of Trade, was authorized to approach his step-brother with the offer of the post of Joint Vice-Treasurer of Ireland, at a salary of £2000 a year. North declined, and took his place on the Opposition benches. A strong supporter of the Stamp Act, he vigorously opposed its repeal by the Rockingham government, and, in May 1766, repulsed a further offer of ministerial office. Two months later, however, when the government was dismissed and replaced by one led by Lord Chatham, he accepted the lucrative post of Joint Paymaster-General. Within six months he was sworn off the

Privy Council, and was occasionally summoned to Cabinet meetings. In March 1767, he was offered the post of Chancellor of the Exchequer, in place of Charles Townshend 'who was proving a difficult colleague' (Thomas, 2004). He declined, and when Townshend died unexpectedly four months later was still reluctant to take his place, despite being personally invited by the King and by the Duke of Grafton, who was acting premier in the absence of Lord Chatham. One reason may well have been financial – the salary was £2500, as against the £3500 he was currently receiving. Eventually, after consulting his 'father', he accepted the post. By then, he was widely seen as a 'coming man'. Townshend himself was reputed to have said a few weeks earlier: 'See that great, heavy, booby-looking, seeming changeling. You may believe me when I assure you as a fact that if anything should happen to me, he will succeed to my place, and very shortly after come to be First Commissioner of the Treasury' (Thomas, 1976, p.20).

Around the same time, Grenville had told a friend: 'North is a man of great promise and high qualifications, and if he does not relax his political pursuits he is very likely to be Prime Minister' (ibid.). North became Chancellor of the Exchequer on 6 October 1767; it was not very long before the appointment was being widely acclaimed as a success. North's six-year experience on the Treasury Board had been excellent preparation for the post, and he quickly showed himself to be both competent and decisive, as well as being utterly loyal to Grafton. The latter, as First Lord of the Treasury, soon excused himself from attending the twice-weekly meetings of the Treasury Board, allowing North to preside over them in his absence. Within three months of his appointment, North also assumed the unofficial role of leader of the House of Commons, a key position when the Prime Minister (and also Lord Grafton, who was acting in his place) was in the House of Lords. He soon established almost complete mastery of the House, after a number of skilful interventions, including handling the dodgy issue of excluding John Wilkes from the Commons, despite his repeated election for the Middlesex constituency in the spring of 1769 (see Chapter 10). By this time, Grafton had replaced Chatham as Prime Minister, and he retained North as his principal spokesman in the House of Commons. George III noted with approval how well he was succeeding in managing the House, and in December 1769, when the Grafton ministry appeared to be tottering, sent North a note saying 'Lord North – I wish to see you about eight this Evening' (Whiteley, p.77). At the ensuing meeting, the King appears to have offered North the reversion in the event of Grafton resigning. North seems to have given a non-committal answer, but five days later wrote to his 'father' 'my pride...has by the late offer been gratified to the utmost of its wish' (Thomas, 1976, p.33).

A month later, when Grafton threw in his hand, George III had little difficulty in persuading North to take up the challenge. The positive reason for asking him was North's mastery of the Commons. The negative one, as the King explained to the outgoing Secretary of State, Sir Harry Conway, was that he was absolutely determined not to go back to either of the three previous Premiers – Chatham, Rockingham and Grenville, all of whom he had found to be unsatisfactory. He would sooner abdicate his Crown, he said (Brooke, 1972, p.158). North became First Lord of the Treasury on 28 January 1770, aged 37, and was to serve for 12 years and 58 days. His premiership may be divided into three periods, each of roughly four years. In the first period – up to 1774 – the country was at peace, and he was seen as a diligent and largely success-ful premier. In the second – until late in 1777 – it drifted into war with the American colonists, and the government was strongly supported by a wave of patriotic fervour. In the final period, up till March 1782, it gradually dawned on Parliament and the public – and sooner than most on the Prime Minister himself – that the War was likely to be lost, and North spent a vast deal of time and effort trying to persuade a highly reluctant King that he should let him resign.

In the first year or two of his premiership, North was concerned, above all, with consolidating his position – in his Cabinet (which was not of his choosing, but was substantially made up of survivors from the Grafton government), in Parliament, and with the King, who, though encouraging, was not yet convinced that North was the ideal answer to his problems. The first test he faced was over the Falkland Islands, where – in June 1770 –Spanish forces had seized a British mili-tary base at Port Egmont, and attempted to assert their sovereignty over the islands. The Cabinet was divided over how to respond, with Viscount Weymouth, the belligerent Secretary of State for the Southern Department, who was the responsible minister, advocating war on Spain unless the British base was reinstated. But North took a coldly realistic view, realizing that the British fleet had been substantially run down since the end of the Seven Years War in 1763. It was now heavily out-gunned by the combined forces of Spain and her Bourbon ally, France, still led by the Duc de Choiseul, who was itching for an opportunity to avenge his country's defeats. North encouraged secret negotiations with the French, which were facilitated by the action of Louis XV in dismiss-ing de Choiseul, who had run foul of his new mistress, Madame du

Barry. The outcome was that the Spaniards evacuated the British base, but received confidential assurances that Britain would quietly relinquish it after a decent interval (in fact, in 1774). Weymouth resigned in disgust, and North won a stunning vote of confidence in the House of Commons by 275 votes to 157. The subsequent government reshuffle, following the departure of Weymouth, enabled him to reshape the Cabinet much more to his own design. Two years later, he was able to bring his step-brother, Lord Dartmouth in, as a third Secretary of State, with responsibility for the American colonies.

In the Commons, North soon established a near impregnable position. This he achieved by his great assiduity, and by his good nature, which assuaged the hostility even of those who opposed his policies. He was a living exemplar of the biblical adage that 'a soft answer turneth away wrath'. It was said of North that though he had plenty of opponents, he never had any enemies. Every day that the House met, he took his place on the Treasury bench, and remained there until it rose, often late into the night. As Peter D.G. Thomas comments:

> This was more than mere form...During his first five sessions as prime minister, from 1770 to 1774, he made about 800 speeches and interventions in debate...He was the leading administration speaker on government business, whether or not he moved the proposals himself, for he was 'the minister', and many of these speeches lasted an hour or more. North never prepared formal orations and seldom spoke from notes, for his prodigious memory enabled him to put the government case and refute points made against it. His speeches were distinguished by clarity. When he spoke every squire understood the subject of debate, whether foreign policy, the national finances, or the constitution, or at least thought he did. (Thomas, 2004)

One of North's most potent rhetorical weapons was humour, which he often turned against himself. Once, when he appeared to have dozed off during a debate, an enraged opponent, who was in the midst of an interminable speech, exclaimed 'Even now, in the midst of these perils, the noble Lord is asleep'. Without opening his eyes, North said wearily: 'I wish to God I was' (Bigham, 1924, p.131). Although he was not a great orator, North was an outstanding parliamentarian, and this was the basic reason why he was able to continue as Prime Minister for so long. It has been noted more than once that – with the exception of Newcastle who served for seven years – none of the eighteenth century

Prime Ministers from the House of Lords remained in power for any length of time. By contrast, all the commoners, apart from Grenville, who upset the King, served for long periods – Walpole nearly 21 years, Pelham 10, North 12 and the Younger Pitt 19. The underlying reason was that MPs – especially the large swathe of country gentlemen with no fixed political allegiances – needed constant sympathetic attention from the Prime Minister, in order to keep them on board. This attention was impossible to apply from the Upper House, and no Prime Minister was ever more approachable and ready to pass the time of day with a cheery word than Frederick North.

North also benefited from the increasing impotence of the Opposition. The death of George Grenville, in November 1770 removed a considerable figure from the House, and North moved swiftly to win the backing of a majority of his followers, who felt bereft without their leader. The Earl of Suffolk became Lord Privy Seal, and Alexander Wedderburn Solicitor-General, while places or pensions were obtained for several other Grenvillites. The remaining two sizeable opposition groups – the followers respectively of Rockingham and Chatham – were only able to act together on spasmodic occasions and were seldom in a position to mount an effective challenge. George III was delighted with North's performance during his first year or two in office, and hastened to express his appreciation. When, in June 1771, his uncle, the Earl of Halifax, was dying, the King wished to appoint him to the Earl's post of Ranger of Bushy Park, which involved a salary and a handsome house, near Twickenham, to the west of London. The post, however, was an 'office of profit under the Crown', and therefore not available to an MP, so North requested that his wife should be appointed instead. For the rest of his life, Bushy House proved a highly agreeable and convenient place for him to relax in the bosom of his family at the weekends, and periodically for longer stretches. An even more significant indication of the King's approval was the bestowal, in June 1772, of the Order of the Garter, a rare distinction for a commoner, Robert Walpole being the only other one to be so honoured throughout the whole of the eighteenth century. Subsequently, North was often referred to during parliamentary debates as 'the noble lord in the blue ribbon' (Thomas, 1976, pp.51–2).

As Premier, North was in receipt of an avalanche of requests for patronage, which he dealt with reasonably conscientiously, and always with great courtesy, though he found it difficult to refuse, in as many words. This sometimes led to misunderstandings, or accusations of broken promises, and eventually he felt constrained to give an explanation to the Commons, as reported in the *London Evening Post* on 25 February 1772:

> It was the etiquette of the Minister, if he could not grant the favour asked of him, at least to send home the person refused in good humour. This was well understood by courtiers; but for such ignorant honest country gentlemen as the Honourable Member, he thought it right to explain, that, when he only nodded, or squeezed the hand, or did not absolutely promise, he always meant No; which produced a great and long laugh. (Thomas, 2004)

On becoming Premier, North retained his post as Chancellor of the Exchequer, and so was in complete charge of the Treasury. This was a heavy call on his time and energy, as Thomas explains:

> The Treasury board met usually twice a week, and this demand on North's time became burdensome...between 1775 and 1782 he missed only 23 of 670 such meetings. In the House of Commons, three days a week were set aside, in form at least, for the two finance committees, supply to decide expenditure and ways and means to meet the cost by taxes and duties. Budget day was already an annual occasion for the presentation of the nation's accounts, and in the early 1770s North made it a great political occasion, and an opportunity for a review of the year's events. (ibid.)

North proved himself adept at handling the nation's finances, and he applied himself, in his early years, to reducing the national debt, which stood at the historically high figure of £140 million. In five years he succeeded in reducing this by £10m, cutting the annual interest burden by £500,000. He mainly achieved this by an ingenious use of the annual lottery, but he also introduced some tax changes which prefigured the more famous tax reforms of the Younger Pitt a dozen years or so later.

Although his government had its ups and downs during its first four years, it was generally seen as successful, and North's personal prestige was high in 1774, when the dormant issue of British taxation of the American colonies again came to a head, and with it the overall right of the British Parliament to legislate for the colonies. North already had a track record as being unsympathetic to the grievances of the colonists. In 1769, when Chancellor of the Exchequer, under Grafton, he had resisted the proposal to rescind the duties on tea imposed by Charles Townshend in 1767. His was the determining vote in a 5–4 decision, which over-ruled the wishes of the Prime Minister. The Americans largely avoided paying the duty through the large-scale smuggling of tea from the Netherlands, but in 1772, in response to an appeal from the East India Company, which had accumulated large stocks of tea which it found difficult to sell, the government approved proposals which would enable the tea to be 'dumped' in North America at prices which would undercut the Dutch smugglers, even after the tea duty had been paid. When this was put to the House of Commons, it faced heavy resistance, with widespread calls for the tea duties to be abolished, but North refused, saying, of the colonists, that 'the temper of the people there is little deserving favour from hence' (Thomas, 1976, p.74).

The American response was the famous 'Boston Tea Party', of 16 December 1773, when, disguised as Indians, a group of dare-devil colonists boarded a British ship, under cover of darkness, and destroyed a valuable shipment of tea belonging to the East India Company. Whether from choice, or because of overwhelming pressure both from the House of Commons and the King, North resolved on a robust response, proposing a series of punitive measures, known to the colonists as the 'Intolerable Acts'. These included the Boston Port Act, which closed the city's harbour until such time as restitution was paid for the destroyed tea. Equally obnoxious to the Americans was the Massachusetts Government Act, sharply reducing the degree of self-government which this colony had previously attained. Then, there was the Quebec Act, which placed all the previously French-controlled territory between the Ohio and Mississippi rivers under the control of the province of Quebec, threatening to close it off to settlement or exploitation by the American colonists. Warned that the Acts might provoke the Americans to armed resistance, North laughed this off, saying that the despatch of 'four or five frigates' would be sufficient to deal with any trouble. The opposition – Rockinghamites and Chathamites – agreed that a firm response was necessary, but were critical of the Massachusetts legislation and urged that some conciliatory move should also be made, notably the repeal of the tea duty. Their arguments went unheard in a House which was becoming gripped with patriotic fervour, as conflict threatened. The 'Intolerable Acts', passed in the spring of 1774, led to the convening of the First Continental Congress, attended by all the colonies except Georgia, which met in Philadelphia on 5 September 1774. This denounced taxation without representation and the maintenance of a British army in the colonies without their consent, adopted a declaration of personal rights, declared a boycott of British imports and petitioned the Crown for a redress of grievances accumulated since 1763. Meanwhile the British Governor of Massachusetts, cowed by the increasing militancy of the local population, submitted his resignation, and was replaced – in an act of intended firmness – by the Commander-in-chief of the British forces in North America, General Sir Thomas Gage. The Earl of Dartmouth, as Secretary of State for the American Colonies, however, made an attempt to achieve conciliation, proposing the sending of a Commission to America 'to examine into the disputes'. North put his step-brother's proposal to the Cabinet, but it was turned down after the King had remarked that sending a commission would look like 'the Mother Country being more afraid of the continuance of the dispute than the Colonies' (Thomas, 1976, p.83).

A week later, North made his own conciliatory move, persuading the Cabinet to agree that Britain 'would promise not to tax the colonies if in return they agreed to pay the cost of their own civil governments, courts of law, and defence' (ibid., p.83). Too late! A year or two earlier this might have sufficed to reconcile the colonists, but the scale of their demands had now grown so great that it was seen almost as an irrelevance. So, the drift to war began, with the British sending over more troops, mainly German mercenaries, and the colonists recruiting their own militias, particularly in Massachusetts. In April 1775, the first skirmishes occurred at Lexington and Concord, Massachusetts, followed in July by the Battle of Bunker Hill, outside Boston, technically a British victory though a pyrrhic one, as the heavy British casualties were twice as high as on the American side. Full-scale war now appeared inevitable, though the British Parliament agreed to the despatch of peace commissioners, who were expected to negotiate with the rebels. When they duly arrived, however, they revealed that they were authorized only to accept the submission of the rebels and to offer pardons to those who repented their actions. In the meantime, the Declaration of Independence had been approved by the Second Continental Congress, in July 1776, and George Washington had been placed in command of a newly raised Continental Army.

So the die was cast, and Lord North, bolstered by a wave of patriotic fervour, which embraced King, country and a clear majority of the House of Commons, prepared for war *à l'outrance*, confident of success. His step-brother, Lord Dartmouth, had no stomach for directing operations against the population for whom he had previously been responsible, and asked to stand down as Secretary for the Colonies, becoming instead Lord Privy Seal. His replacement was a distinguished soldier, Lord George Germain, previously known as Lord George Sackville. Sackville had been unjustly court-martialled and disgraced for alleged disobedience during the Battle of Minden, in 1759. His reputation had, however, subsequently been rehabilitated. North recognized that he himself had no interest in, nor aptitude for, military strategy and left the direction of the war in Germain's hands. His intention was to repeat the winning formula in the Seven Years War, when the Elder Pitt had directed the war effort, and the Duke of Newcastle had taken charge of the other Prime Ministerial duties, notably – as First Lord of the Treasury – raising sufficient funds to pay for the military and naval campaigns. Germain may have lacked the dynamic energy of the Elder Pitt, but he proved himself to be a sound strategist and an efficient administrator. If the campaigns he planned did not yield the success he hoped for it was due more to the shortcomings of the generals in charge, and in particular their failure to press home their advantage on several occasions after winning significant victories.

For the first two years of the war, the British forces generally held the upper hand, and American morale sank, until it was revitalized by Washington's successful Trenton-Princeton campaign, launched on Christmas night 1776. In the summer of 1777, Germain launched his master-stroke, sending General Burgoyne with a powerful army down the Hudson Valley from Canada to link up in New York, with another army led by General Sir William Howe, brother of Admiral Lord Howe, who was commanding the British fleet. The objective was to cut off the rebellious New England colonies from the southern states, where loyalist sentiment was more strong, enabling the British to re-establish themselves there, before concentrating all their forces to subdue the North. Unfortunately for the British, this did not go according to plan. Burgoyne met with greater and more effective resistance than expected, as he slowly made his way down the Hudson, and Howe, impatient of waiting for him, set off southwards himself, and occupied the American capital of Philadelphia. After suffering several defeats, and despairing of being reinforced by Howe, Burgoyne surrendered his entire army, when it became surrounded at Saratoga, on 17 October 1777.

This proved to be the turning point of the war – though few people realized it at the time, apart from Lord North. He despaired of victory, certainly under his own leadership, and during the next four years, on literally dozens of occasions, begged George III to allow him to stand down. One of his most fervent appeals was in March 1778, when he suggested that the King should send for Lord Chatham in the desperate hope that he would be able to repeat his achievements during the Seven Years War. But the King, remembering only too well the fiasco of his premiership during 1766–68, refused to countenance this. A few weeks later Chatham collapsed, making his final speech in the House of Lords (see Chapter 9), and died shortly after. Unabashed, North then tried to pass the poisoned chalice to a member of his own Cabinet, writing to the King that 'The person best qualified for that station appears to him to be Lord Suffolk'. No sooner was this suggestion made, than Suffolk keeled over and died at the age of 39 (Cannon, 1974, p.178). Meanwhile, North continued to dominate the House of Commons, successfully defending the government policies against increasing clamour from the opposition – from Chathamites (now led by Lord Shelburne), critical of the conduct of military operations, and Rockinghamites, who were openly calling for recognition of American independence. There were rare defeats in parliamentary votes, most notably on a famous motion by John Dunning, on 6 April 1980, that 'The Influence of the Crown has Increased, is Increasing, and Ought to be Diminished'. This was passed by 233 votes to 215, and North, once again, offered his resignation, only to see it refused. In practice, there was little risk of defeat on a confidence motion, until such time that the House became convinced that the war was definitively lost. This was still a year or two ahead.

The costs of the war placed an enormous strain on government finances, and put an end to North's earlier successful efforts to run down the National Debt. Like Newcastle before him, during the Seven Years War, North succeeded in getting the bills paid, partly by tax increases but mainly by negotiating a series of large loans, though the rate of interest demanded increased as the years of war went on. North's own finances were also under pressure, as Lord Guilford continued to make only the meanest of provisions for him. By September 1777, his debts totalled some £16,000, and the King got to know of this, and wrote to him, offering to pay them off. His letter concluded: 'You know me very ill if you do not think that of all the letters I have ever wrote to You this one gives me the most pleasure, and I want no other return but Your being convinced that I love You as well as a Man of Worth as I esteem you as a Minister' (Whiteley, p.169). The following year he helped to put North's finances on a firmer permanent basis by appointing him as Lord Warden of the Cinque Ports, with a salary of £1000 a year when Prime Minister, and a nominal £4000 thereafter. Peter D.G. Thomas comments: 'These rewards had the political consequence that North felt himself unable to resign without the King's permission; and that he was never able to obtain. The bond had become a chain' (Thomas, 1976, p.168).

What was the basis of this 'bond' between King and Prime Minister? There is little doubt that the King felt more comfortable dealing with North than with any other of his premiers, even Lord Bute. He was more successful than any of the others in getting his policies through the House of Commons, and he was much the most agreeable to deal with. North treated him with great respect, but was never obsequious. His opponents regarded him as a mere creature of the King, willing to accept anything the monarch demanded. In fact, his views genuinely coincided with the King's on a wide range of issues, and could be characterized, in more modern terms, as generally right-wing or reactionary. Their instinctive reactions were often similar, if not identical. The question is did the 'bond' go any further than that? Did the King have any inkling that North might be his own half-brother? We shall never know, but – in any event – their friendship went back a very long way. They had been brought up in the same princely household, and Prince George might well have looked up to the young Frederick as a sort of 'elder brother' figure, even if no blood relationship was suspected.

The surrender of the British army at Saratoga, in October 1777, not only unnerved North, but greatly encouraged the Comte de Vergennes, the French foreign minister. Already France had been covertly helping the rebels, but he now recommended Louis XVI to declare war on Britain, and send an army and navy to fight on the American side. Spain, too, entered the war in the hope of recouping its loss of Florida in the Seven Years War, despite an unsuccessful attempt by North to buy it off with an offer to cede Gibraltar. Finally, in an act of gross folly, Britain itself declared war on the Netherlands, thus bringing all three of the strongest European maritime powers into the conflict on the other side. Hitherto, the greatest advantage which Britain held was its control of the sea, which enabled it to transport its troops along the American coast, so that they could strike at any time and place against the rebel forces. Now it lost this advantage, and the French fleet, under Admiral de Grasse, was able to perform the same service for the Americans, and in particular for the 6000-strong army under General Rochambeau, which the French had shipped across the Atlantic in 1780. After Saratoga, the British ceased all operations in New England, and fighting was restricted to the southern states, and the West Indies. British efforts were also undermined by the loss of control of the English Channel to the combined fleets of France, Spain and the Netherlands. There was a lively fear of a Franco-Spanish invasion, and this meant that the dispatch of further troop reinforcements to North America could not be contemplated.

In the four years following Saratoga, despite periodic British successes in the more southern states, hopes of a final British victory over the Americans began to fade, and the government's majorities in crucial parliamentary divisions gradually declined to about half the level previously achieved. The young Charles James Fox effectively became the leader of the Rockinghamites in the Commons, and he and Edmund Burke made a formidable debating team harrying the government. In June 1780, in an attempt to broaden his government, North approached Rockingham with a proposal that he and his leading supporters should form a coalition with him. But Rockingham's terms, which included negotiating a peace with the Americans on the basis of independence, were quite unacceptable to the King, even if, which was unlikely, North had been able to bring himself to agree. Instead, in September 1780, North risked calling a general election, a year before it was due under the Septennial Act. Although he lost some seats, the result was reasonably satisfactory for him, and in the first division in the new Parliament the ministry had a comfortable majority, with 212 votes to 130. The election was a costly affair for the government, which expended an estimated £62,000 (Whiteley, p.188) in the customary inducements to electors and the patrons of 'pocket' boroughs to ensure the election of its own supporters. Such expenditure was normally met from secret service funds, but there was a shortfall of some £30,000, and –believing he had the King's full authority – North borrowed this amount in his own name from the royal banker, Henry Drummond, and spent a further £2754 of his own money.

Meanwhile, on the other side of the Atlantic the conflict was gradually approaching its endgame. In October 1781 a British army under Lord Cornwallis found itself cooped up in the port of Yorktown, and besieged by superior forces led by Rochambeau, Washington and Lafayette. Expected help from a British fleet, laden with reinforcements, which set sail from New York failed to arrive, after it had been defeated in a battle with the French Admiral de Grasse, whose ships then began to bombard the British positions. A despairing Cornwallis then surrendered his entire army, virtually bringing the war to an end, though a British fleet led by Admiral Rodney was later able to defeat de Grasse in the Battle of the Saints, in April 1782. When news arrived in London of Cornwallis's surrender, a stricken North cried out 'Oh God, it's all over' – a judgment which was shared by most of his Cabinet and by a clear majority of parliamentarians. Germain, however, was determined to continue the war, while George III resolutely set his face against conceding independence to the Americans. It took another five months before he was prepared, with the greatest reluctance, to face reality. During this time the opposition made a series of determined attempts to force the North government out of office, which were beaten off with steadily declining majorities. The last one to be put to a vote, on 8 March 1782 was defeated by a mere nine votes, and North then received a deputation from 'a group of independent MPs', who informed him that they were withdrawing their support from him, being 'of opinion that vain and ineffectual struggles tend only to public mischief and confusion'. Realizing that defeat was inevitable in a further no-confidence motion due on 20 March, and wishing to avoid the opprobrium of being condemned by the House of Commons, North at last summoned up the resolution to insist on his resignation. He wrote what has become a famous letter to the King, gently explaining to him his constitutional responsibilities, saying, *inter alia*:

> Your Majesty has graciously and steadily supported the servants you approve, as long as they could be supported. Your Majesty has firmly and resolutely maintained what appeared to you essential to the welfare and dignity of this country, as long as the country itself thought proper to maintain it. The Parliament have altered their sentiments, and as their sentiments whether just or erroneous must ultimately prevail, Your Majesty, having persevered so long as possible, in what you thought right, can lose no honour if you yield at length, as some of the most renowned and most glorious of your predecessors have done, to the opinion and wishes of the House of Commons. (Thomas, 1976, p.132)

North had been loyal, perhaps over-loyal, to the King, but he never had any doubt that his greater loyalty was to Parliament. When he announced his resignation to the House, on 20 March, in a speech of great dignity, he thanked MPs for:

> the very kind, the repeated and essential support he had for so many years received from the Commons of England, during his holding a situation to which he must confess he had at all times been unequal. And it was...the more incumbent upon him to return his thanks in

that place because it was that House which had made him what he had been. (Cannon, 1974, p.182)

The King did not take kindly to North's determination to resign, and accepted it only with the greatest reluctance after an interview of over an hour. According to Horace Walpole, 'the King parted with him rudely without thanking him, adding "Remember, my Lord, that it is you who desert me, not I you"' (Thomas, 1976, p.132). Thereafter, he often treated North in a spiteful or vindictive way, notably over the payment of the election expenses incurred in 1780. He refused to honour the full debt of £30,000 owed to his banker, Henry Drummond, paying only £13, 000, and insisting that North should accept responsibility for the balance. (It was only several years later, in 1786, that he relented, and reluctantly paid off the debt, which the impoverished North had been unable to discharge).

At the time of his resignation, North was still only 49, and was the leader of a substantial body of MPs, the second largest grouping in the Commons. His prospects of staging a comeback, and enjoying a renewed period of power, after a decent interval, must have appeared quite good. In fact, although he continued to be active politically, almost until his death, aged 60, in 1790, he was to enjoy only a brief period of less than nine months in office, in the so-called 'Fox–North coalition', led by the Duke of Portland, in 1783 (see Chapter 13). Thereafter, he continued to cooperate with Charles James Fox, in opposing the government of the Younger Pitt, and proved himself to be still one of the most effective debaters in the House, until 1788, when his 'father' finally died, aged 86, and he inherited the earldom of Guilford. Now, at last, he became a very rich man, with property in five counties. But by then his health had badly deteriorated, and in his last years he became totally blind. Cosseted by his loving family, he continued to receive constant visits from a host of friends, who still enjoyed his highly congenial company, both at his London home in Grosvenor Square and at Bushy Park. The historian Edward Gibbon was later to recall: 'The house in London which I frequented with the most pleasure was that of Lord North; after the loss of power and of sight, he was still happy in himself and his friends' (Whiteley, p.15). Early in 1792, he became fatally ill, and dropsy was diagnosed. He died on 5 August 1792, at Grosvenor Square, shortly after confiding to his daughter Catherine that he feared that his posthumous reputation would be irredeemably tainted by his responsibility for the loss of the colonies. It proved to be a prescient prediction.

So, was Lord North the worst ever British Prime Minister? Having now surveyed the careers of all 51 premiers over three centuries, from Walpole to Blair, this author, at least, is convinced that he was not. He can think of a number of stronger candidates, both from the eighteenth century and later, for that dubious honour. What is certain is that North was the wrong person to be Prime Minister during most of the 12 years that he held that office. In 'normal' times, he would have made an effective premier, with a distinctly conservative bent, as he in fact showed during his first four years in office. What he was assuredly not cut out to be was a war leader. It is arguable that had Rockingham been Prime Minister during these years the war might have been prevented. If Chatham had been premier it would have been prosecuted with more vigour and perhaps with greater success. What is equally certain, with the benefit of hindsight, is that independence for the 13 colonies was inevitable, and would have come at some point during the second half of the century, with or without a war. A serious clash of interest with the metropolitan power was bound to come, and it would have been impossible to withhold independence from such a thrusting and enterprising people as the American colonists. This judgment does not absolve North from his own serious responsibility in provoking the conflict, notably for having blocked the repeal of the tea duties, which were the proximate cause of the war. But this was a responsibility which he shared with a majority of the Cabinet, with the mass of parliamentary and public opinion and, above all, with George III, who was the most pig-headed and inveterate opponent of any concession, however timely, being made to American demands. A descendant of Lord North's, the ninth Earl of Guilford, asked one of his biographers, Professor Charles Daniel Smith, 'if it was true that my ancestor was responsible for the loss of the American colonies?' Smith replied; 'Well, let's put it this way: he had a lot of help!' (Smith, p.11).

Works consulted

Bigham, Clive (1924), *The Prime Ministers of Britain 1721–1924*, London, John Murray.

Brooke, John (1972), *King George III*, London, Constable.

Cannon, John (1969), *The Fox-North Coalition*, Cambridge, CUP.

Cannon, John (1974), 'Lord North (1770–82)', in Herbert Van Thal, ed., *The Prime Ministers*, Volume I, London, Allen & Unwin.

Simms, Brendan (2007), *Three Victories and a Defeat: The Rise and Fall of the First British Empire, 1714–1783*, London, Allen Lane.

Smith, Charles Daniel (1979), *The Early Career of Lord North the Prime Minister*, London, The Athlone Press.

Thomas, Peter D.G. (1976), *Lord North*, London, Allen Lane.

Thomas, Peter (1998), 'Frederick North, styled Lord North 1752–90, Second Earl of Guilford', in Robert Eccleshall and Graham Walker, eds., *Biographical Dictionary of British Prime Ministers*, London, Routledge.

Thomas, Peter D.G. (2004), 'Frederick North, second Earl of Guilford, known as Lord North, 1732–1790', in *Oxford Dictionary of National Biography*, Oxford, OUP.

Whiteley, Peter (1996), *Lord North: The Prime Minister who Lost America*, London, The Hambledon Press.

12
William Petty, Second Earl of Shelburne – Too Clever by Half

The MARQUIS of LANSDOWN.

Published as the Act directs by J. Sewell &c. 1783

John Quincy Adams was probably the cleverest man ever to be President of the United States, but also the most disliked. This was largely responsible for abridging his political career, and he served only one term at a period when the norm was two. William Petty, the second Earl of Shelburne, has a good claim to be regarded as his nearest British equivalent. Born in Dublin, on 2 May 1737, his parents, who were first cousins, were John Fitzmaurice (later Petty) and Mary Fitzmaurice, both of whom were descended from a family which had dominated the western Irish county of Kerry, since the twelfth century. The head of the family when William was born was his grandfather, the first Earl of Kerry, who ruled the roost with unbridled tyranny. William's father, who was an MP in both the Dublin and Westminster Parliaments, changed his surname in 1751, after inheriting great wealth and large estates, both in England and Ireland, from his uncle, Henry Petty. He became an Irish peer, as the first Earl of Shelburne, in 1753, and Baron Wycombe, in the peerage of Great Britain, in 1760, which gave him a seat in the House of Lords. William clearly felt that his mother was the dominant partner in the marriage, saying of her that she was a foolish woman, but:

> one of the most passionate characters I ever met with, but good natured and forgiving when it was over – with a boundless love of power, economical to excess in the most minute particulars, and persevering, by which means she was always sure to gain her ends of my father…. If it had not been for her continual energy my father would have passed the remainder of his life in Ireland and I might at this time be the chief of some little provincial faction. (Norris, 1963, p.3)

William grew up as a neglected son. 'A poor school [Dr Ford's Academy, in Dublin], the intermittent attentions of a cheap French Huguenot tutor, and a year of penurious idleness in London at the age of fifteen were almost the sum of his early formal education' (ibid.). The care and attention which he was denied at his home, which he characterized as 'domestic brutality and ill-usage' (Cannon, 2004), was, in part at least, compensated by his aunt, Lady Arabella Denny. 'Shelburne believed that it was due to her that he was able to read, write and speak, and attributed his later success to her…she instilled in him an exaggerated respect for methodical habits (though he lacked these himself) and a strong sense of duty' (Norris, p.3).

William's parents, newly enriched by their great inheritance, at least found the money to send him to Christ Church, Oxford, where he matriculated on 11 March 1755. He now held the courtesy title of Viscount Fitzmaurice, and stayed there for a further two years, imbibing, according to his own reminiscences, an eclectic mix of 'natural law and the law of nations, some history, part of Livy, and translations of Demosthenes', a mixture enlightened by 'Blackstone's early lectures and a good deal of indiscriminate reading in religion' (ibid., p.3). This led him into a great deal of scepticism concerning orthodox Christianity, 'and in later years he held to an austere Deism strongly coloured by dislike for the Anglican clergy' (ibid., p.4). He left Oxford, without taking a degree, and his experience left him with a passionate intellectual curiosity, but also a conviction that he was poorly educated, and he long continued to feel an inferiority complex towards many less gifted but more polished contemporaries. Deeply discontented with his lot, he later wrote 'it became necessary for me to take some resolution for myself; home detestable, no prospect of a decent allowance to go abroad, neither happiness nor quiet' (Cannon, 2004). He determined to join the Army, and his father was persuaded by Henry Fox, his political mentor and a distant relative, to purchase him a commission in the twentieth Regiment, then commanded by Colonel James Wolfe, a very able officer, who was later to meet a glorious death leading his troops to a famous victory at Quebec in 1759.

In the Army, the young Lord Fitzmaurice thrived, not least because of the support he received from Wolfe who encouraged him to continue his private studies in philosophy, as well as a range of military subjects, and he became a popular figure in the regiment. He took part in the raid on Rochefort, in 1757, one of the first engagements in the Seven Years War. When Wolfe left for Canada, he was transferred to the third (Scots) Guards, and posted in Germany, where he distinguished himself at the battles of Minden and Kloster Kampen. He was decorated for bravery and, in 1760, was recommended by the British commander, the Marquis of Granby, for promotion to Colonel and appointment as *aide-de-camp* to the new King, George III. In the same year, his father received his barony, which meant that he relinquished his parliamentary seat at Wycombe, on entering the House of Lords. While still serving in Germany, Fitzmaurice was elected unopposed to take his place as the MP for Wycombe, and was re-elected for the same seat in the general election of March 1761, both for this seat, and for the constituency of Kerry in the Irish Parliament in Dublin. He was never, however, to sit in the House of Commons, for two months later, in May 1761, his father died, and Fitzmaurice inherited both of his father's titles, and took his seat in the House of Lords. Henceforth, he was known as the Earl of Shelburne.

At the age of 24, Shelburne now appeared as a very grand figure indeed. One of the richest men in the country, with splendid residences at Bowood House, in Wiltshire, Wycombe Abbey in Buckinghamshire and Lixnaw in County Kerry, his royal appointment and his high military rank, the world seemed to be at his feet. But the political career to which he aspired proved to be a chequered one. This was partly due to flaws in his character, but largely to ill luck, and the misfortune that his earliest political associates turned out to be two of the most unpopular figures of the time – the Earl of Bute and Henry Fox. The former was despised as a royal favourite, and the latter deeply distrusted as an opportunist, and for having made a large personal fortune through holding the office of Paymaster-General (see Chapters 5 and 6). Shelburne also undoubtedly suffered from not having sat in the Commons, and learning there the tough trade of competitive politics before being promoted to the more sedate benches of the Upper House.

He was also the victim of envy. One of the more influential of the younger Whig leaders was the Duke of Richmond, who took against Shelburne because he had been promoted over the head of the Duke's younger brother, Lord George Lennox, in obtaining his colonelcy. Richmond convinced himself – wrongly – that this had been the result of political intrigue, and resigned his post as a Gentleman of the Royal Bedchamber in protest. He then proceeded to blacken Shelburne's reputation with his fellow Whig grandees, including the Duke of Devonshire and the Marquess of Rockingham. This meant that Shelburne, a natural Whig, was put on the wrong foot, from the outset, with what must have seemed his likeliest future political allies.

For the moment, however, he was involved with Bute and Fox, who had been his father's political sponsors. Bute, who became Prime Minister in May 1762, was anxious to recruit Henry Fox as Leader of the House of Commons, in order to force through the peace treaty terms which he was negotiating with France, about which the current leader, George Grenville, was distinctly lukewarm. He used Shelburne as a go-between with Fox, who was playing hard to get. Holding the highly lucrative post of Paymaster-General, Fox's main concern was to secure a cast-iron assurance that he would receive a peerage, preferably an earldom, as soon as he had completed his mission in the Commons. Bute and George III were ready to concede this, but assumed that Fox would be willing to relinquish the Paymastership when he went up to the Lords. This was not Fox's intention, and he was later annoyed with Shelburne for putting it about that it was, describing him as 'a perfidious and infamous liar' (Norris, p.12). Fox, however, did not for long hold this against him. More serious for Shelburne was that he upset the King on a number of occasions. The first was as early as March 1761, when he applied to become Controller of the Royal Household. George III evidently regarded this as highly presumptuous for a young man of 24 who had only recently become his *aide-de-camp*, and Shelburne was forced to make abject apologies through Bute. The King, and Bute, were also irritated when he made a speech deploring any continuation of the war in Germany and voted against a motion which Bute had moved in the House of Lords. Despite this, Bute was eager to appoint Shelburne to a ministerial post, and Fox urged him 'to get your harness on immediately' (Cannon, 2004). Shelburne, however, evidently regarded the post he had in mind as too insignificant, and declined to accept. Throughout his career, as a very wealthy man, he was completely indifferent to the 'emoluments' of office, and this made him reluctant to accept any post which was not completely to his liking, and all too ready, if he did not get his way, to resign. Despite his refusal to join Bute's government, he was long to remain an object of suspicion to the leading Whigs, who regarded him as an acolyte of the King's favourite. This suspicion was further aroused when he purchased Bute's house in Berkeley Square (now known as Lansdowne House) as his London residence.

When Bute resigned as Premier in April 1763, he, Bute, continued to enjoy the King's confidence, and was largely responsible for recruiting ministers for the government of his successor, George Grenville. He greatly valued Shelburne for his high intelligence and his formidable debating skills in the House of Lords, and recommended his appointment as Secretary of State for the Southern Department, which would have meant displacing the Earl of Egremont, Grenville's brother-in-law, and a much more experienced politician. It was not to be:

> The King refused to consider it and Grenville, under no illusion but that it was intended to use Shelburne as Bute's agent and spy in the new government, compromised by offering the Board of Trade. Shelburne's first reaction was to refuse, but... he demanded the full powers of policy and patronage which had been enjoyed by the Earl of Halifax at the Board of Trade between 1752 and 1761. Egremont objected to this, and as a compromise Shelburne was allowed cabinet rank. But when Shelburne kissed hands for his first office on April 20, 1763, it was as the subordinate of the Secretary of State. Far from ruling the cabinet for Bute, Shelburne was only a hostage in the Grenville camp. (Norris, p.13)

It was an inauspicious start, and things only got worse during the barely four months which ensued before he resigned in a huff. During this brief period, he amply demonstrated 'his inability to work with others in a ministerial team. He was touchy and interfering as a subordinate, uncooperative as an equal and secretive when in command' (Stuart,

1981, p.247). Shelburne had shown himself to be a skilled and assiduous administrator, thoughtful and forward-looking in his policies, but arrogant and highly impatient in his dealings with his colleagues. They were unsurprised, and – on the whole – relieved, when he threw in his hand, leaving office on 2 September 1763. Two months later he strongly opposed a government motion to expel John Wilkes from the House of Commons, and Grenville complained to George III, who promptly dismissed him as his *aide-de-camp*, describing him as 'a worthless man' (Cannon, 2004). Shelburne, however, continued with his army career, eventually rising to the rank of General, in 1783. Yet it seems to have been very much a part-time commitment, and he never again saw any military action. Shelburne had collected a small but devoted parliamentary following, based, initially, on the Members he returned for the two 'pocket boroughs' he controlled, Wycombe and Calne. It included such highly able figures, as Colonel Isaac Barré, John Calcraft and Richard Rigby. More generally, however, his reputation among politicians had sunk to a low level. He was regarded as awkward, sententious, insincere, self-seeking and – above all – devious. He was dubbed the 'the Jesuit of Berkeley Square', a comment not on his religious views, which were very far from Catholicism, but on his alleged methods, with an oblique reference to his association with the Earl of Bute. Yet his evil public reputation was in almost complete contrast to how he was viewed by those closest to him. As Charles Stuart was to write in a perceptive essay: 'Everything we can learn of Shelburne, from his published letters and papers, from his first wife's diary or from his friends shows him to have been, in private life, considerate, unselfish and amiable with, above all else, a wholly disinterested and dedicated regard for truth' (Stuart, 1981). Shelburne became somewhat less maladroit in his public life as he grew older, but he was never able to live down the largely unjustified reputation he early acquired. Give a dog a bad name...

For the next three years, Shelburne was in opposition, and fell under the spell of the Elder Pitt. He was to remain a follower and close collaborator with him until Pitt – now Chatham – died in 1778. But he was never personally close to him, to Shelburne's great regret. In his old age, he was to write:

> I was in the most intimate political habits with him for ten years, the time when I was Secretary of State included, he Minister [*i.e.* Prime Minister], and necessarily was with him at all hours in town and country, without drinking a glass of water in his house or company, or five minutes conversation out of the way of business. (Norris, p.17)

Meanwhile, he occupied himself with making extensive improvements to his various properties, employing Capability Brown to construct a lake at Bowood and Robert Adam to enlarge the house, and modernizing his somewhat run-down estates at Wycombe. On 3 February 1765, aged 27, he married the 19-year-old Lady Sophia Carteret, the only child of Earl Granville, the former John Carteret, and great rival to Sir Robert Walpole, and to his successors, the Pelham brothers. This marriage further augmented his extensive landholdings, bringing to him large estates near Bath, centred on Lansdowne Hill, from which he – much later – took his title, on becoming the Marquess of Lansdowne. The marriage lasted only six years, Lady Sophia dying in childbirth in January 1771, at the age of 25. They had had two sons, one of whom was to die in childhood. According to John Norris:

> Lady Shelburne's diary shows her to have been amiable and intelligently observant of the world of affairs. She was apparently devoted to her husband, tolerating his restlessness and conforming to his odd evangelical enthusiasms. His letters to her are surprisingly cold in tone, but when she died...he sank into a depression and had to go abroad for a season to recover. (Ibid., p.6)

George Grenville's government was dismissed by the King in the summer of 1765, and the new Premier, Lord Rockingham, offered Shelburne his former post back, as President of the Board of Trade. He declined, citing 'a real consciousness of my own inability in so active an office, to which the domestic habits I have lately fallen into add not a little' (Cannon, 2004). In truth, Shelburne was by now a pretty unconditional supporter of Pitt, and was unwilling to serve in an administration from which he was excluded. His loyalty was rewarded a year later, when Pitt, now translated to the House of Lords as the Earl of Chatham, was asked to form a government, and proposed him as Secretary of State for the Southern department, where his responsibilities also included India, Ireland and America. This was the most senior post in the government, after Chatham and the Duke of Grafton, who was First Lord of the Treasury. Shelburne, who was now 29, was not to make a success of it.

During the first six months or so, Chatham very carefully supervised Shelburne's work. The position changed dramatically during the spring of 1766, when he retired to Bath, and later to his country estate, suffering from a severe nervous breakdown, and virtually abandoning his prime ministerial duties. Of all the ministers, Shelburne was politically closest to him and the most clearly in accord with his views. Now, he felt himself alone, and progressively fell out with all his colleagues. His greatest difficulties were with the Chancellor of the Exchequer, Charles Townshend, who was determined to raise significant sums of money by taxing the North American colonists. Shelburne, who had voted against both the Stamp Act, when it was introduced in 1765, and the Declaratory Act of 1766 (see Chapter 7), was convinced that Townshend's proposals would unnecessarily inflame American opinion, and vainly sent a message to Chatham asking him to intervene. Eventually, against Shelburne's opposition, the cabinet agreed on the imposition of import duties on china, glass, paper and, most famously tea. Shelburne went into a sulk, and for a time boycotted cabinet meetings. He was to clash again with Townshend over revenues from India, where there was general agreement that the East India Company should not enjoy all the gains accruing from the newly conquered territories, but that at least part of it should go to the British government. Shelburne, who had a financial interest in the company, nevertheless proposed taking a hard line against it, calling for 'a searching review which would lead to a measure of government control and a substantial subsidy to the exchequer' (Cannon, 2004). Townshend favoured a softer approach, suggesting direct negotiations with the company's directors, and his view carried the day. Townshend's sudden death in September 1767 ended his rivalry with Shelburne, but the feud continued with his elder brother, Viscount Townshend, who was Lord Lieutenant of Ireland, which came under Shelburne's authority. The two men were constantly at odds, with Shelburne, who favoured a more 'liberal' approach to Irish problems, continually over-ruling his decisions.

As well as his colleagues, Shelburne succeeded, once again, in alienating the King, who wrote to Chatham that 'he and Grafton regarded Shelburne as "a secret enemy" and suggesting his removal' (ibid.) Chatham did not agree, but Shelburne suffered the humiliation of seeing the American colonies taken away from him, and given to a newly appointed Secretary of State for the Colonies, Lord Hillsborough. Difficulties also arose over determining the government's attitude to Wilkes's election for the Middlesex constituency in the 1768 general election, with the King and most ministers in favour of ejecting him, while Shelburne strongly opposed this step. The King evidently hoped that Shelburne would resign, but he refused to do so, putting his faith in Chatham's return. When Chatham himself eventually resigned in October 1768, Shelburne followed suit, leaving Grafton to reorganize the government without his participation.

Shelburne was now 31, and left office a deeply chastened man. He now embarked on what turned out to be a period of 13 years in opposition, 12 of them against the predominantly Tory government led by Lord North. He held himself aloof from the main Whig opposition, led by Rockingham, but became the most influential figure in the much smaller group of Chathamite supporters, and their acknowledged leader after Chatham's death in 1778. Shelburne has been described as 'perhaps the most brilliant intellectual in politics in the second half of the eighteenth century after Burke' (O'Gorman, 1974, p.185). O'Gorman goes on to say:

> He took few ideas for granted and subjected prevailing ideas and institutions to constant analysis...He must have been one of the very few eighteenth-century statesmen to have enjoyed the services of what the twentieth century would term a 'think tank' in the little coterie of intellectuals which he patronised at Bowood, and to have established a formal secretariat to facilitate his political activities. (Ibid.)

His circle at Bowood included the eminent utilitarians, Jeremy Bentham, Richard Price and Joseph Priestley, while among his friends were Benjamin Franklin, who spent five years in London representing the colony of Pennsylvania, Dr Samuel Johnson and Sir Joshua Reynolds. On a visit to Paris in 1771, following the death of his first wife, he met a number of the leading *Philosophes*, including D'Holbach, Turgot, Trudaine and, in particular, Morellet, whose views on free trade greatly influenced him.

During his lengthy period in opposition, Shelburne thought long and deeply about the problems facing Britain, and evolved a programme of reforms which, in many respects, were a great deal more radical than those espoused by the Rockingham Whigs. An exception was Shelburne's approach to the conflict with the American colonies, by far the most contentious issue throughout the period of Lord North's government. Shelburne argued consistently for a conciliatory approach to the Americans, for a cessation of hostilities and a negotiated settlement on generous terms. In a speech, in January 1775, supporting a motion of Chatham's to withdraw British troops from Boston, he condemned 'the madness, injustice and infatuation of coercing the Americans into a blind and servile submission'. Yet he was strongly against the recognition of American independence, saying – even after the surrender at Yorktown – that 'he would never consent, under any given circumstances, to acknowledge the independency of America' (Cannon, 2004). 'Without America', he argued, 'Britain would be but a petty state' (ibid.). Shelburne's solution was a 'federal union' between a largely self-governing America and the United Kingdom, under the British Crown. This somewhat resembled the dominion status achieved by Canada, Australia and New Zealand a century or more later. Had he been in a position to offer this to the Americans some years before, it is highly likely that they would have accepted it, which would have brought the war to an end far sooner, or even prevented it in the first place. Even after peace had been negotiated and independence ceded, Shelburne continued to argue for a free trade area with the newly formed United States, but by then he was out of power, and his voice was unheeded.

Partly through his support for John Wilkes, Shelburne was drawn into close contact with a group of Radicals in the City of London. Subsequently, he advocated a series of 'economical reforms', loosely based on their demands and designed, in part, to reduce the power of the Crown, and government ministers, to corrupt the electoral system. Thus, Shelburne advocated the reduction of the parliamentary term from seven to three years, and a moderate measure of electoral reform, based on awarding a third member to each county (where the franchise was generally wider than in the boroughs and therefore more 'democratic', though that is not a term which he would have used). He also advocated the abolition of a great range of 'fees' (some dating from Medieval times) paid to government officials, in addition to their salaries, a policy he had started to implement in his own ministry, during his two brief periods in office.

By 1778, when Shelburne had been a widower for seven years, his younger son, William, died aged nine, and soon afterwards, his engagement was announced to Frances Molesworth, described as 'a young, attractive and wealthy heiress' (Cannon, 2004). But, according to Horace Walpole, it was not long before she began complaining that 'Shelburne did nothing but talk politics to her', and the engagement was called off. In 1789, however, he married Lady Louisa FitzPatrick, daughter of the Earl of Upper Ossory, who was 18 years his junior. Her family were close to Charles James Fox, and this alliance might have brought Shelburne closer to the Whig mainstream, but Lady Louisa's brothers took a great aversion to him, so the link bore no political fruit. She and Shelburne had two children, the elder of whom, Henry, third Marquess of Lansdowne, was to have a distinguished political career as a senior member of several Whig governments in the first half of the nineteenth century. Lady Louisa was praised by Jeremy Bentham for 'her beauty, her reserve and her kindness' (Norris, p.6). The marriage was to last only 11 years, before she died at the age of 34. 'Shelburne felt her death in 1789 perhaps more than he had done that of his first wife. It left him alone in the world in his later middle age, when he was in the political wilderness without the distraction of pubic affairs (ibid.). On 22 March 1780, Shelburne was to fight a duel, in Hyde Park at 5 a.m., with a Scottish MP, Lieutenant-General William Fullarton, who had taken exception to 'some characteristically sharp remarks' which Shelburne had made in a parliamentary debate (Cannon, 2004). Shelburne was lightly wounded in the groin, but was admired for his courage, and the incident brought him much acclaim, with several towns conferring their freedom upon him, because the Scots were even more unpopular than he was.

During the 12 years of Lord North's ministry, the two largest opposition groups were able to work together only spasmodically, due largely to personal differences between Rockingham and both Chatham and Shelburne, and the deep distrust in which the latter was held by the Rockinghamites. These were more important than the actual policy differences between them. Like Chatham, Shelburne placed little store on party allegiances, while the Rockinghams regarded them as essential. Rockingham and his followers were convinced that the King was bent on securing unlimited power, and felt that he could only be constrained by a disciplined party with a consistent policy, which they aimed to impose on the monarch by virtue of their parliamentary power. Their objective, in contemporary terms, was 'to storm the closet' – that is, to force the King to appoint ministers of their, and not his own choosing, and accept whatever policies they proposed. Shelburne, by contrast, believed that the Royal Prerogative to choose his own ministers was an essential element of the 'Glorious Revolution' settlement, creating a balanced division of power between King and Parliament. It was only after the surrender of Lord Cornwallis's army, at Yorktown in October 1781, that the two groups came together to launch a determined effort to oust the government of Lord North.

It took five months for them to achieve this objective, and when North – faced with imminent defeat in a confidence vote – insisted on resigning, the King had no alternative but to seek a new Prime Minister from among the opposition. Rockingham and Shelburne were the only feasible choices. Despite his earlier hostility to Shelburne, the King found him greatly preferable, partly because of his continued opposition to American independence. George III offered the post to Shelburne, but realizing that he could not command a majority in the Commons, he declined. The King, with the greatest reluctance, and only after vainly exploring other possibilities, finally agreed to Rockingham forming a government, but refused to deal with him personally, insisting on using Shelburne as an intermediary, and that he should hold a senior post. He, in fact, became Home Secretary (replacing the former Southern Department), and the King underlined his new confidence in him by appointing him to the Order of the Garter. Charles James Fox was appointed Foreign Secretary (replacing the Northern Department), Lord John Cavendish, a leading Rockinghamite, became Chancellor of the Exchequer and Edmund Burke, Paymaster-General.

The new government was an uneasy coalition between Rockinghamites and Chathamites. Rockingham had much the larger parliamentary following, but Shelburne enjoyed the confidence of the King, who regarded him as the joint head of the government, and wanted to channel patronage through him rather than through the First Lord of the Treasury. During the brief three months of Rockingham's premiership, Shelburne was constantly at odds with him over patronage and other issues, and with Fox over the conduct of peace negotiations with the Americans and their European allies. With the backing of the King, who treated Rockingham with disdain and who was violently hostile to Fox, Shelburne gradually strengthened his position. The main legislative battle was over the issue of 'economical reform'. Burke's Bill to reform the Civil List, removing or reducing a large number of sinecures, pensions or fees, was the centre-piece. The King was willing to let the Bill proceed, but insisted that he – rather than Parliament – should be responsible for implementing parallel reforms in the Royal Household. Shelburne, whose obsequiousness to the King now knew few bounds, managed to amend the Bill accordingly. He also began to forge alliances with former close supporters of Lord North, such as Henry Dundas, Charles Jenkinson and John Robinson. His greatest catch, however, was the young William Pitt, then only 22, but already seen as a rising star.

The main business of the Rockingham government was to attempt to negotiate peace with the American colonists, and with their three allies – France, Spain and Holland. Fox assumed that as Foreign Secretary, he would be the minister responsible, but Shelburne's department was responsible for the colonies, and he too claimed responsibility. The ludicrous outcome was that they both sent separate representatives to Paris, to negotiate with Benjamin Franklin, the US plenipotentiary in France. The two men were also divided over the terms to offer the Americans. Fox, backed by Rockingham, believed that independence should be granted unconditionally at the outset of the official talks: Shelburne, acutely aware of the King's continuing reluctance to face reality, argued that recognition should be held back, and used as a bargaining counter during the negotiations to extract concessions from the US, notably over the treatment of 'loyalists' who had supported Britain during the war. At two successive Cabinet meetings, held on 26 and 30 June 1782, in the absence of Rockingham, who was away ill, Fox was narrowly outvoted on this issue, and petulantly announced that he would resign, as soon as Rockingham returned. Unfortunately for him, Rockingham died the following day (see Chapter 8). The Rockinghamites quickly met and chose the young Duke of Portland as their new leader, proposing him as the next Prime Minister. Yet George III was having nothing of this; he had already been in close touch with Shelburne, even before Rockingham's death, and now asked him to form a new government. Fox refused to serve, and hoped that his fellow Rockinghamites would follow his example, and thus abort Shelburne's appointment. It was not to be – Lord John Cavendish, the Chancellor of the Exchequer, Edmund Burke and a few more junior ministers decided to quit, but the rest agreed to stay. The decisive voice was that of Fox's uncle, the Duke of Richmond, who agonized over his conflicted loyalties, but eventually held on to his post, as did most of his colleagues. Fox was deeply disappointed, but a clear majority of the Rockinghamite MPs rallied to his side, and went into opposition.

So Shelburne became Prime Minister on 4 July 1782, at the age of 45. His government was substantially the same as Rockingham's, except that Lord Grantham replaced Fox as Foreign Secretary and the now 23-year-old William Pitt came in as Chancellor of the Exchequer. Shelburne rewarded some of his own followers with more junior posts: Isaac Barré replaced Burke as Paymaster-General and his new ally, Henry Dundas, became Treasurer of the Navy. Thomas Townshend, later Lord Sydney, took over Shelburne's post as Home Secretary, and also acted as Leader of the Commons. Yet in this latter role, he proved scarcely adequate, and he was soon effectively replaced by William Pitt, the only minister capable of matching such formidable opposition debaters as Fox, Burke and North. Pitt soon became Shelburne's closest collaborator, and was seen by many – including George III – as his likely successor. The parliamentary position of Shelburne's government was hazardous from the first. He had no assured majority, and it was estimated that, of the three largest factions in the Commons, Shelburne 'would have 140 followers, North 120 and Fox 90' (Cannon, 1969, p.30). This left over 200 Members uncommitted, but strongly suggested that if Shelburne wished to remain in power he should seek to make an arrangement with either Fox or North. Isolated in the House of Lords, and by his congenital inability to work on a basis of mutual confidence with his ministerial colleagues, Shelburne remained woefully ignorant of the flow of parliamentary opinion, and only realized very late in the day the necessity of dealing with one or other of his rivals.

The principal task of his government was to pursue the peace negotiations with the US, and its allies, in the hope of being able to present a peace treaty which would be acceptable to a majority of the House of Commons. This was no easy mission, as the war was well and truly lost, and the British negotiating position was very weak. It was, however, somewhat improved by the British victory over the French, in the final battle of the war, when Admiral Rodney defeated the Comte de Grasse in the Battle of the Saintes, securing Britain's precarious position in the West Indies. In the event, the Americans got their way on virtually every issue, securing unconditional recognition, a very favourable territorial settlement, giving them control of all the land between the Mississippi, the Ohio and the Great Lakes, with only Canada remaining in British hands and without promising restitution to 'loyalists' who had lost their property during the war. In addition, Britain restored Senegal and Gorée to France, and ceded Tobago, while the two countries restored to each other the various islands which they had occupied during the war. To Spain, Britain ceded Florida and Minorca, though it kept control of Gibraltar, which had survived a determined Spanish siege. It was not a very appetizing proposition to put to the House of Commons, and Shelburne began to sniff danger when it appeared that Lord North's followers, in particular, were enraged by the failure to secure the position of the 'loyalists'. Believing, however, that North was a pure creature of the King, he got George III to send him an admonitory letter. The King duly obliged, beginning:

Lord North has so often whilst in office assured me that whenever I could consent to his retiring he would give the most cordial support to such an administration as I might approve of... my strongest wishes that he will give the most active support... to the administration formed with my thorough approbation on the death of Lord Rockingham, and that during the recess he will call on the country gentlemen who certainly have great attention for him to come early and show their countenance by which I may be enabled to keep the constitution from being entirely annihilated, which must be the case if Mr. Fox and his associates are not withstood... (Cannon, 1969, p.28)

It was obtuse, in the extreme, for the monarch to write such a letter to his former Prime Minister so soon after he had mortified him by refusing to foot the bill for government expenses during the 1780 general election (see Chapter 11). North wrote back an evasive reply, saying:

> that it was true that he had, while in office, received the support of several independent country gentlemen, but he did not know whether he could venture to ask them to support the present ministry, and he was afraid that 'he might give them some offence if he were to attempt it'. (Ibid.)

North was at the same time receiving unexpected attentions from another quarter. His great parliamentary critic during his ministry had been Charles James Fox, but Fox now approached him saying that he did not believe there were any irreconcilable differences between them, and that they and their followers should work together to ensure the defeat of Shelburne, over the peace preliminaries, which had been agreed with the Americans in November 1782. Their opposition, and that of their supporters, came from different sources. Fox thought that Shelburne had grossly mishandled the negotiations by unrealistically resisting recognition of independence for far too long, while North and his friends bitterly resented that the 'loyalists' had been let down. What potentially united the two factions was the desire to get back into office, and this was to prove sufficiently strong to overcome hesitations on both sides. Meanwhile, Shelburne was finding it increasingly difficult to keep his government together. There were serious divisions within the Cabinet over both 'economical' and parliamentary reform, as well as on policy towards both Ireland and India, while many ministers constantly complained about his failure to consult. In January 1783, the Duke of Richmond and Lord Keppel, the First Lord of the Admiralty, resigned, and Shelburne, for the first time, began to scent the possibility of defeat. Very late in the day, he concluded that it would be necessary to conclude a deal with either North or Fox to secure the acceptance of the peace terms. He made contact with North's supporters, who insisted that he should be brought into the government as the price for giving their support. Shelburne might have been willing, but the Younger Pitt, who was now the main prop of the government, declared that he would find this utterly unacceptable. He blamed North for the eclipse of his father, and said, in effect, 'it is either him or me'. So Shelburne sent Pitt to see Fox to find out what his terms would be. The interview did not last long: Fox insisted that Shelburne would have to stand down, and

Pitt left the room, saying 'I did not come here to betray Lord Shelburne' (see Chapter 14). On 14 February Fox and North met, and formally agreed on an alliance.

It was soon put to the test, the peace proposals being presented to Parliament on 18 February. In the Lords, Shelburne offered 'a rather rambling and theatrical defence but carried the day, in a very full house, by seventy votes to fifty-nine' (Cannon, 2004). In the Commons, there was much confusion, but eventually the government was defeated, on a procedural motion, by 224 to 208. This was a rather better result for Shelburne than might have been expected; he was backed by a majority of the independent Members of the House. Yet despite defections, and a great deal of cross-voting among the different factions, the agreement between Fox and North largely held firm. The House met three days later, to vote on a motion of censure on the government. The debate was dominated by a magnificent speech by Pitt extolling Shelburne's virtues, but to no avail – the government lost by a similar margin, 207 votes to 190. Unwilling to recognize his own shortcomings, Shelburne blamed the King for letting him down, bitterly complaining that he had betrayed him by surreptitiously helping his enemies. There were no grounds for his suspicions, and the main reason for his failure was his neglect in building up a sufficient basis of party support for himself. As Cannon puts it: 'He had always professed contempt for parties and political organisation, and was to pay dearly for it' (Cannon, 1969, p.31). He submitted his resignation two days later, but remained in office until 26 March, when the King finally acknowledged that he had no alternative to appointing a government dominated by Fox and North (see Chapter 13).

He had been Prime Minister for a mere 266 days, and – at the age of 45 – might well have expected further opportunities to serve in government during the remaining 23 years of his life, during all of which he remained active in politics. It was not to be. As Cannon comments, 'No politician who held office with Shelburne wished to do so again' (ibid., p.59). Even the Younger Pitt, who owed so much to Shelburne's patronage, was not prepared to risk including him in his government, which came into power in December 1783 and remained in office for 17 years. Perhaps he had a bad conscience about this: at the end of 1784 he recommended George III to advance him in the peerage, and Shelburne became the first Marquess of Lansdowne. As such, he continued to plough his lonely furrow in the House of Lords, becoming progressively more radical as he grew older. He welcomed the French Revolution, and was strongly opposed to Britain joining with Austria and Prussia in attempts to suppress it. Thereafter, he consistently campaigned for a compromise peace agreement, and fiercely opposed the repressive legislation introduced by Pitt during the 1790s. This brought him closer to Charles James Fox, and when – much later in 1801 – George III fell ill and a regency was threatened, the Prince of Wales had the two men pencilled in as Secretaries of State in the government which he hoped to form under Lord Moira (Cannon, 2004). George's recovery within a few weeks aborted this prospect and Lansdowne remained in opposition, making his last speech on 23 May 1803, opposing the resumption of war with Napoleon. He died two years later at the age of 68.

Despite his high intelligence and manifold gifts, his political career had been a failure, and he was only too aware of this. It was partly due to ill luck, but more to faults in his personality and judgment. His parents and his grandfather had much to answer for. Their brutality and neglect helped to mould his suspicious and secretive nature, which made him such a difficult colleague to deal with. Moreover, in many respects his ideas were ahead of his time, and were more appreciated by later generations. One of his greatest admirers was Benjamin Disraeli, who devoted several pages of his novel *Sybil* to a panegyric of the man he called 'the ablest and most accomplished minister of the eighteenth century'. Somewhere between this soaring assessment, and the scorn of many of Lansdowne's political contemporaries, will lie a truer estimate of his abilities and achievements.

Works consulted

Bigham, Clive (1924), *The Prime Ministers of Britain 1721–1924*, London, John Murray.

Black, Jeremy (1998), 'William Petty, Second Earl of Shelburne', in *Biographical Dictionary of British Prime Ministers*, London, Routledge.

Cannon, John (1969), *The Fox-North Coalition*, Cambridge, CUP.

Cannon, John (2004), 'Petty, William, second earl of Shelburne and first marquess of Lansdowne (1737–1805)', in *Oxford Dictionary of National Biography*, Oxford, OUP.

Norris, John (1963), *Shelburne and Reform*, London, Macmillan.

O'Gorman, Frank (1974), 'The Earl of Shelburne (1782–83)', in Herbert Van Thal, ed., *The Prime Ministers*, Volume II, London, Allen & Unwin.

Stuart, Charles (1931), 'Lord Shelburne', in eds. Hugh Lloyd-Jones etc., *History & Imagination: Essays in honour of H.R. Trevor-Roper*, London, Duckworth.

13

William Henry Cavendish-Bentinck, Third Duke of Portland –Twice a Figurehead Premier

The Duke of Portland* had the singular distinction of leading both a predominantly Whig and a Tory administration. Twenty-five years separated his two governments, and in each case he was a mere figurehead,

---

* Portland was Prime Minister in both the eighteenth and nineteenth centuries. This chapter is an adapted version of that which appeared in my earlier volume, *Nineteenth Century British Premiers: Pitt to Rosebery* (2008).

the government being dominated by more powerful nominal subordinates. In between his two brief premierships, however, Portland played a prominent political role.

William Henry Cavendish-Bentinck was born on 14 April 1738, the eldest son and third child of the second Duke of Portland and of Margaret Cavendish-Holles-Harley, granddaughter of Robert Harley, Earl of Oxford, a prominent minister under Queen Anne. William's great-grandfather, Hans William Bentinck, had come over from the Netherlands with William III, in 1689, and was his closest friend and most influential adviser, being created Earl of Portland, and awarded extensive estates in several English counties. The title was upped to a dukedom by George I in 1716, and the family holdings were further enlarged, when the second Duchess inherited Welbeck Abbey and an income of £12,000 a year from her mother and her cousin, the third Earl of Oxford. The second Duke is described by the historian, A.S. Turberville, as 'retiring, unambitious, inconspicuous, a much less remarkable personality than his wife...but wise, gentle and kindly' The Duchess was a much stronger personality, who outlived her husband by 23 years, and – through her control of the family purse-strings – was something of a restraining influence on her elder son up till and even after his first premiership.

William was educated at Westminster School and Christ Church, Oxford, qualifying Master of Arts in 1757. He seems to have been an adequate but not outstanding student, and at the age of 19 set out for the Grand Tour, spending three years, mostly in Italy, but also visiting Hamburg, Prussia and Warsaw. Judging from his portraits, an exceptionally handsome young man, known by his courtesy title as the Marquis of Titchfield, he soon acquired a reputation as a philanderer and rapidly got into debt. His parents gave him an allowance of £2500 a year, which they regarded as more than adequate for his needs, but he wrote plaintively to his father asking for this to be increased to £5000. When this was refused, he addressed himself to his two elder sisters, one of whom, Elizabeth, was married to Viscount Weymouth, with no greater success. William aspired to a diplomatic career, hoping for a cushy post in a European capital, but his family doubted if he had sufficient experience, and his sister Elizabeth wrote to him suggesting that a political career might be more appropriate. Her husband controlled the Herefordshire constituency of Weobley, and, in March 1761, shortly before his twenty-third birthday, and even before his return from the continent, he was elected unopposed as one of its two MPs.

He sat in the Commons for exactly one year, and there is no record of any activity on his part. But in March 1762, his father, who had played no part in politics, died. The young Lord Titchfield became the third Duke, immediately taking his seat in the House of Lords, and attaching himself to the largest of the Whig factions, led by the ageing former Prime Minister, the Duke of Newcastle. Newcastle's protégé, the Marquess of Rockingham, was poised to take over and Portland, in turn, became his protégé and close associate.

A poor and infrequent speaker, Portland may appear to have been an indifferent recruit to Newcastle's ranks, but his high social standing made him a prize catch. Dukes (other than royal dukes) were thin on the ground and to find one who was young, personally agreeable, keen and prepared to give generously of his time and money in organizational activities, including the financing of elections, was an unlooked for opportunity. In a very short space of time, Portland was accepted as one of the leading Whig peers.

On his return from the continent, he was also seen as a highly eligible bachelor, but before settling down he embarked on love affairs with two ladies who would have been unlikely to commend themselves to the Dowager Lady Portland as suitable marriage mates for her son. One was a beautiful young widow, Maria Walpole, the illegitimate daughter of Sir Edward Walpole, and niece of the writer, Horace Walpole. Married to the Earl of Waldegrave, who was twice her age, she was left with three young children while still in her early twenties. Portland wooed her passionately, but she set her cap at even higher prey. As Horace Walpole put it, in his Memoirs, 'the young Duke of Gloucester, who had gazed at her with desire during her husband's life, now openly shewing himself her admirer, she slighted the subject and aspired to the brother of the crown'. She became his mistress, and later his wife, much to the fury of George III, who introduced the Royal Marriages Act into Parliament, shortly afterwards, one of his own brothers, the second Duke of Cumberland, also having contracted an unsuitable match (Turberville, 1939, p.44).

Disappointed by Maria, Portland now directed his attention to Anne Liddell, the estranged wife of the Duke of Grafton, who was himself to be Prime Minister in 1768–70. He lavished presents on her, including two horses, and her surviving letters to him reveal that she more than reciprocated his feelings. Suddenly, however, Portland's side of the correspondence grew more distant, and, in March 1766 he wrote announcing his engagement to Lady Dorothy Cavendish, daughter of the fourth Duke of Devonshire. Judging from her portrait, the future Duchess of Portland was a great deal less attractive than either of her rivals, and she was certainly less vivacious. She was, however, universally seen as a suitable match and their marriage, which took place the following November, seems to have been a happy one. The advantage to Portland was obvious, He was marrying into one of the greatest aristocratic and political families of the realm and his new brother-in-law, the fifth Duke of Devonshire, obligingly lent him Burlington House, in Piccadilly, as his London residence, an ideal venue for political entertaining (Turberville, pp.44–51). As for the Duchess of Grafton, she did not remain broken hearted for long. She soon took up with the Earl of Upper Ossory, bearing him a son in 1768 and marrying him as soon as her marriage to Grafton had been dissolved by Act of Parliament in 1769. (It is intriguing that another future Prime Minister, Harold Macmillan, was to marry a Lady Dorothy Cavendish, daughter of the ninth Duke of Devonshire, over 150 years later, in 1920).

What sort of man was the Third Duke of Portland, and what beliefs and principles underlay his political career? First and foremost, he was an almost perfect exemplar of the creed of *noblesse oblige*, as was illustrated by a letter he addressed to his wastrel younger brother, Lord Edward Bentinck, urging on him his duty to accept nomination as a Member of Parliament:

> Since I have been able to exercise my reason, I never could persuade myself that men were born only for themselves. I have always been bred to think that Society has its claims on them, & that those claims were in general proportioned to the degrees of their fortunes, their situation, and their abilities... (Turberville, p.68)

Secondly, Portland was a strong party man, and the party he had chosen was the Whig party, which he saw as the natural protector of the Bill of Rights of 1689. This prescribed a limited monarchy, and parliamentary government, and it was the duty of the Whig aristocracy, in Portland's view, to ensure that this doctrine prevailed. Throughout the reigns of the first two Georges, they had successfully carried out this mission, but the young George III, who ascended the throne in 1760, had lost little time in challenging it, effectively turning out of office a Whig government led by the Duke of Newcastle, and substituting one led by a royal favourite, the Earl of Bute.

Portland, a mild-mannered man, was nevertheless capable of strong emotions and conceived a deep aversion to Bute and a keen distrust of the King. For his part, George refused to accept that he was acting against either the letter or the spirit of the Bill of Rights. He believed that his right to appoint or dismiss ministers at his will was underwritten by this Act, and that it was only the laziness of his great grandfather, George I and his grandfather, George II, which had allowed this power to be usurped by a Whig oligarchy. He was doing no more, he believed, than reclaiming the powers awarded to William III by the 1689 Act.

Despite, his Whig principles, Portland was no democrat and in general held highly conservative views. He was opposed to parliamentary reform, to Catholic emancipation and the abolition of slavery. This might have brought him into conflict with Charles James Fox, the undisputed leader of the Whigs in the House of Commons, but in fact the two men acted in almost complete harmony for many years and were only driven apart by the impact of the French Revolution, in the years after 1789. The basis of Portland's influence was his position as a great territorial magnate, with estates in Buckinghamshire, Cumberland, Hampshire and Soho. Yet he was constrained by two factors – his relationship with his mother, and his own spendthrift ways. The Dowager Duchess of Portland loved her elder son dearly, but was fiercely protective of her own rights. The Cavendish interest, including large estates in Nottinghamshire and Derbyshire and a grand London residence, which she had inherited from her mother, remained hers until her death in 1785, while Portland only controlled the Bentinck inheritance until then. The Dowager chose, however, to make her home at Bulstrode, in Buckinghamshire, the main Bentinck residence, allowing her son, in exchange, to live in Welbeck Abbey, the Nottinghamshire base of her branch of the Cavendish family, conveniently close to Portland's new Cavendish in-laws, the Devonshires, at Chatsworth. There were periodic conflicts between mother and son over the control and management of the different estates and in addition sharp political differences, as the Dowager was an intimate friend of Lady Bute and had many close contacts with courtiers of the King. In addition, Portland's brother-in-law, Lord Weymouth, who had provided him with his parliamentary seat, was a Tory, who served for many years, without distinction, in Lord North's government.

Portland was a benevolent landlord and was regarded as an 'easy touch' by many of his large circle of friends and dependents. He was continually bailing out Lord Edward Bentinck, described by Horace Walpole as his 'idle and worthless younger brother', and lent as much as £56,000 to his rakish friend George Byng (Lord Torrington), which he never got back. In addition, he recklessly spent large sums of money in the general election of 1768 in a determined attempt to win parliamentary seats in Cumberland, where he was a large landowner, from the control of the notorious 'boroughmonger', Sir James Lowther. In the short-term, he was notably successful, doubling the number of seats he directly controlled in the House of Commons, from four to eight, but in the long-term it was ruinous to his finances. Lowther retaliated by launching a lawsuit against Portland, challenging the legality of his Cumberland holdings which had been granted to his great grandfather by William III. Lowther was immensely wealthy and boasted 'I would at any time spend £20,000 to make the Duke of Portland spend fifteen, for I know I can hold out longer than he can, and my meaning is to ruin the Duke of Portland.' The case dragged on for ten years, at enormous expense, and though Portland eventually prevailed, 'it proved a joyless victory, which resulted in the sale of most of his Cumberland estates' (Wilkinson, 2003, p.24). Wilkinson points out that, though Portland was by most measures a very wealthy man, his assets palled in comparison with those of other territorial magnates. Prior to his mother's death, in 1785, his net income was some £9000 a year, which then rose to £17,000. 'These figures should be compared with fellow grandees, such as the Duke of Devonshire and the Marquis of Rockingham, whose net incomes were in the region of £40,000 p.a.' (Ibid., p.61).

Portland did not have long to wait to win ministerial office. In July 1765, three years after he succeeded to the dukedom, the King ejected George Grenville, Bute's successor, from office, and turned once again to the Whigs to form a government. The Marquess of Rockingham became Prime Minister at the age of 35 and invited Portland, then 27, to become Lord Chamberlain, outside the Cabinet. The duties were not very arduous, and were largely routine, such as the organization of 'state ceremonies, the preparation of apartments for royal visits, the redecoration of ballrooms, the purchase of new furniture and similar topics' (Turberville, p.88). Portland found it all rather boring, but proved efficient at his post, and when the King dismissed the Rockingham government, after just over a year, he was one of a number of ministers asked to stay on in the new government led by the Earl of Chatham (the elder Pitt). Portland was not an admirer of Chatham, whom he referred to as 'Lord Cheat'em', and had no qualms in resigning after a few months, when Rockingham called on his supporters to quit the government. In opposition, he stayed close to Rockingham and remained so for the ensuing 16 years until Rockingham was again asked to form a government, in March 1782. This was in succession to Lord North, whose 12 years in office came to an end with the collapse of the British position in the American War of Independence. Rockingham nominated him as Lord Lieutenant, or 'viceroy' of Ireland, but less than three months after his arrival in Dublin the sudden death of the Prime Minister brought the government to an abrupt end.

The Rockinghamites met to appoint a successor, whom they optimistically assumed would be asked by George III to form a new government. Much the most able of the Whig peers was the Duke of Richmond, an illegitimate descendant of Charles II, who had served with distinction in both the Rockingham governments and would dearly have loved to be chosen. Yet, in Horace Walpole's words, quoted by Turberville, 'with a thousand virtues, he was nevertheless exceedingly unpopular'. One reason was his ardent advocacy of Parliamentary reform, which did not go down well with many of the Whig magnates, who feared the loss of their 'pocket' boroughs. What, asked Turberville, of the party's

> most active and brilliant representative in the Lower House – Fox? It is exceedingly doubtful whether this most intensely aristocratic of all political connexions would ever have selected a commoner as its head: but there was a fatal objection apart from that – Fox was anathema to the King. It was Fox himself who proposed the solution which found general favour – the election of the Duke of Portland. (Turberville, p.180)

So it was that one of the least qualified people ever to lead a British political party was chosen. As his grandson, the nineteenth century diarist, Charles Greville, also quoted by Turberville, put it:

> My grandfather was a very honourable, high-minded but ordinary man; his abilities were very second-rate, and he had no power of speaking, and his election to the post of leader of the great Whig party only shows how aristocratic that party was … they would never have endured to be led by a Peel or a Canning. (Ibid., pp.180–1)

George III never seriously considered asking Portland to become Prime Minister and hastened to appoint the Earl of Shelburne, formerly a close associate of the Elder Pitt, who asked Portland to stay on as Lord Lieutenant of Ireland. Soon afterwards, however, he resigned, joining the bulk of the Rockinghamites in opposition, and beginning a long and harmonious partnership with Fox, who was the undisputed Whig leader in the Commons. As recounted in Chapter 12, Shelburne's ministry did not last long, being defeated in February 1783, in a House of Commons vote on the American peace terms, due to the coming together of the forces of Fox and of Lord North MP, the former Tory Prime Minister.

The King, with great reluctance, agreed that they should form the next government, but insisted that someone else should be Prime Minister. His preference was the young William Pitt, then only 23, but he was unwilling and in any case was unacceptable to both Fox and North, who both insisted that Portland should be chosen. He agreed to take office, but the new government, installed on 2 April 1783, was totally dominated by Fox, as Foreign Secretary, and North as Home Secretary, both being in the House of Commons. In effect, Portland's role was principally to act merely as Leader of the House of Lords, but he enjoyed excellent relations with both of his nominal subordinates, and seemed quite comfortable to be seen as a figurehead.

From the outset, George was determined that the government, to whom he refused all patronage, should be of brief duration and his resolve was only strengthened when it proposed to him a generous formula for clearing the debts of the spendthrift Prince of Wales and substantially increasing his official allowance. The King expressed his 'utter indignation and astonishment' at so large a sum being proposed (far larger than *he* had enjoyed as heir apparent), and charged the Duke with 'neglecting the interests of the Sovereign and of the public to gratify the passions of an ill-advised Young Man'. Portland replied with an emollient letter proposing a compromise, which the King accepted, and – untypically – apologized to Portland for his earlier ill temper. Despite this apparent reconciliation, George was still determined to remove the Portland government at the earliest opportunity, which – as described in Chapter 14 – occurred when Fox enthusiastically pushed through the Commons a Bill, drafted by Edmund Burke, sharply curtailing the independence of the East India Company and transferring its powers of patronage to parliamentary commissioners. In a plot carefully contrived with the former (and future) Lord Chancellor, Lord Thurlow and with the Younger Pitt, the latter's cousin, the second Earl Temple, was authorized to tell members of the House of Lords that the King would regard any of them who voted for the Bill as his 'personal enemy'. Rumours of what was afoot reached the government and Portland referred obliquely to them in his speech proposing the Second Reading of the Bill in the Lords. Perhaps there was nothing to be done about it, but Portland badly mishandled the situation, making no serious attempt to persuade peers of the merits of the Bill and then bungling the parliamentary procedure for its approval. The Bill was defeated by 19 votes, but the government, which still enjoyed a large majority in the Commons, refused to resign. It was then unceremoniously dismissed by the King, who sent personal messengers at midnight to the homes of

Portland, Fox and North to demand the return of their seals of office. Portland's premiership, which came to an end on 18 December 1783, had lasted a mere 260 days. The King's intervention was described, by the leading historian of this period, as 'indefensible according to both the constitutional theory and practice of his own day' (Cannon, p.xiii). Portland received no blame from his colleagues for his maladroit performance. He was regarded by them as a martyr for the Whig cause, and 'it became impossible to conceive of the return of the whigs without his reinstatement [as Prime Minister]' (Wilkinson, 2004).

Such a return seemed probable late in 1788, when the first bout of madness of George III appeared to open the way to the appointment of his son (later George IV), a bosom friend of Fox and other leading Whigs, as Prince Regent. The King's recovery, the following March, before a regency bill had been passed, forestalled this possibility and the main body of the Whigs were to remain in the wilderness for many years to come. Portland, however, was restored to office, though not to the premiership, some five years later.

The French Revolution, in 1789, had opened up deep divisions within the Whig Party, with Fox enthusiastically welcoming it, and Edmund Burke reacting sharply against. Portland's initial reaction was mildly favourable, but as the excesses mounted up, he, together with many other Whig aristocrats, began to fear for his property if French revolutionary ideas were to cross the Channel. When war broke out with France, in 1792, he became even more concerned and succumbed to the patriotic fervour whipped up by Pitt's supporters. He was, however, deeply reluctant to break with Fox, who was opposed to the war, and for long refused to respond to feelers from Pitt to join his government, as Lord Loughborough, the leading Whig lawyer, had done, in becoming Lord Chancellor in January 1793. It was another 18 months before he was prepared to take the plunge, finally, as recounted in Chapter 14, becoming Home Secretary in July 1794. He was accompanied by four other conservative Whig defectors, who joined the cabinet at the same time and he succeeded in bringing over to the government side more than half of the Whig representation in the Commons. This greatly bolstered Pitt's majority and left Fox in charge of a diminishing rump of largely demoralized supporters.

The Portlandites also obtained numerous peerages and other honours, as well as appointments to non-cabinet posts, of which the most important was the Lord Lieutenancy of Ireland. This went to Earl Fitzwilliam, Rockingham's nephew and a close friend of Portland's. On his arrival in Dublin, Fitzwilliam embarked on a purge of government officials, replacing supporters of Pitt with Irish Whigs and without obtaining Cabinet approval, expressed his sympathy for Catholic emancipation. Portland was horrified and immediately recalled Fitzwilliam, offering, however, as a token of friendship, to resign as Home Secretary and telling Fitzwilliam that the King had agreed to his appointment to a Cabinet post as compensation for his dismissal, provided he affirmed his support for the ministry. With all the pride of a leading Whig magnate, Fitzwilliam rejected this offer out of hand and his friendship with Portland was at an end. As Home Secretary, Portland continued to be responsible for Irish affairs and following the unsuccessful United Irish uprising, led by Wolfe Tone, in 1798, took a leading role in the moves to incorporate the Irish Parliament into the British Parliament at Westminster. This was only achieved by the massive employment of patronage and outright bribes to Irish MPs to induce them to vote their own Parliament out of existence. This policy was carried through by the men on the spot in Dublin, the Marquis of Cornwallis, as Lord Lieutenant, and Viscount Castlereagh MP, as Chief Secretary. When Portland left office, in 1801, there were substantial funds missing from the Home Office accounts, which was promptly covered up. For nearly 200 years, Portland, who was known to be in financial difficulties at the time, was suspected of having diverted the money (more than £30,000) for his own purposes. It was only with the release of the Home Office secret service papers, in the 1990s and sharp detective work by the historian, David Wilkinson, that it was revealed that the missing money had, in fact, been illegally transmitted to Dublin to grease the palms of Irish Protestant legislators (Wilkinson, 2003, pp.148–58).

Portland's Whiggish instincts did not long survive his recruitment to the Pitt government and his previous animus against Pitt, who had usurped his premiership a dozen years earlier and against George III, soon evaporated. Indeed, he became a fervent admirer of Pitt, whom he found a considerate colleague and of the King, with whom he developed good relations and whom he came to see as a model patriotic monarch. For all intents and purposes, Portland became a Tory, though he never described himself as such, and his record as Home Secretary showed him to be one of the most hard-line of Pitt's ministers. He was largely responsible for introducing and implementing the oppressive legislation directed against alleged supporters of the French Revolution and of parliamentary reform and he did not scruple to use secret service informers and *agents provateurs* to harry their activities. Nor did he show himself sympathetic to those suffering from serious food shortages, following a series of bad harvests, setting his face against proposals to fix food prices or make government purchases of imported grain. Only on two occasions, in 1795 and 1800, did he relent, in the face of strong pressure from other ministers.

When Pitt resigned, along with other leading cabinet ministers, in February 1801, in protest against George III's vetoing of Catholic emancipation, Portland did not join them. He carried on as Home Secretary in Henry Addington's government, later switching to become Lord President of the Council, a position he retained in Pitt's second ministry, formed in May 1804. The following year, he relinquished the post to make room for Addington (now Lord Sidmouth), but remained in the Cabinet as Minister without Portfolio. He went into opposition when Lord Grenville formed his 'Ministry of All the Talents', on Pitt's death in February 1806, becoming the nominal leader of the Pittites, who were excluded, or excluded themselves, from the government because of their incompatibility with the Whigs, who formed the largest element in Grenville's team. The Pittite group included such strong characters as George Canning, Spencer Perceval, Lord Hawkesbury (the future Lord Liverpool) and Viscount Castlereagh, whose mutual rivalry was assuaged by their common agreement to unite under the emollient Duke.

Portland was now an elderly man and his health was far from good and it looked as though his ministerial days were at an end. Yet when, in early 1807, George III once again came into conflict with his ministers on the issue of Catholic emancipation), Portland wrote an ill-advised letter to the King urging him to stand his ground. Grenville and his leading colleagues agreed to withdraw their Bill granting the rights of Catholics to hold senior positions in the Army and Navy, but refused to promise the King never to raise the issue again. Thereupon, he peremptorily dismissed them and appealed to Portland to take Grenville's place. With evident misgivings, Portland complied, forming what was effectively a Tory government, with the leading positions all filled by Pittites. On paper, at least, it was a strong team, with Spencer Perceval as Chancellor of the Exchequer, George Canning as Foreign Secretary, Lord Hawkesbury (shortly to succeed to the Earldom of Liverpoool) as Home Secretary and Viscount Castlereagh MP as Secretary for War and the Colonies. In practice, it proved a great deal weaker than the sum of its parts. This was because of the lack of direction which it received from Portland, who attended cabinet meetings only spasmodically, and hardly ever the House of Lords, where he remained silent throughout his premiership. Wilkinson did not put it too bluntly, when he wrote: 'Portland was worse than useless as prime minister. Not only did he fail to direct policy, he also bungled the lesser role of conciliator' (Wilkinson, 2003, 164–5). Contemporary comment, especially from Whig supporters, who felt betrayed by him, was even more unkind. Wilkinson quotes, at length, a poem published in the *Morning Chronicle*, and beginning:

> He totters on a crutch;
> his brain by sickness long depressed,
> has lost the sense it once possessed,
> though that's not losing much. (Ibid., p.137)

The government faced serious problems, not least in promoting the war against Napoleon, where the campaign in Spain and Portugal was going badly and the expedition to the Dutch island of Walcheren, with the aim of seizing Antwerp, planned by Castlereagh, went disastrously wrong. They were compounded by a scandal involving the King's brother, the Duke of York, who was Commander-in-Chief, and whose mistress was accused of selling army commissions. The worst feature of Portland's government, however, was the intrigues conducted by individual ministers against their colleagues. The main culprit was George Canning, who – sensing that the Portland ministry would not last long – endeavoured to manoeuvre himself into a position where he would be well placed to succeed him. His main rival was likely to be Perceval, but the man he had in his sights was Castlereagh, and he approached Portland, threatening to resign if Castlereagh was not removed from the War Office and replaced by Lord Wellesley, the elder brother of General Sir Arthur Wellesley, later the Duke of Wellington. Portland agreed, in principle and squared the matter with the King, but insisted that the change could not be made until after the outcome of the Walcheren expedition was known and that until then the decision should be kept from Castlereagh so as not to undermine him. He also suggested that the bad news should ultimately be conveyed to Castlereagh by Earl Camden, the Lord President of the Council, who was his uncle, and who nobly offered to give up his own post in his nephew's favour, in order to soften the blow. Yet when the time came, after the failure of the Walcheren expedition, his nerve failed him and shortly afterwards Portland had an apoplectic seizure while on his journey from London to Bulstrode and was taken out of his carriage 'speechless and insensible. He made a partial recovery of both mind and speech, but no hopes were entertained of his ultimate restoration to health' (Turberville, p.301). His family wanted Portland to retire immediately, and when Perceval also recommended him to do so, he decided to call it a day, a decision which alarmed Canning, as he thought it had come too early for his own chances of the succession. When Castlereagh learned of Canning's conduct, he was outraged, and immediately demanded satisfaction. The two men met on Putney Heath for a duel, in which Canning was slightly wounded and the scandal added to the ignominy of the collapse of Portland's government.

Portland resigned on 4 October 1809, after a premiership of two years and 187 days. This was more than three times as long as his first premiership, but whereas he had played a useful role as a mediator the first time round, he was almost a complete passenger in his second administration. Perceval went on to form a government from which both Canning and Castlereagh were excluded and the former had to wait another 13 years before he was restored to office. Portland agreed to continue in Perceval's cabinet as Minister without Portfolio, but died three weeks later, after a second apoplectic attack, on 30 October 1809, aged 71. He left debts of £500,000 and it was only by effecting painful economies, including the sale of the main Bentinck estate at Bulstrode, that his son, the fourth Duke, who eschewed any political participation, was able to mend the family fortunes.

Portland's long political career had seldom risen above the level of mediocrity. As opposition leader in the 1780s, he lent respectability to the otherwise somewhat raffish Whigs and his patience and affability helped to hold the party together in a difficult period. A conscientious, if reactionary, Home Secretary between 1794 and 1801, he would probably have been wiser to bow out of politics at that stage, and devote his evidently waning powers to the management of his still extensive estates. Yet a misguided sense of duty, and a desire to please the King, to whom he was now devoted, forced him to carry on. His historical importance lies chiefly in his action in 1794 of bringing the more conservative Whigs over to Pitt. He thereby paved the way for a reconstituted Tory party, which was to become the dominant political force in the first three decades of the nineteenth century.

Works consulted

Cannon, John (1969), *The Fox-North Coalition*, Cambridge, Cambridge University Press.

Derry, John W. (1990), *Politics in the Age of Fox, Pitt and Liverpool*, Basingstoke, Macmillan.

Smith, E. Anthony (1973), 'The Duke of Portland', in Herbert Van Thal (ed.), *The Prime Ministers*, Volume I, London, Allen & Unwin.

Stephens H.M. (H.M.S) (1885), Article in *Dictionary of National Biography*.

Turberville, A.S. (1939), *A History of Welbeck Abbey and its Owners*, Volume II, London, Faber and Faber.

Wilkinson, David (2003), *The Duke of Portland: Politics and Party in the Age of George III*, Basingstoke, Palgrave Macmillan.

Wilkinson, David (2004), Article in *Oxford Dictionary of National Biography*.

14
William Pitt, the Younger – Peacetime Prodigy, Less Successful in War

If ever anybody was pre-programmed to be Prime Minister, it was
William Pitt the Younger.* He was born, in Kent, on 28 May 1759 – the

---

* Like Portland, Pitt was Prime Minister in both the eighteenth and nineteenth centuries. This chapter is an adapted version from that which appeared in
my earlier volume, *Nineteenth Century British Premiers; Pitt to Rosebery*, (Palgrave-
Macmillan, 2008).

very year in which his father gained lasting renown as a war leader in the Seven Years War. The elder Pitt (later Lord Chatham) was not, then, actually Prime Minister, but he planned and directed Britain's military and naval operations, which saw France driven out of its possessions in both Canada and India and worsted in conflicts in West Africa and the West Indies. Although his subsequent term as Prime Minister, in 1766–68, was a disappointment, his achievements in 1759, combined with his passionate patriotism, rare incorruptibility and soaring oratory established him as Britain's outstanding eighteenth century political leader.

The elder Pitt came from a well-established landed family, with a tradition of public service, whose fortune derived from his grandfather, Thomas Pitt, a trader in India, who became Governor of Madras. William the Elder married Hester Grenville, whose brother, George Grenville, was also to be Prime Minister (in 1763–65), so the young William grew up in a family which was deeply political on both sides. William was the second son and fourth child (out of five) in the family, but from the outset his father had marked him out as the one to carry forward the flame of his own burning ambition. Partly because of his delicate health, but also because of the elder Pitt's unpleasant memories of Eton, which he described as 'a stultifying and brutal place' (Turner, p.6), William was educated at home by a private tutor, but his father took a very active role in his instruction. He coached him in oratory, getting him to translate, verbally and at sight, passages from Greek and Latin authors and hearing him recite. By the age of seven, William was already looking forward to following in his father's footsteps. Very quick to learn he was judged at 14 to be the equal or superior of most 18-year-olds and started to study at Pembroke Hall, Cambridge, with the Rev. George Pretyman (whom he was much later to nominate as Archbishop of Canterbury, only to be over-ruled by George III) as his tutor. His health soon broke down and he spent much of the next three years at home, suffering, among other ailments, from gout. His doctor, Anthony Addington (father of his successor as Prime Minister, Henry Addington), prescribed a bottle of port every day as a cure. It seemed to work, but it left William with a heavy dependence on alcohol, which was to do him no good in the long run.

As an undergraduate, he lived a solitary life, meeting few people other than his tutor, Pretyman. He proved a diligent student of Latin and Greek, showed a taste for mathematics and learned French, but no other modern languages and showed little interest in contemporary culture. In 1776, still aged only 17, he graduated as a Master of Arts, without taking an examination. He stayed on in Cambridge and his social life at last took off, bringing him into contact with a group of well-bred young men, several of whom were later to become his political associates. One of these was William Wilberforce, the famous campaigner for the abolition of the slave trade, who left a record of Pitt's life at Cambridge, describing him as being always 'remarkably cheerful and pleasant, full of wit and playfulness' (Ehrman, Vol. I, pp.17–18). This view was corroborated by others, including Pretyman and he was undoubtedly very popular with his fellows but at the same time he was remarked as being gawky and awkward and painfully shy with strangers. He was in no doubt that politics was his vocation and travelled frequently to London to listen to parliamentary debates, on one occasion being introduced to Charles James Fox, the leading Whig orator, who commented favourably on his lively intelligence. He attended the House of Lords on 7 April 1778, to hear his father's last speech, a passionate appeal to make peace with the American rebels, and when the Earl collapsed before reaching his peroration, helped to carry him out of the Chamber. Chatham died a month later and – in the absence of his elder brother, John, who was on military service overseas – Pitt was left to make the funeral arrangements and attempt to sort out his father's tangled financial affairs. He was deeply in debt, having – unlike most of his contemporaries – refused to enrich himself from his ministerial duties, and though Parliament voted to pay off the debts and to establish an annuity of £4000 attached to the Earldom (which went to his brother), Pitt received no legacy and himself went into debt, which – with ups and downs – continued for the rest of his life.

It was necessary to earn a living and Pitt now started eating dinners at Lincoln's Inn, with the intention of working at the bar. He qualified in June 1780, and in August went to work on the Western circuit. In September, however, a general election was called and he hastily returned to Cambridge, where he was nominated as a candidate for one of the University seats. He was just over 21 years old and wrote enthusiastically to his mother that it was 'a seat of all others the most desirable, as being free from expense, perfectly independent and I think in every respect extremely honourable' (Turner, p.13). The only disadvantage was that Pitt, despite his long residence in Cambridge, had very little support. He came bottom of the poll, in fifth place with less than 14 per cent of the votes. In order to secure election at such an early stage, it would be necessary, he concluded, to surrender some of the independence he (like his father) so craved. When he was approached by a notorious 'boroughmonger', Sir James Lowther, to take over, with all expenses paid, the representation of Appleby (in Westmorland) – one of his string of 'rotten boroughs', which had become immediately vacant – he accepted with little hesitation. Lowther was an admirer of his father, and as Pitt explained to his mother:

> No Kind of Condition was mentioned, but that if ever Our Lines of Conduct should become opposite, I should give Him an Opportunity of chusing another Person. On such Liberal Terms, I should certainly not hesitate to accept the Proposal, than which Nothing could be in any respect more agreeable. (Ehrman, I, p.26)

Accordingly, on 8 January 1781, Pitt was returned unopposed at a by-election, without setting foot in the constituency.

The Parliament to which Pitt was elected was divided as much by faction as by party. The historical division between Whigs and Tories had become somewhat blurred during the 20 years that George III had occupied the throne. The long domination of the Whigs throughout the reigns of the first two Georges, which had seen the Tories steadily decline in both numbers and influence, was a thing of the past. The Whigs still saw themselves as the guarantors of the Glorious Revolution of 1688–89, believing in a limited monarchy, the supremacy of Parliament, a vigorous and basically anti-French foreign policy, free trade and relative religious tolerance. Led by an oligarchy of enlightened aristocrats, they tended to be arrogant, self-satisfied and to behave as though they were born to rule. The main Whig factions were led by three peers – the Marquess of Rockingham, the Earl of Shelburne and the Duke of Portland, with Charles James Fox the dominant figure in the House of Commons.

The Tories, representing primarily the gentry, were strong supporters of the royal prerogative and the Church of England, tending to believe in the divine right of monarchs, and were long tainted by suspicions of Jacobitism, though this was less of a factor after the failure of the 1745 uprising of Bonnie Prince Charlie. They were also protectionist, and more isolationist in international affairs, putting their trust in the British Navy to keep the nation out of danger. Their long eviction from power was ended by the accession of George III, who distrusted the Whig oligarchs and was determined to assert his own personal role. In 1762, he installed a Tory, the Earl of Bute, a personal favourite, as Prime Minister, but his ministry lasted for less than a year. There followed four short-lived Whig governments, one of them led by the elder Pitt as Earl of Chatham, but in 1770, George succeeded in imposing a second Tory administration. This was led by Lord North MP, a much more substantial politician than Bute, who was to continue in office for 12 years. When Pitt was elected, his long rule was nearing its end, and he was largely discredited by the disasters of the American War of Independence.

Pitt's entry into Parliament aroused great interest, almost entirely because of his father, to whom he bore much physical resemblance, with his long, thin face and tall body, though at six feet his was longer and more ungainly than his father's. He also made much of his adherence to his father's principles, of putting patriotism before party advantage and of refusing to enrich himself at the public expense. He did not disappoint the high expectations: after hearing his maiden speech, which made a deep impression on the Commons, Edmund Burke declared 'he is not a chip of the old block, he is the old block himself' (Duffy, p.4).

Like the Elder Pitt, William described himself as an 'independent Whig', and loosely attached himself to the faction led by the Earl of Shelburne, who had been one of the two Secretaries of State in his father's administration. He proved himself an incisive critic of the North government, making a powerful speech, on 12 June 1781, in favour of Fox's motion for peace with the American colonies. A year later, with his reputation as an up-and-coming force already well established, and the government clearly on its last legs, he rashly declared that he would 'never accept a subordinate situation' in any successor administration. North resigned a few days later and the Marquess of Rockingham was summoned to form a new Whig government, in which Shelburne became Home and Fox, Foreign Secretary. Pitt was offered the post of Vice-Treasurer of Ireland, which his father had briefly held in 1746. It carried a salary of £5000, which Pitt could well have done with, but he felt trapped by his earlier words and declined, choosing instead to support the new government from outside. Pitt now moved swiftly to assert himself as an advocate of electoral reform, moving a resolution to appoint a select committee to consider the state of representation, supporting one to shorten the duration of parliaments and a bill to check bribery. Pitt's efforts failed, but he resolved to return to the charge on a more auspicious occasion. Meanwhile, the Rockingham government lasted a mere three months, the Prime Minister dying suddenly of influenza in July 1782. The King chose Shelburne as his successor and Fox, who had quarrelled with him over the peace negotiations with America and France, declined to serve under him and resigned his post, as did Burke, who had been Paymaster-General. Shelburne, the bulk of his Cabinet being peers, was desperate to recruit debating strength in the Commons to counter these two formidable adversaries and offered Pitt the post of Chancellor of the Exchequer. This was not then as senior a post as it subsequently became, as the First Lord of the Treasury (i.e., the Prime Minister) was primarily responsible for financial and fiscal affairs; nevertheless it was a stunning promotion for a man of 23 with no previous ministerial experience.

Pitt's period as Chancellor lasted a mere eight months, during which he made his mark by reorganizing customs duties, cutting out wasteful expenditure and reducing the extent of jobbery in public offices. Meanwhile, Shelburne, a highly intelligent man but lacking in political skills, was having great difficulty in seeking approval for the peace terms which had finally been negotiated with the Americans. An unholy alliance was formed between the followers of Fox, the leader of the 'advanced' Whigs and the main critic of the American War and the Tory Lord North, who had been responsible for its conduct. Shelburne realized that he would have to break up this alliance if his policy and his ministry were to survive. He made overtures to some of North's supporters who, however, insisted that North should be included in the government, which Pitt was not prepared to countenance. Shelburne then sent Pitt to see Fox to invite him to rejoin the government. Fox refused, saying that for a new coalition to be formed, Shelburne would have to resign. Pitt stormed out, saying, 'I did not come here to betray Lord Shelburne', and the two men, who previously had been mutual admirers, were never to meet in private again (Turner, p.43). The Commons passed a censure motion against the peace terms, by 207 to 190 votes, on 22 February 1783 and Shelburne resigned two days later, much to the King's chagrin. In the final Commons debate, Pitt had made an extraordinarily eloquent appeal on Shelburne's behalf and castigated the opportunism of the two previously sworn enemies, Fox and North, who were clearly putting themselves forward as joint heads of a new government. 'If this ill-omened marriage is not already solemnised', he said, 'I know a just and lawful impediment, and, in the name of public safety, I here forbid the banns' (Duffy, p.10).

George III made a last desperate effort to avoid giving office to the pair, one of whom was his most inveterate critic, and the other whom he felt had abandoned him by insisting on resigning after the collapse of the British position in North America. He offered the premiership to the 23-year-old Pitt, on Shelburne's recommendation and renewed the offer twice more over the succeeding six months. In Duffy's words, Pitt's 'refusals show a great degree of political maturity and *judgment* in being able to control his ambition'. Pitt was clear in his own mind that he could not hope to form a viable government without being able to command a majority in the House of Commons, and this he could only do with the cooperation, or at least the acquiescence, of Lord North, a man he held 'responsible for the misuse of Crown influence to corrupt Parliament, and for the confrontation with the colonies which had hastened the death of his father, who had exhausted himself in battling against it, and resulted in the loss of America' (Duffy, pp.12–13).

Eventually, the King had to agree to the Fox–North coalition, which was nominally led by a Whig grandee, the Duke of Portland, with Fox resuming his tenure of the Foreign Office and North becoming Home Secretary. It took office on 2 April 1783, but from the beginning George III was determined to overthrow it at the earliest opportunity, and refused point-blank to sustain the government with the powers of royal patronage normally put at the disposal of his ministers. The King, however, had to act with some circumspection, as the new government enjoyed a comfortable majority in the House of Commons. He seized his opportunity towards the end of the year, when the government introduced legislation to bring the East India Company, which governed territories whose population greatly exceeded that of Britain itself, under closer control. It proposed that the management and patronage of the company should be transferred to parliamentary commissioners appointed for a four-year term. The King and Pitt, thought that Fox would use the extensive patronage of the Company to the government's advantage, to compensate for the royal patronage which it lacked. They also recalled that Fox's father, Henry, the first Lord Holland, had used the patronage at his disposal, when he had been Paymaster-General in 1757–65, to build himself a large fortune, and were determined to block the Bill.

Fox appeared to have little difficulty in getting it through the Commons, and though George was insistent on his right to veto legislation, this power had not been used since the reign of Queen Anne, and it was widely thought to have fallen into desuetude. In a plan cooked up with Lord Thurlow, a former and future Lord Chancellor, in which Pitt was complicit, it was resolved to use the House of Lords to defeat the measure. The King authorized Lord Temple, a cousin of Pitt's, to tell peers that anybody who voted for the India Bill 'was not only not his friend, but would be considered by him as an enemy' (Duffy, p.18). The Lords duly obliged, defeating the Bill, on 17 December 1783, by 95 votes to 76. Both Pitt and George III had expected the government to resign immediately, but it decided to cling to office, not least because it secured 2–1 majorities in votes in the House of Commons attacking the use of the King's name and those who advised its use in the Lords. The King waited a further day, and then sent messengers at midnight to Portland,

Fox and North requiring them to surrender their seals of office. Pitt was appointed First Lord of the Treasury on 19 December, with Lord Thurlow as Lord Chancellor, but few other men of any standing were prepared to associate themselves with a government which had been brought to power in such an underhand way and Pitt was attacked for forming a government of mediocrities. Few people expected it to survive for long and it was quickly dubbed the 'mince pie government', on the assumption that it would not last beyond Christmas. In such inauspicious circumstances began a premiership which was to last for over 17 years (and almost 19 years, in all, including Pitt's second ministry in 1804–06). Pitt was aged 24 years, 205 days – almost nine years younger than any other British Prime Minister – his closest rival, the third Duke of Grafton, being just over 33 on his appointment in 1768.

Pitt endured a scary few months, being repeatedly defeated in votes in the House of Commons, but – to Fox's exasperation – refused to resign, secure in the knowledge that he retained the King's confidence. During this period, however, his personal stock rose sharply, due to the skill with which he defended himself in parliamentary debates. The burden on him was considerable, as his entire cabinet was made up of peers, and he had to act as the government's spokesman on every conceivable issue. Pitt's reputation also grew outside Parliament, partly because of his forbearance in declining to appoint himself to a sinecure office, the Clerkship of the Pells, worth £3000 a year, which was in the Prime Minister's gift. He also gained from public revulsion at an attack on his carriage by a Foxite mob on his return from receiving the Freedom of the City of London. Salvation came with the dissolution of Parliament in March 1784 – three-and-a-half years before the end of its term. Pitt knew that the odds were overwhelming that he would emerge with a comfortable majority from the election. He had already made deals with 'borough mongers', and the full weight of royal patronage (and Treasury money) was at his disposal. Indeed, throughout the eighteenth century, no sitting government was ever to lose an election. It was the King who gave ministers their marching orders, not the electors, who were few in number and largely influenced by a relatively small number of aristocratic landowners. The general election of 1784 was no exception: no detailed breakdown of the results has survived, but it was generally estimated that the government secured a majority of around 120 in a House of 558. The opposition was divided between about 130 MPs committed to Fox and 70 to North, who had been the main loser in the election and whose support subsequently fell away (Derry, p.52). For Pitt, the election brought another cause for satisfaction: he was able to exchange his 'pocket' borough of Appleby for his first love – Cambridge University – where this time he came top of the poll and was easily elected, retaining the seat for the rest of his life.

With his solid parliamentary majority and the renewed support of the King, Pitt no longer seemed vulnerable and he settled in for a long innings in Downing Street, though nobody foresaw that it would prove quite as long as it did. His cabinet was still devoid of parliamentary talent and he himself chose to retain the office of Chancellor of the Exchequer throughout his premiership, but he was able to bring along two close associates of high ability, who were eventually to fill the most senior posts. These were his cousin, William Grenville, son of a former Prime Minister, who was to rise successively to Home and Foreign Secretary and Henry Dundas, a formidable political 'fixer' from Scotland, who became his chief 'trouble shooter', and was also to be Home Secretary and later Secretary for War and the Colonies. His main handicap was that the King insisted on choosing the ministers himself, and ruled that Lord Thurlow, a man whom Pitt found highly uncongenial and disloyal, should continue as Lord Chancellor. Thurlow's relationship to George III was much closer and warmer than his own, which Pitt resented but was unable to do anything about.

Across the floor of the House of Commons, he had regularly to face Fox, now the undisputed leader of the Whigs, and his only rival and perhaps superior, as a parliamentary orator. Always credited by history with both his forenames, he was invariably known as Charles or Charley during his lifetime. Ten years older than Pitt and himself the second son of a distinguished political father, Fox was also known for his precocity, having first been elected to Parliament at the age of 19. This was two years below the legal limit, but in the less rule-bound ways of the eighteenth century, nobody objected when he took his seat. His own political career was to be blighted by Pitt's rise to power and by George III's unrelenting hostility. He was effectively to be the leader of the opposition (though the title did not then exist) for 23 years, and his sole periods in Cabinet office were three stints as Foreign Secretary, each lasting only a few months, in 1782, 1783 and 1806. On more than one occasion, Pitt sought to include Fox in his government but Fox demanded that they should both serve under a nominal superior, such as Portland, while Pitt invariably insisted on retaining the premiership. The two leaders' long rivalry prefigured that of Gladstone and Disraeli nearly a century later and they were an equally contrasting pair, both in appearance and character. Pitt was tall, stiff and withdrawn; Fox fat, warm and gregarious. Pitt was cautious, calculating and conservative;

Fox radical, impulsive, untidy. Pitt's political judgment was excellent, and he never (except on Ireland much later in his career) attempted to push hard for policies that had little chance of being acceptable to Parliament or – more importantly in his eyes – the King. Fox's *judgment* was poor, and though he was capable of wild opportunism, consistently pursued policies calculated to alienate the King. Fox was dissolute – a gambler and womanizer, who eventually contracted a happy marriage with a former courtesan, Elizabeth Armistead. Pitt was highly disciplined, had little apparent interest in women, and has – on the basis of rather slender evidence – become something of a gay icon (see page 239, below). Nearly everybody loved 'Charley', whose charm was a by-word. Except for a few bosom friends, with whom he was able to unbend in moments of alcoholic revelry, Pitt was respected but not greatly liked. They had some causes in common – electoral reform and the abolition of the slave trade – and in other circumstances their complementary talents could have drawn them together and made a formidable team. But raw ambition drove them apart in 1782–84 and they were never to be reconciled. Indeed, Pitt revealed a vindictive streak in his character, following his sweeping victory in the 1784 election, when he persisted for several months in an attempt to get Fox unseated from his Westminster constituency on – by eighteenth century standards – relatively minor evidence of irregularities. He was only finally dissuaded from this course when he was defeated on the issue by a House of Commons vote. (It was by no means unusual for the government to lose parliamentary votes, at a time of weak or non-existent party discipline, and when those in general support of the government, or even cabinet ministers, felt no particular obligation to deliver their votes except on major issues.)

Pitt's over-riding objective during his first years in office was to restore national confidence, and the declining economy, after the setbacks and disasters of the American War. His purpose was to stimulate trade – particularly with Europe to offset the loss of North American markets (which was to prove only temporary) – to improve the public finances and to usher in a period of political stability. On any reckoning, he was largely successful in his endeavours and within a relatively short time, not only King George but a large proportion of the 'political' class, came to view him as the indispensable head of government. One of Pitt's principal tools was his annual budgets but he did not make a name for himself, at least in his earlier years, as a tax pioneer. He relied on traditional forms of taxation and did not noticeably expand the tax base, concentrating as Ehrman convincingly argues (Ehrman, Vol. I, pp.250–6) primarily on increasing the yield from existing taxes, by improving methods of collection and by cracking down more effect-ively on smuggling. His most important innovation, in 1786, was to establish a sinking fund, with the objective of eventually paying off the national debt, which had doubled to around £213 million as a con-sequence of the American War. Pitt's proposal was well received, and steady progress was to be made in reducing the debt over the first half dozen years, but the outbreak of war with France in 1793 meant that it rapidly resumed its upward trend. Pitt was also active in cutting out wasteful expenditure, and, wherever possible, reducing or terminating the award of pensions and sinecures, though he was not above using such means for *political* purposes, including to strengthen the govern-ment's position in the House of Lords.

Pitt was also successful in his efforts to promote trade, though he suffered a setback in 1785, when he was forced to withdraw proposals for free trade between England and Ireland. He had more success with a commercial treaty, negotiated with France, in 1786, which led to a sharp increase in trade between the two traditional enemies. Pitt was to return to his earlier campaign for electoral reform, introducing a bill, in April 1785, which provided for a very modest extension of the franchise in county constituencies, while granting one million pounds to com-pensate the electors of 36 rotten boroughs which were to be disfran-chised, while the 72 seats thus made available were to be transferred to London, Westminster and the more populous counties. Neither the King nor several of his ministerial colleagues approved of the meas-ure, and nor did Lord North and his followers, though Fox supported the Bill. The King did not try to prevent its introduction, but insisted that it should be introduced in Pitt's personal capacity rather than as a government measure. Pitt made a powerful speech seeking leave to introduce the Bill, but it was defeated by 248 to 174 votes. A disap-pointed Pitt decided to cut his losses, and never again raised the issue, indeed opposing reform bills introduced by private members on three occasions in the 1790s and 1800s. So parliamentary reform had to wait nearly another half century until the 'great' Reform Bill of 1832. Nor did Pitt's enthusiasm for reform extend to support for the repeal of the Test and Corporation Acts. These two measures, dating from the mid-seventeenth century, had the effect of excluding Protestant dissenters (later known as Nonconformists) from membership of municipal cor-porations or from holding a wide range of public offices or commissions in the army and navy. Although these acts were only enforced in a spas-modic manner, they remained a standing grievance, particularly to the business community, in which many dissenters had gained prominence.

Pitt appeared to have no strong views on the subject and consulted the Archbishop of Canterbury, who informed him that only two out of 16 bishops favoured reform (Hague, p.239). Unwilling to alienate the Church of England, Pitt threw his weight against the proposed repeal, which was duly defeated, in March 1787, by 176 votes to 98. Pitt was a strong supporter of the abolition of the slave trade and encouraged his friend Wilberforce to bring motions before the House of Commons to secure this objective. On one occasion, in April 1792, he made what was regarded as one of the greatest speeches of his career in support of Wilberforce's demand for 'immediate' abolition but the House preferred to adopt an amendment tabled by Dundas, substituting the word 'gradual', which stripped the motion of any practical effect. William Hague describes Pitt's inability to secure the final abolition of the trade as his 'greatest failure'. He writes:

> The sincerity of his opposition to this dreadful trade was all too plain, but so is the fact that he lost the energy, focus and will to pursue the matter to a successful conclusion ... The fact that abolition was so speedily secured by Grenville and Fox soon after Pitt's death suggests that he too could have secured it if he had marshalled his forces to do so. (Hague, p.589)

By the late 1780s, an increasingly frustrated Fox followed the course pursued by earlier opposition leaders in the reigns of George I and George II, by transferring his allegiance to the court of the Prince of Wales, who was at daggers' drawn with his father. More intelligent and much more cultured than the philistine King, the future George IV was far from being an admirable character. Dissolute, vain, extravagantly self-indulgent, lacking in judgment and profoundly untrustworthy, Fox and his fellow Whigs would have been well advised to keep him at arms-length. Instead, Fox and he became bosom companions, and few doubted that the first act of young George if he were to succeed his father would be to dismiss Pitt from power and restore Fox and Portland to their former posts. In 1788 George III was 50 years old, and had already reigned for 28 years. Given the average expectation of life, it was not fanciful to suppose that before long the Prince of Wales would ascend the throne. His – and Fox's – opportunity seemed to have arrived in November 1788, with the Regency crisis, brought on by the onset of George III's first serious attack of porphyria, a little understood hereditary illness, whose symptoms included temporary insanity. The King's principal doctor, Warren, declared that he was incurable and unlikely to live for long. The Whigs, in Fox's absence on holiday in Italy, were persuaded by Richard Sheridan, the Irish play-wright and leading Foxite MP, to demand the immediate installation of the Prince as regent. Pitt, sensing the great danger he was in, played for time, insisting that all the relevant precedents should be studied and that an Act of Parliament should be passed setting out the terms of the regency. He also consulted his own former doctor, Anthony Addington, who gave a much more favourable prognosis, saying that he had seen worse cases than the King make a full recovery. Pitt's regency bill sharply curtailed the powers of the regent, in particular, preventing him from granting peerages and making official appoint-ments (except on a temporary basis), and placing the King's person and property wholly in the Queen's hands. Fox, who had hastened back to London, in a poor physical state, stricken with dysentery, then made a crucial blunder. The self-proclaimed `tribune of the people` declared in the House of Commons that the Prince had an hereditary right to the regency, implying that Parliament had no business in seeking to define the limits. Pitt immediately seized his chance, whispering to his neighbour 'I'll unwhig the gentleman for the rest of his life', and pro-ceeded to point out that this went directly against the long-standing Whig principle of parliamentary sovereignty. Despite, the disloyalty of his Lord Chancellor, Thurlow, who was negotiating behind his back with the Foxites and the Prince, to ensure that he kept his own post in the event of a change of government, Pitt was able to rally his Cabinet and a majority of the House of Commons, who adopted the Bill on 5 February 1789. It then went to the Lords, but further progress was made unnecessary by the King's sudden recovery.

The outcome of the Regency crisis was as great a triumph for Pitt and a disaster for Fox, as the overthrow of the Fox–North coalition in 1783. The King's inveterate hostility to Fox became even greater and his grati-tude to Pitt knew few bounds. He sought to make him a Knight of the Garter, which Pitt declined, suggesting instead that the honour went to his elder brother, the second Earl of Chatham, who was currently First Lord of the Admiralty. A couple of years later, he finally overcame Pitt's reluctance to accept a sinecure office, appointing him as Warden of the Cinque ports, worth £3000 a year, and with a fine residence, Walmer Castle, to go with it. Pitt's stout defence of the King's position, against the intrigues of his eldest son, also increased his own standing with the public. Unlike his two Hanoverian predecessors, who were disliked as foreigners who made little effort to endear themselves to their new countrymen, George III was widely popular, despite his authoritarian tendencies. He looked and behaved like an English country squire, and fully shared the tastes and prejudices of a majority of his subjects.

Pitt's advantage over Fox was consolidated by the general election of 1790, where his supporters improved even further on their major success in 1784, with 340 seats going to the government, 183 to the opposition and 35 'others' (Turner, p.118). Meanwhile, Pitt had begun to make his mark on the international stage, reducing his ineffectual Foreign Secretary, the Marquis of Carmarthen (later, Duke of Leeds) to little more than a cipher. He chanced his arm by ordering mobilization in 1787, when France threatened to intervene in the Netherlands on the side of the Republicans in their struggle for power with the *Stadhouder*, the Prince of Orange. Together with the King of Prussia, who was the Prince's brother-in-law, he threatened a military riposte, and Prussian troops actually crossed the Dutch border, whereupon the Republicans' resistance collapsed. The French then hastily backed down, and Pitt was able to claim a triumph without firing a shot. Three years later, he was able to repeat the trick with Britain's other traditional enemy – Spain – over the Nootka Sound dispute. This concerned the establishment of a British trading post on Vancouver Island, in territory long claimed by Spain. The Spanish reacted by stopping a British ship and arresting the traders, while demanding that the British should recognize Spanish sovereignty over the entire west coasts of the American continents. The British cabinet prepared for war, and called on Spain to compensate the arrested traders. Spain proved obdurate until it transpired that its long-time ally and fellow Bourbon kingdom, France, distracted by the early phases of the Revolution, was in no mood to go to war on its behalf. It then smartly climbed down, agreed to compensate the traders and conceded that British subjects could enter areas not actually settled by the Spanish and fish in the Pacific.

Pitt had followed up his Dutch success by concluding a 'Triple Alliance' between Britain, Holland and Prussia, and now aspired to expand this into a general 'Concert of Europe', whose purpose would be the peaceful settlement of disputes and the confirmation of European boundaries as they had existed in 1787. In particular, he aimed to associate Austria and Russia with the project, which would leave France isolated if it declined to participate. This grand design, which prefigured the system imposed after the Congress of Vienna in 1815, collapsed at its first test, in 1791, when Catherine the Great of Russia proclaimed the annexation of the fortress of Ochakov (Odessa), which had been captured during a war with Turkey. Britain and Prussia sent an ultimatum to Catherine that she should return it to the Turks, and Pitt prepared to send British fleets to the Black and Baltic seas to add to the pressure. But the Austrians declined to join in and Catherine showed herself to be unexpectedly obdurate. Pitt also faced strong parliamentary and cabinet opposition and – deeply humiliated – sent a message to the Prussians to withdraw the ultimatum, telling Joseph Ewart, the British Ambassador to Berlin, 'with tears in his eyes, that it was the greatest mortification he had ever experienced' (Ehrman, II, p.24). His projected 'Concert' was dead and two years later he looked on helplessly as Russia, Prussia and Austria proceeded to the second of their three partitions of Poland. The Duke of Leeds resigned as Foreign Secretary, in protest against his handling of the Ochakov affair, which caused Pitt no anguish, as it enabled him to promote his cousin, and close associate, William Grenville, in his place.

The storming of the Bastille on 14 July 1789 marked a watershed in Pitt's long premiership. Before then he had been a highly successful peacetime Prime Minister and a moderate reformer. Later he was to be a markedly less successful war leader and what might be most accurately described as a moderate reactionary (if that is not a contradiction in terms), though it was to be nearly another four years before Britain was actually at war with France. Initially, Pitt welcomed the early stages of the French Revolution, as did the great majority of Britain's political class. It came in the midst of the hundredth anniversary celebrations of the 'Glorious Revolution' of 1688–89, and the general feeling was that France was at last catching up with Britain and would develop into a constitutional monarchy with enhanced liberties for its citizens. Even as disorders spread, Pitt remained sanguine, as he believed that this would weaken France as a great power, which would be to the British advantage. His attitude hardened after the September massacres of 1792 and the execution of Louis XVI the following January, yet he still resisted pressure to join Austria and Prussia in their war against France. Eventually, it was France which declared war, in April 1793, after Britain had objected to its invasion of Holland.

Meanwhile, serious splits developed within the opposition. Fox had welcomed the Revolution unequivocally, exclaiming after the fall of the Bastille, 'How much the greatest event it is that ever happened in the world!, and how much the best!'. Many of his younger supporters, including a future reformist Prime Minister, Charles Grey, were inspired to seek to revive the movement for parliamentary reform, which was largely dormant since the failure of Pitt's Bill in 1785. They founded a body called Friends of the People, and argued for much more thorough-going changes, including Household suffrage. This, however, fell well behind the demands of more rank-and-file bodies, such as the London Correspondence Society, led by a shoemaker, Thomas Hardy. These included universal male suffrage, the abolition of the property quali- fication for MPs, equal electoral districts, the payment of MPs, annual parliaments and the secret ballot. These demands horrified the more conservative Whigs, including Portland, who regarded their advocates as no better than 'Jacobins', and feared for the defence of their own property. They were even more appalled by the publication, in 1791, of Thomas Paine's *Rights of Man*. The earliest and most painful defector from Fox was Edmund Burke, formerly his closest friend and collabor- ator. Showing extraordinary prescience, Burke, at an early date, foresaw all the more nefarious consequences of the Revolution – the growth of fanaticism, the descent into chaos and civil war, the destruction of liberty and the military adventurism, which would plunge Europe into a generation of war. He spelled out his fears in his pamphlet, *Reflections on the Revolution in France*, published in November 1790, and advocated immediate action to forestall them. Pitt himself was by no means con- vinced and for more than another two years maintained a policy of strict neutrality towards the events in France.

Once war was joined, however, in 1793, he became fully committed to conducting it to a successful conclusion. This did not, in his view, neces- sarily involve the restoration of the monarchy, which most of his allies wished to proclaim as a war aim, but it did mean that France should cease to be a constant threat to the security of its neighbours. Pitt was emphatic that only he should lead the government but was anxious to strengthen its position by recruiting heavyweight figures from the opposition who were prepared to sever their connections with Fox. An opportunity had already arisen, in January 1793, when Thurlow had finally exhausted Pitt's – and the King's patience – by attacking the government's fiscal policies in the House of Lords. Pitt successfully demanded his resigna- tion and was able to replace him as Lord Chancellor by the Whigs' lead- ing lawyer, Lord Loughborough. Detailed negotiations then followed with Portland and other leading Whigs, but they were not yet already to abandon Fox. Eighteen months later, however, in July 1794, Pitt pulled off a considerable coup, when Portland, who became Home Secretary, and four of his leading colleagues, joined the cabinet, bringing a large parliamentary following with them. The Portlandites drove a hard bar- gain: 'The alliance could not have been arranged without Pitt's generous offer of five places in the cabinet, five peerages and one promotion in the peerage, a pension for Burke, two offices in the royal household, the lord lieutenancy of Middlesex and the promise of the lord lieutenancy of

Ireland' (Turner, p.118). Some of Pitt's supporters criticized him for ceding too much, fearing that he would lose control over his own cabinet, 6 of whose 13 members were now his former political opponents. But Pitt was careful to keep the main portfolios connected to the war effort in the hands of his own loyalists, and the effect of the whole exercise was to hamstring the opposition. Portland was able to bring 62 MPs over to the government's side, 'leaving the Foxites in the Commons as a small and isolated party of about fifty-five members' (Turner, p.132). In any event, the cabinet, as a whole, seldom played a significant role in determining war policy. Pitt was in the habit of settling decisions with his two closest collaborators – Grenville, the Foreign Secretary, and Dundas, War Secretary, and provided these three were of one mind there was little chance of their being successfully challenged. The only other person of great influence was the King, who liked to be consulted and was not bashful about making his own suggestions. On some occasions he was to over-rule Pitt, but most of the time the Prime Minister got his own way.

Pitt's reputation as a reformer did not long survive the onset of war. Backed by his new Home Secretary, Portland, he introduced a series of repressive measures which, while ostensibly aimed at would-be violent supporters of the French Revolution, were, in practice, employed against the essentially peaceful advocates of electoral reform, such as the leaders of the London Correspondence Society, who were actually arraigned in a treason trial which carried the threat of the death sentence. Fortunately, a London jury had the good sense to acquit them, though in Edinburgh one man was hanged on similar charges, and others imprisoned or sent to Botany Bay. Pitt himself took part in the cross-examination of several of those arrested, but was highly embarrassed when he was subpoenaed to appear as a witness in the trial of the noted radical, John Horne Tooke. Here he was forced to admit the similarity between the views attributed to Tooke and his own advocacy ten years earlier. Pitt's measures, which included the suspension of *habeus corpus* for several periods, were bitterly opposed in the Commons by Fox and his depleted band of supporters, but were carried by large majorities. Fox denounced them as a concerted attack on liberty, but the historian John Derry attempted to put them in perspective when he wrote:

But Pitt and Portland did not preside over anything like a reign of terror. Something like a total of 200 prosecutions over a period of ten years hardly merits such a description. Many of the cases ended in acquittal or the charges being dropped and the proceedings discontinued. The pressure of convention and the weight of public opinion achieved more in damping down radicalism than either the Seditious Meetings Act or the Treasonable Practices Act. With the ascendancy of loyalism and the popular identification of radicalism with Jacobinism, radicals suffered more from the prejudices of the community than from the force of law. (Derry, p.97)

Pitt's war strategy closely paralleled that of his father during the Seven Years War, utilizing Britain's naval supremacy to facilitate attacks on France's overseas possessions, while subsidizing European allies to bear the brunt of military operations on the continent. Consistently, however, he failed to match the achievements of the elder Pitt. While most of the French possessions in the Caribbean were over-run, British troops had great difficulty in consolidating their conquests and were decimated by tropical diseases. They had more success in their operations against France's allies, Spain and Holland, conquering Trinidad from the former and the Cape Colony and Ceylon (Sri Lanka) from the latter. On the continent, however, direct British military operations – against Toulon, the Vendée (in support of French royalists) and Flanders – all ended in disaster. Nor did Britain's allies – either in the First coalition (1792–97), or the Second (1798–1801), fare any better. Whereas his father had had the good fortune to ally himself with a military genius – Frederick the Great – none of the Younger Pitt's more numerous allies revealed conspicuous fighting qualities, their armies being regularly rolled over by French generals, from Carnot to Bonaparte. They then hastened to make peace, often on humiliating terms, leaving the British to fight on alone. The British troops, also, were poorly led, notably by Frederick, Duke of York, the favourite son of George III, whose ineffectiveness as commander during the Flanders campaign has been immortalized in the famous song, *The Grand Old Duke of York*. Virtually the only successes Pitt had to celebrate were periodic victories by the Navy, a deserved recompense for the assiduity he had shown in modernizing and expanding the fleet throughout the 1780s.

Pitt was to prove persistently optimistic in his conduct of the war but failed – despite his Herculean labours – to pursue a consistent path, while his organization of public business was chaotic. Nor did his close personal alliance with Grenville and Dundas remain untroubled. The former was critical of his readiness to strike at France at any time and at any place, whenever an opportunity arose, believing that the available forces should be concentrated and only used in carefully planned and well-resourced campaigns which offered a good prospect of success. He also became exasperated at Pitt's continuance in paying subsidies to Prussia at a time when it was proving to be an inactive and unreliable ally, much more interested in carving up Poland, in successive partitions, with Austria and Russia, than in fighting against the French. Dundas proved an efficient organizer but was inclined to defeatism and favoured an essentially defensive policy, giving priority to forestalling the probably exaggerated fears of a French invasion. Pitt had never anticipated a prolonged war, believing that the French economy would quickly collapse under the strain and was distressed to find that it was the British economy which appeared to suffer most, with recurrent food shortages, labour unrest and the national debt reaching unprecedented heights. Periodically he was tempted to seek a negotiated peace but George III was reluctant to agree. On two occasions, however, in 1796 and 1797, serious talks began, with Pitt essentially offering a deal on the basis of the return of the conquered French colonies in exchange for a withdrawal from the Low Countries. This was not sufficient bait to attract even the more moderate members of the *Directoire*, which replaced the terror regime in 1795. Pitt's wisdom in sticking to these conditions may be questioned. Certainly, Fox and Pitt's friend Wilberforce, firmly believed that a continuation of the war was not in Britain's interest and that a perfectly reasonable settlement could have been reached if the British negotiators had been more flexible. It could also be argued that the continuation of the war led to what Britain most feared – a permanently aggressive and expansionist France, which was assured by the rise to power of Napoleon, a direct result of his victories in the War of the Second Coalition, which Pitt organized after 1798.

Pitt wore himself out and largely destroyed his health through his wartime exertions, becoming more and more dependent on alcohol. While attempting to supervise every detail of the war effort, he was also singlehandedly running the Treasury, having retained his post as Chancellor of the Exchequer throughout his premiership. He found it increasingly difficult to finance the war, balancing tax increases with very extensive borrowing, but he continued to show tenacity and ingenuity in introducing his annual budgets. One of these, in 1798, was to introduce Income Tax for the first time. Intended only as a temporary measure, and initially raising far less than he had envisaged, it was eventually to become the principal resource on which subsequent Chancellors of the Exchequer have depended to fill the coffers of the state. He continued to carry a heavy load as Leader of the House of Commons, all his senior ministers, with the exception of Henry Dundas, being in the Lords, which meant that he had continually to speak for the government on a very wide range of subjects.

He was an increasingly isolated figure. Both his sisters, to whom he was devoted, had died in childbirth, his younger brother, James, a naval captain, had perished at sea, and his brother-in-law, Edward Eliot, who became his closest companion, died in 1791. Devoted associates of his youth, such as William Wilberforce, gradually drifted away, and he found it difficult to cultivate new friends. Although he remained throughout his career a masterly presence in the House of Commons, he did not use it as a means to build up a circle of close personal supporters. He was the object of immense respect, but little warmth, among his fellow MPs. A much-quoted account by the great parliamentary diarist, Sir Nathaniel Wraxall, describing his first appearance in the House as Prime Minister, is revelatory of the general disdain with which he treated them:

> From the instant that Pitt entered the doorway, he advanced up the floor with a quick and firm step, his head erect and thrown back, looking neither to the right nor the left, not favouring with a nod or a glance any of the individuals seated on either side, among whom many who possessed £5,000 a year would have been gratified even by so slight a mark of attention. It was not thus that Lord North or Fox treated Parliament.

With a few of his ministers he enjoyed greater intimacy, particularly Henry Dundas, who became his main drinking companion and whose home, close to his own house at Holwood in Kent, he often visited. Also nearby lived Lord Auckland, the former William Eden, a distinguished former ambassador, who had negotiated Pitt's commercial treaty with France. Pitt spent much time at his home in the autumn of 1796, relaxing with Auckland and his extensive family, not least his eldest daughter, the attractive 19-year-old Lady Eleanor Eden. Pitt made no declaration but apparently Eleanor and both her parents assumed he was working up to a proposal of marriage, a prospect which gave them enormous pleasure. Rumours began to spread and even reached the newspapers, and in January 1797 Pitt felt constrained to send an embarrassed letter to Auckland, disclaiming any such intention, and saying that, however, desirable such a union would be, there were 'decisive and insurmountable' obstacles. Auckland apparently concluded that these were of a temporary and financial nature and wrote back suggesting that Pitt should come round 'and talk about the whole at leisure and again and again' (Hague, p.391). Pitt was therefore forced to write a further and less circumspect letter, making it brutally clear that his mind was 'unalterably' fixed.

This episode, which caused a considerable stir, is discussed in detail by Pitt's most exhaustive biographer, John Ehrman and more recently by former Tory leader William Hague. Both are disinclined to believe that Pitt's main motivation in backing off was the chaotic state of his financial situation (over which he exercised none of the conscientious care which he lavished on the nation's finances as First Lord of the Treasury), though this could have been a subordinate factor. Both conclude that, when it came down to it, Pitt simply could not face the prospect of marriage, either with Eleanor or any other woman, given his apparent lack of carnal interest in the opposite sex. Ehrman does not believe that he was actively homosexual. 'If he had any homosexual "potential" it would seem to have been very mild', he writes, 'and it is much more likely that he had no strong sexual inclinations at all' (Ehrman, I, p.109). Ehrman does, however, add that 'If there was a homosexual relationship in Pitt's life, Canning might appear the most obvious candidate' (Ehrman, III, p.94). The future Foreign Secretary, and briefly Prime Minister, was one of a number of young junior ministers – among them Castlereagh, Huskisson. Perceval and the future Lord Liverpool – with whom Pitt enjoyed friendly and relaxed relations, but Canning was clearly his favourite and he was reported to be in a 'trance' when he attended his young protégé's wedding. That there was mutual affection is clear, but there is only the slightest evidence that it took a physical form. Ehrman quotes Pitt as having told his niece, Lady Hester Stanhope, many years later, that he must stay 'a single man for my King and country's sake'. 'He stood apart', he concludes, 'untouched as a priest stands untouched at the centre of his avocations; a priest in this instance of politics and government!' (Ehrman, III, p.97).

Lonely, in failing health, depressed by the continued lack of success in the war, as the eighteenth century drew to its end, Pitt began to show occasional signs of losing his grip. In May 1798, he provoked a duel with an opposition MP, George Tierney, after carelessly impugning his patriotism in a parliamentary exchange. It took place on Putney Heath, both men fired twice, but neither was injured, Pitt firing his second shot into the air. More seriously for his survival as Prime Minister, he failed to keep George III regularly informed of the government's intentions. This had fatal consequences in 1801, when Pitt proposed to his Cabinet colleagues that legislation should be brought in to enable Catholics to vote in parliamentary elections and to be appointed to public office. Intended as a *quid pro quo* for the Union of the British and Irish Parliaments, which had been approved the previous year (though only after extensive bribery of Irish MPs to vote their own chamber out of existence), the proposal fell foul of several of Pitt's colleagues, notably the Lord Chancellor, Lord Loughborough. He hastened to inform the King of what was proposed and George angrily declared that he could not approve the measure which was a breach of his Coronation oath to defend the Protestant religion. Pitt feeling himself morally bound to proceed with the legislation, in the light of informal assurances which had been given to Irish Catholics, promptly offered his resignation to the King. Perhaps he hoped that George would not accept it and would acquiesce in Catholic emancipation in order to keep the services of the man who had loyally served him for 17 years. But George had grown tired of Pitt's growing independence, and – crucially – now had an acceptable candidate for the premiership in view and was no longer fearful of opening the way to Fox, whose influence in Parliament had sharply declined since the defection from him of the Portland Whigs. He turned to Henry Addington, the popular Speaker of the House of Commons and a friend of Pitt's, many of whose ministers (but not Grenville or Dundas) were willing to serve under him. Pitt himself was happy to lend his support to Addington, whom he probably thought was in a better position than himself to seek a peace treaty with France, which he now believed to be necessary.

Addington duly succeeded in negotiating the Peace of Amiens, within a year of assuming the premiership. Described by Canning as 'the peace everybody was glad of and nobody was proud of' (Derry, p.121), it broke down after 14 months, after both sides had breached its terms, Napoleon by invading Switzerland and the British by refusing to evacuate their troops from Malta. War resumed in May 1803, and Addington quickly revealed himself as a less than inspiring war leader. Agitation soon arose for the return of Pitt, celebrated in a song composed by Canning as 'The Pilot that weathered the Storm', and Addington twice attempted to recruit him to his government. Pitt made it clear, however, that he would come back only as Prime Minister, and in May 1804, Addington, bowing to the inevitable, tended his resignation. George welcomed Pitt back with a clear conscience, his new Prime Minister having promised him that he would not raise the subject of Catholic emancipation again during the King's lifetime.

The government which Pitt formed, in May 1804, was not the one he intended. He had wanted to form a 'grand coalition', uniting all the significant parliamentary factions in a patriotic government pledged to resist the threat of a French invasion which, with Napoleon massing his forces outside Boulogne, seemed a much more serious threat than at any time since 1793. In particular, he wished to include Fox and his supporters, as well as those of his cousin, Grenville, from whom he had become estranged, partly because of the pledge he had given the king over Catholic emancipation, and who, together with Fox, had led the opposition to the Addington ministry. The King was perfectly prepared to accept Grenville in the government, but drew the line at Fox, whereupon Grenville himself refused to participate. The result was that Pitt's government was largely composed of Addington's ministers, plus a few of his own strong supporters, notably George Canning. Dundas, who had been ennobled as Viscount Melville, returned as First Lord of the Admiralty, but was soon forced to resign when he, by the casting vote of the Speaker, was impeached for alleged malversation of funds during his earlier service as Treasurer of the Navy. Tears were reported to have rolled down Pitt's cheeks 'in one of the rare occasions on which he lost control of his feelings in public... at the destruction of his old and loyal colleague' (Derry, p.131). Melville was ultimately acquitted, but his removal was a heavy blow to Pitt, an exhausted, seriously ill and depressed man, who showed little of the resilience of 20 years earlier, when he had formed his first administration.

With infinite difficulty, Pitt now managed to construct the Third Coalition, luring Austria and Russia to put large armies into the field, with Prussia also limbering up. In October 1805, Nelson's great victory at Trafalgar, destroying the cream of the French and Spanish fleets and removing the threat of invasion, restored Pitt's spirits and his customary over-optimism, only for these to be smashed by Napoleon's comprehensive defeats of the Austrians and Russians at Ulm and Austerlitz. When news of Austerlitz reached Pitt, in December 1805, he pointed to a map of Europe and said: 'Roll up that map; it will not be needed these ten years', a prescient estimate of how long it would take before Napoleon's final defeat at Waterloo. A month later, on 23 January 1806, Pitt was dead. The cause was long suspected to be cancer, but, according to Hague, who consulted expert medical opinion, the most probable cause was a peptic ulcer. 'Two hundred years later he would have been cured in a few days by therapy with antibiotic and acid-reducing drugs. In 1806, there was nothing that could be done for him' (Hague, p.577).

The Younger Pitt was a new kind of Prime Minister, compared to whom the great majority of his predecessors were amateur dilettantes. No premier before, and few since, has dedicated his life so completely to his calling, working exceptionally long hours, suppressing most of his other interests and possible sources of pleasure, and establishing such a command over the political scene. He was able to expand the informal, if not the formal powers of the premiership, establishing his authority, at least to a limited extent, over other departments than the Treasury, which was the only one where the writ of previous premiers had actually run, though most of them had had considerable influence over foreign policy and defence issues. Partly because he had to deal with an exceptionally opinionated and stubborn monarch, whom he was reluctant to challenge directly, Pitt was never able to establish his own right to appoint, shift or dismiss ministers, nor to be accepted as the only minister to have direct access to the King and the sole right to advise him. Nevertheless, the fact that he was known to seek these objectives made it easier for his successors to pursue them from more pliable monarchs, though it was not until the end of the reign of Queen Victoria that these were unequivocally conceded.

Though not particularly efficient in his own working methods, being notoriously unwilling to reply to letters and tending to postpone decisions on routine matters until they reached crisis point, he was concerned to improve the overall performance of the administration and was always on the lookout for improvements, if not fundamental reforms, to be introduced. He was always exceptionally cautious, if not conservative, in constitutional matters, and became more so as he grew older, tending to conform to George III's own view that the British constitution, as defined by the legacy of the Glorious Revolution, was a perfect instrument and should not be tampered with. Pitt was singularly concerned about his own reputation, wishing to be seen as a selfless public servant, always putting the national interest above any narrow party or factional interest and utterly incorrupt in all his dealings. These principles he claimed to have inherited from his father and he could certainly be said to have followed them exceptionally closely, even to the extent of leaving behind him massive debts – largely caused through his being systematically swindled by servants and tradesmen – which had, like his father's, to be posthumously redeemed by a vote of the House of Commons. He was a far more successful politician than his father, and much better at handling his relations with George III than the Elder Pitt had been with either him or George II. Pitt was not a party man, and never called himself a Tory, though history has so assigned him and the modern Conservative Party has recognized him as one of its founding fathers. He could fairly lay claim, nearly 200 years before Harold Wilson, to the title of the Great Pragmatist and was the first Prime Minister who actively sought to mould public opinion to reinforce his position in Parliament and with the Court.

He was perhaps a less great man than his father, and infinitely less capable as a war leader. Indeed, one modern historian, A.J.P. Taylor, has argued that it was wrongheaded of Pitt to get involved in war in the first place. 'What was the war about?', Taylor asked. 'Pitt claimed to be fighting for the liberties of Europe. What he was fighting for was the liberties of princes and for the aristocracy. The decision to go to war with revolutionary France in 1793 was a catastrophe for free principles' (Taylor, p.22). This was, of course, the view that Fox took at the time, and it is one of history's great might-have-beens to ponder what would have happened if he, rather than Pitt, had been George III's choice as his Prime Minister.

Works consulted

Ayling, Stanley (1991), *Fox*, London, John Murray.

Derry, John W. (1990), *Politics in the Age of Fox, Pitt and Liverpool*, Basingstoke, Macmillan.

Duffy, Michael (2000), *The Younger Pitt*, London, Longman.

Ehrman, John (1969), *The Younger Pitt: I The Years of Acclaim*, London, Constable.

Ehrman, John (1983), *The Younger Pitt: II The Reluctant Transition*, London, Constable.

Ehrman, John (1996), *The Younger Pitt: III The Consuming Struggle*, London, Constable.

Hague, William (2004), *William Pitt the Younger*, London, HarperCollins.

O'Gorman, Frank (1997), *The Long Eighteenth Century*, London, Arnold.

Oxford Dictionary of National Biography, London, 2004, Oxford University Press.

Taylor, A.J.P. (2000), *British Prime Ministers and Other Essays*, London, Penguin.

Turner, Michael J. (2003), *The Younger Pitt: A Life*, London, Hambledon and London.

Epilogue

So, who were the 14 men who led British governments between 1721 and 1800 and what was their background? Thirteen of them held the post of First Lord of the Treasury; the exception was the Elder Pitt (Lord Chatham), who wished to divest himself of any departmental responsibilities and took instead the non-executive post of Lord Privy Seal. Of the 14, 12 were aristocrats, including four dukes, four earls and a marquess. The other two, Walpole and the Elder Pitt, derived from the upper reaches of the gentry, though both ended their careers as earls.

Eleven of the 14 were educated at 'public' schools, five each at Eton and Westminster and one at St. Paul's. Shelburne attended a minor school in Dublin, while Devonshire and the Younger Pitt had private tutors. All but Devonshire and Rockingham went on to universities, seven to Oxford, four to Cambridge and one to Leyden, in the Netherlands. Fewer than half of the premiers had an occupation outside politics, apart from managing family estates. Wilmington, Grenville and the Younger Pitt were lawyers and the Elder Pitt and Shelburne, soldiers.

The average age at which they became Prime Minister was 47, the eldest being Wilmington, at 69, and the youngest, Pitt the Younger, at 24. Even apart from Pitt, the eighteenth century was notable for producing youthful premiers – the only other Prime Ministers to achieve the top office below the age of 40 all date from this period – Grafton (33), Rockingham (35), Devonshire (36) and North (37).

Although party allegiances were less clear-cut in the eighteenth century, 11 of the 14 can be classified as Whigs, and three as Tories. As the latter included two long-serving premiers, in Lord North and the Younger Pitt, the Tories were longer in office than these figures would suggest – holding power for 30 out of the 79 years between 1721 and 1800.

Of the Prime Ministers, nine were from the House of Lords and five from the Commons. Yet the five commoners were in power for no less than 65 out of the 79 years. As noted in Chapter 11, it was far easier to govern from the Commons than from the Lords. Of the five commoners, all but one (Grenville) had lengthy periods in power. Of the Lords, only Newcastle managed to hang on for more than three years. The longest single term of office, that of Walpole, was 20 years and 314 days; the shortest was Rockingham's second ministry – 96 days. Four of the Prime Ministers were to die while in office – Wilmington, Pelham, Rockingham and the Younger Pitt (during his second term, in 1806).

In my two earlier volumes, on Prime Ministers of the nineteenth and twentieth centuries, I included a somewhat tentative rank-ordering, based on the overall influence of their careers rather than concentrating narrowly on their periods in power. On a similar basis, here is my estimate of their eighteenth century predecessors:

1. Walpole
2. Pitt the Elder (Chatham)
3. Pelham
4. Pitt the Younger
5. Rockingham
6. Grenville
7. Newcastle
8. North
9. Shelburne
10. Portland
11. Devonshire
12. Grafton
13. Bute
14. Wilmington

Appendix

Prime Ministers of the Eighteenth Century

Name	Party	Age at First Appointment	Dates of Ministries	Total Time as Premier
1. Sir Robert Walpole, first Earl of Orford, born 26 Aug. 1676, died 18 Mar. 1745. Married (1) Catherine Shorter, 30 Jul. 1700, (2) Maria Skerritt, Mar. 1738, 3 sons, 4 daughters	Whig	44 years, 107 days	3 Apr. 1721 to 11 Feb. 1742	20 years, 314 days
2. Spencer Compton, first Earl of Wilmington, born 1673, died 2 Jul. 1743. Unmarried, may have had illegitimate children	Whig	c. 69 years	1 Feb. 1742 to 2 Jul. 1743	1 year, 136 days
3. Henry Pelham, born 25 Sep. 1694, died 6 Mar. 1754. Married Lady Catherine Manners, 29 Oct. 1726, 2 sons, 6 daughters	Whig	48 years, 336 days	27 Aug. 1743 to 6 Mar. 1754	10 years, 191 days
4. Thomas Pelham-Holles, Duke of Newcastle, born 21 Jul. 1693, died 17 Nov. 1768. Married Lady Henrietta Godolphin, 2 Apr. 1717, no children.	Whig	60 years, 288 days	16 Mar. 1754 to 11 Nov. 1756, 29 Jun. 1757 to 26 May, 1762	7 years, 205 days
5. William Cavendish, fourth Duke of Devonshire, born 1720, died 20 Oct. 1764. Married Charlotte Boyle, Baroness Clifford, 17 Mar. 1748, 3 sons, 1 daughter	Whig	c. 36 years	16 Nov. 1756 to 29 Jun. 1757	225 days

Continued

Name	Party	Age at First Appointment	Dates of Ministries	Total Time as Premier
6. James Stuart, third Earl of Bute, born 25 May 1713, died 10 Mar. 1792. Married Mary Wortley Montagu, 24 Aug. 1736, 5 sons, 6 daughters	Tory	49 years, 1 day	26 May 1762 to 8 Apr. 1763	317 days
7. George Grenville, born 14 Oct. 1712, died 13 Nov. 1770. Married Elizabeth Wyndham, May 1749, 4 sons, 5 daughters	Whig	50 years, 14 days	16 Apr. 1763 to 10 Jul. 1765	2 years, 85 days
8. Charles Watson-Wentworth, second Marquess of Rockingham, born 13 May, 1730, died 1 Jul. 1782. Married Mary Bright, 26 Feb. 1752, no children.	Whig	35 years, 61 days	13 Jul. 1765 to 30 Jul. 1766, 27 Mar. to 1 Jul. 1782	1 year, 113 days
9. William Pitt, the Elder, first Earl of Chatham, born 15 Nov. 1708, died 11 May, 1778. Married Hester Grenville, 16 Nov. 1754, 3 sons, 2 daughters	Whig	57 years, 257 days	30 Jul. 1766 to 14 Oct. 1768	2 years, 76 days
10. Augustus Henry Fitzroy, third Duke of Grafton, born 28 Sep. 1735, died 14 Mar. 1811. Married (1) Anne Liddell, 29 Jan. 1756, (2) Elizabeth Wrottesley, 24 Jun. 1769, 7 sons, 9 daughters	Whig	33 years, 16 days	14 Oct. 1768 to 28 Jan. 1770	1 year, 106 days
11. Frederick North, styled Lord North, second Earl of Guilford, born 13 Apr. 1732, died 5 Aug. 1792. Married Anne Speke, 20 May, 1756, 4 sons, 3 daughters	Tory	37 years, 290 days	28 Jan. 1770 to 27 Mar. 1782	12 years, 58 days

Continued

Name	Party	Age at First Appointment	Dates of Ministries	Total Time as Premier
12. William Petty, second Earl of Shelburne, 1st Marquess of Lansdowne, born 2 May 1756, died 7 May 1805. Married (1) Lady Sophia Carteret, 3 Feb. 1765, (2) Lady Louisa Fitz Patrick, 19 Jul. 1779, 3 sons, 1 daughter	Whig	45 years, 63 days	4 Jul. 1782 to 26 Mar. 1783	266 days
13. William Cavendish-Bentinck, third Duke of Portland, born 14 April 1738, died 30 Oct. 1809. Married Lady Dorothy Cavendish, 8 Nov. 1766, 4 sons, 2 daughters	Whig, then Tory	44 years, 353 days	2 Apr. 1783 to 18 Dec. 1783, 31 Mar. 1807 to 4 Oct. 1809	3 years, 82 days
14. William Pitt, the Younger, born 28 May 1759, died 23 Jan. 1806. Unmarried.	Tory	24 years, 205 days	19 Dec. 1783 to 14 Mar. 1801, 10 May 1804 to 23 Jan. 1806	18 years, 343 days

Index

Note: Page numbers in **bold** refer to chapter titles